The Divine Office

Edward J. Quigley

THE DIVINE OFFICE

A STUDY OF THE ROMAN BREVIARY

BY

REV. E.J. QUIGLEY

1920

PREFACE

In the studies preliminary to ordination, the greatest time and attention must be given to the study of Dogmatic and Moral Theology. Certain subjects, such as liturgy, are always in danger of being shortened or of occupying a very small space in a college course. After ordination, priests find that these subjects are things of daily and hourly interest and importance. Who is it that does not know that the study of the Mass and the Missal, of the Breviary, its history and its contents are studies useful in his daily offering of sacrifice and praise?

I hope that this book may serve as an introductory manual to the study of the Breviary. It may be useful to junior students in colleges, in giving them some knowledge of the Church's Hours, which they assist at in their college choirs. It may assist them to know and love the official prayers of the Church, and may help to form devout habits of recitation, so that, when the obligation of the daily office is imposed on them, they may recite it digne, attente et devote. The "texts and intentions" may be an aid to them, and to students in Holy Orders, in the great and glorious work of pious prayer.

Perhaps, this book may be a help to priests. It is an attempt to bring into one handy volume many matters found in several volumes of history, liturgy, theology, and ascetic literature. Much of it they have met before, but some of it may be new and may enable some to pray more fervently and to aid them in the difficult work of saying each Hour and each part of an Hour with attention and devotion. Some of the pages may be to them instructive, and may give them new ideas on such points as the structure of the Hours, the Collects, the Te Deum, the Anthems of the Blessed Virgin, etc.

No book is faultless. Of this one, I can say with the Psalmist, "I studied that I might know this thing, it is a labour in my sight" (Psalm 72). And I can say it with St. Columban, *Totum, dicere volui in breve, totem non potui.* In the book I quote Cardinal Bona. In his wonderful *Rerum Liturgicarum* (II., xx., 6) he wrote what I add as a finish, to this preface: —

"Saepe enim volenti et conanti vel ingenii vires vel rerum antiquarum notitia vel alia subsidia defuerunt; nec fieri potuit quin per loca salebrosa in tenebris ambulans interdum offenderim, Cum aliquid incautius et neglentius a me scriptum offenderit, ignoscat primum lector, deinde amica manu corrigat et emendat et quae omisi suppleat. "

E. J.Q.

ROCKCORRY, CO. MONAGHAN.

CONTENTS

PART I.

GENERAL QUESTIONS.

PART II.

RULES FROM MORAL AND ASCETIC THEOLOGY FOR THE
RECITATION OF THE BREVIARY.

Who are bound to say the office?
Must every holder of a benefice read the office?
What sin is committed by the omission of a notable part?
What sins are committed by the omission of the whole office?
What must a person do who has a doubt about omissions?
Does a person, who recites by mistake, an office other than that
  prescribed fulfil his obligation?
What causes justify an inversion of the hours?
Is it a sin to say Matins of following day before finishing Compline
  of the current day?
What is the time fixed for recitation of the Office?
When may a priest begin the recitation of Matins and Lauds for the
  following day?
What is true time as regards recitation of the office?
Are priests bound to recite Matins and Lauds before Mass?
At what time should the little hours be said?
Where should the office be recited?
What kind of verbal pronunciation should be attended to?
May the recitation be interrupted?
May Matins be separated from Lauds without cause?
Is intention required in reading the hours?
Is attention required? external? internal? superficial attention,
  literal attention?
Opinions of theologians on necessary attention.
Distractions, voluntary and involuntary.
Does a person reciting the hours sin, if he have distractions?

Causes excusing from reading the hours.
Scruples and the direction of the scrupulous.

ART. I. RULES FOB PIOUS RECITATION OF HOURS.

1. The words read.
2. To whom we speak.
3. We pray in the name of the church.
4. Our associates on earth.
5. The purpose of our prayer.
6. It gives glory to God and draws down his blessings.
7. It brings help to those who recite it fervently.

ART. II. THE MEANS TO ADOPT OF PIOUS RECITATION.

A. *Before Recitation.*

1. Purify conscience.
2. Mortification of passions.
3. Guarding the senses.
4. Knowledge of the work that is to be done.

B. THE IMMEDIATE PREPARATION FOR THE RECITATION.

1. Reading the Ordo Recitandi officium.
2. To recollect ourselves.
3. To invoke God's aid.
4. To unite ourselves with Christ.
5. (a) Christ our model in prayer.
   (b) Our prayers to be offered through him.
   (c) Church wishes this and practices it ever.
   (d) Lives of saints show how they united with Christ in prayer.
   (e) Remembrance of the sublime work we engage in.
   (f) To propose general, special and particular intentions.

ART. III. AIDS DURING THE RECITATION OF THE HOURS.

(a) Suitable place.
(b) Respectful and devout attitude.
(c) Slow, deliberate pronunciation.

(d) Distractions.
(e) To apply the mind to what is read.
(f) To read without critical judgments.
(g) To think of Christ's Passion.
(h) To think of the presence of God and of our Angel Guardian.

ART. IV. AFTER SAYING THE OFFICE.

1. Thanks to God.
2. Ask his pardon for faults.
3. Say the *Sacro-sanctae*.
4. The Sacro-sanctae.

PART III

THE CANONICAL HOURS.

CHAPTER I.—MATINS (TITLE XIII).

Parts Pater Noster and Ave (Title XXXII)
  Credo   (Title XXXIII)
  Domine labia mea—Deus in
  Invitatory   (Title XIX)
  Hymns   (Title XX)
  Antiphons   (Title XXI)
  Psalms   (Title XXII)
  Canticles
  Replies of Biblical Commission on Psalms
  Versicles and responds   (Title XXIV)
  Absolutions and blessings (Title XXV)
  Lessons   (Title XXIV)
  Responses   (Title XXIV)
  Rubrics and Symbolism
  Te Deum   (Title XXXI)
  Texts and Intentions

CHAPTER IV.—VESPERS AND COMPLINE PAGE (TITLE XVII-XVIII).

Vespers.
  Etymology, structure, antiquity.
  Reasons for Hour
  Texts and intentions

Compline.
  Etymology, structure, antiquity
  Reasons for Hour
  Suffrages of the Saints (Title VII)
  Anthems of Blessed Virgin
  Texts and intentions

The Little Office of the Blessed Virgin (Title XXVII)

PART IV.

HEORTOLOGY.

CHAPTER I.—A. PROPER OF THE TIME.

Advent
Christmas
St. Stephen; St. John; Circumcision; Epiphany;
  Septuagesima; Lent; Easter and Paschal Times;
  Ascension; Whit Sunday; Trinity Sunday

B. PROPER OF THE SAINTS.

December; January; February; March; May;
  June; July; August; October; November

ROGATION DAYS AND LITANIES

NOTE A. Breviary Hymns.
NOTE B. Particular Examen.
NOTE C. Bibliography.

PART I.

GENERAL QUESTIONS.

THE DIVINE OFFICE

CHAPTER I.

IDEA OF THE BREVIARY.

Etymology. —The word, Breviary, comes from an old Latin word, *Breviarium*, an abridgment, a compendium. The name was given to the Divine Office, because it is an abridgment or abstract made from holy scripture, the writings of the Fathers, the lives of the Saints. The word had various meanings assigned to it by early Christian writers, but the title, Breviary, as it is employed to-day—that is, a book containing the entire canonical office—appears to date from the eleventh century. Probably it was first used in this sense to denote the abridgment made by Pope Saint Gregory VII. (1013-1085), about the year 1080.

Definition. —The Breviary may be defined as "the collection of vocal prayers established by the Church, which must be recited daily by persons deputed for that purpose. "

Explanation of the Definition. —"Prayers, " this word includes not only the prayers properly so called, but also, the whole matter of the divine office. "Vocal, " the Church orders the vocal recitation, the pronunciation of each word. "Established by the Church, " to distinguish the official prayers of obligation from those which the faithful may choose according to their taste. "Which must be recited, " for the recitation is strictly obligatory. "Daily, " the Church has fixed these prayers for every day of the year, and even for certain hours of the day. "By persons deputed for that purpose, " therefore, persons in holy orders recite these prayers not in their own name, but as representatives of the universal Church.

Different Names for the Breviary. —This book which is, with us, commonly called the Breviary, has borne and still bears different names, amongst both Latins and Greeks.

Amongst the Latins, the recitation of the Breviary was called the Office (*officium*), that is, the duty, the function, the office; because it is, *par excellence*, the duty, function and office of persons consecrated to God. This is the oldest and most universal name for the Breviary and its recitation. It was called, too, the Divine Office (*officium divinum*), because it has God for its principal object and is recited by persons consecrated to God. It is called the ecclesiastical office (*officium ecclesiasticum*), because it was instituted by the Church. Other names were, *Opus Dei; Agenda; Pensum servitutis; Horae; Horae Canonicae.*

Which books were employed in olden times in reciting the Office?

Before the eleventh century the prayers of the Divine Office were not all contained in one book, as they are now in the Breviary, which is an abridgment or compendium of several books. The recitation of the Office required the Psaltery, the Lectionary, the Book of Homilies, the Legendary, the Antiphonarium, the Hymnal, the Book of Collects, the Martyrology, the Rubrics. The Psaltery contained the psalms; the Lectionary (thirteenth century) contained the lessons of the first and second nocturn; the Book of Homilies, the homilies of the Fathers; the Legendary (before the thirteenth century), the lives of the saints read on their feast days. The Hymnal contained hymns; the Book of Collects, prayers, collects and chapters; the Martyrology contained the names with brief lives of the martyrs; the Rubrics, the rules to be followed in the recitation of the Office. To-day, we have traces of this ancient custom in our different choir books, the Psalter, the Gradual, the Antiphonarium. There were not standard editions of these old books, and great diversities of use and text were in existence.

Divisions of the Divine Office. —How is the daily Office divided? The Office is divided into the night Office and the day Office. The night Office is so called because it was originally recited at night. It embraces three nocturns and Lauds. The day Office embraces Prime, Terce, Sext, None, Vespers, and Compline.

Parts or Hours of the Office. —How many parts or hours go to make up the Office? Rome counts seven, and seven only; and this is the number commonly counted by liturgists and theologians. They reckon Matins and Lauds as one hour.

The old writers on liturgy ask the question: "Why has the Church reckoned seven hours only? " Their replies are summarised well by Newman: "In subsequent times the hours of prayer were gradually developed from the three or (with midnight) the four seasons above enumerated to seven, viz. : —by the addition of Prime (the first hour), Vespers (the evening), and Compline (bedtime) according to the words of the Psalm—'Seven times a day do I praise thee, because of thy righteous judgments. ' Other pious and instructive reasons existed, or have since been perceived, for this number. It was a memorial of the seven days of creation; it was an honour done to the seven petitions given us by our Lord in His prayer; it was a mode of pleading for the influence of that Spirit, who is revealed to us as sevenfold; on the other hand, it was a preservative against those seven evil spirits which are apt to return to the exorcised soul, more wicked than he who has been driven out of it; and it was a fit remedy of those successive falls which, scripture says, happen to the 'just man' daily. " (*Tracts for the Times*, No. 75. "On the Roman Breviary. ")

> "Matutina ligat Christum qui crimina purgat,
>   Prima replet sputis. Causam dat Tertia mortis.
>   Sexta cruci nectit. Latus ejus Nona bipertit.
>   Vespera deponit. Tumulo completa reponit.
>   Haec sunt septenis propter quae psallimus horas."

> "At Matins bound; at Prime reviled;
>   Condemned to death at Tierce;
>   Nailed to the Cross at Sext; at None
>   His blessed Side they pierce.
>   They take him down at Vesper-tide;
>   In grave at Compline lay,
>   Who thenceforth bids His Church observe
>   The sevenfold hours alway."

(Gloss. Cap. I. De Missa)

Thus, this old author connects the seven hours with the scenes of the Passion. Another author finds in the hours a reminder and a warning that we should devote every stage of our lives to God. For the seven canonical hours, he writes, bear a striking resemblance to the seven ages of man.

The Divine Office

Matins, the night office, typifies the pre-natal stage of life. *Lauds*, the office of dawn, seems to resemble the beginnings of childhood. *Prime* recalls to him youth. *Terce*, recited when the sun is high in the heavens shedding brilliant light, symbolises early manhood with its strength and glory. *Sext* typifies mature age. *None*, recited when the sun is declining, suggests man in his middle age. *Vespers* reminds all of decrepit age gliding gently down to the grave. *Compline*, night prayer said before sleep, should remind us of the great night, death.

CHAPTER II.

SHORT HISTORY OF DIVINE PRAISE IN GENERAL AND OF THE BREVIARY IN PARTICULAR.

From all eternity the Godhead was praised with ineffable praise by the Trinity—the three divine Persons. The angels from the first moment of the creation sang God's praises. *Sanctus, sanctus, sanctus, Dominus Deus, Sabaoth. Plena est omnis terra gloria ejus* (Isaias vi. 3).

Cardinal Bona writes that Adam and Eve blessed and praised God, their Creator. For God created the first human beings, and "created in them the knowledge of the Spirit of God that they might praise the name which He has sanctified and glory in His wondrous acts" (Ecclesiasticus xvii. 6-8), Every page of the Old Testament tells how the chosen race worshipped God. We read of the sacrifices of Cain, Abel, Enoch, Noe; of the familiar intercourse which the great patriarchs, Abraham, Isaac, Jacob had with God. Recorded, too, are the solemn songs and prayers of Moses thanking God for His guidance in the freedom from the slavery of Egypt (Exodus xv.). David, under God's inspiration, composed those noble songs of praise, the Psalms, and organised choirs for their rendering. He sings "Evening and morning and at noon I will speak and declare and He shall hear my voice" (Psalm 54, v. 18); "I rose at midnight to give praise to Thee" (Psalm 118, v. 162); "Seven times a day I have given praise to Thee" (Psalm 118, v. 164).

The Prophet Daniel, a captive in Babylon, prayed thrice daily, his face turned to Jerusalem. The Israelites, captives in Babylon with Nehemias, "rose up and read in the book of the Law of the Lord their God, four times in the day, and four times they confessed and adored the Lord their God" (II. Esdras ix. 3). Hence, the Jewish day, made up as it was with sacrifices, libations, oblations, purifications, and public and private prayer, was a day of prayer. In these public meetings they sang God's praises, sang of His glory and of His mercy. Sometimes they spoke with loving familiarity, sometimes they prayed on bended knee, sometimes they stood and pleaded with outstretched hands, pouring out the prayers inspired by God Himself.

In the New Law our Saviour is the model of prayer, the true adorer of His Father. He alone can worthily adore and praise because He alone has the necessary perfection. Night and day He set example to His followers. He warned them to watch and pray; He taught them how to pray; He gave them a form of prayer; He prayed in life and at death. His apostles, trained in the practices of the synagogue, were perfected by the example and the exhortations of Christ. This teaching and example are shown in effect when the assembled apostles were "at the third hour of the day" praying (Acts ii. 15); when about the sixth hour Peter went to pray (Acts x. 9). In the Acts of Apostles we see how Peter and John went at the ninth hour to the temple to pray. St. Paul in prison sang God's praises at midnight, and he insists on his converts singing in their assembly psalms and hymns (Ephes. v. 19; Col. Iii. 16; I. Cor. xiv. 26).

What form did the public prayers, which we may call the divine office, take in the time of the Apostles? It is impossible to say. But it is certain 10 that there were public prayers, 20 that they were offered up daily in certain determined places and at fixed hours, 30 that these public prayers consisted principally of the Psalms, hymns, canticles, extracts from Sacred Scripture, the Lord's Prayer, and probably the Creed, 40 that these public prayers varied in duration according to the will of the bishop or master who presided.

"The weekly commemoration of Christ's resurrection, the yearly recurrence of the memory of the great facts of Christ's life, the daily sanctification of the hours of the day, each led the Christian to draw upon the hours of the Psalter, and when, gradually, fixed hours for daily prayer passed beyond the home circle and with groups of ascetics entered the public churches, it was from the Psalter that the songs of praise were drawn, and from the Psalms were added a series of canticles, taken from the books of the Old and the New Testaments, and thus, long ages before any stereotyped arrangement of the Psalms existed, assigning particular Psalms to particular days or hours, the Psalms were feeding the piety of the faithful and teaching men to pray" (*The New Psalter*—Burton and Myers). In this matter of public prayer, it is hard for us to realise the "bookless" condition of the early Christians and their difficulties. It was twenty-five years after the Ascension before the first books of the New Testament were written, and many years must have elapsed before their wide diffusion; hence, in their bookless and guideless condition the early Christians were advised to use the Psalms in their new devotional life (Ephes. v. 19; Col. iii. 16; St. James, v. 13).

The first clear evidence of a division of the Psalter for use in the Western Church is found in the work of St. Benedict (480-543). He had spent his youth near Rome, and keeping his eye on the Roman usage he assigned the Psalms to the various canonical hours and to different days of the week. The antiphons he drew from existing sources, and of course the canonical hours were already in existence. In his arrangement, the whole Psalter was read weekly, and the whole Bible, with suitable patristic selections, was read every year. He also arranged the Sunday, Festal and Ferial offices. For the recitation of the offices of a saint's day, St. Benedict arranged that the Matins shall have the same form as a Sunday office—*i. e.*, three nocturns, twelve lessons and responsories, but the psalms, antiphons and lessons are proper to each saint. This arrangement interrupted the weekly recitation of the whole psalter, and caused great difficulty in later times; for when the feasts increased in number the ferial psalter fell almost into complete disuse.

St. Benedict's arrangement of the psalms and his other liturgical regulations spread rapidly, but the Roman secular office never adopted his arrangement of the psalms, nor his inclusion of hymns, until about the year 1145. In some details each office shows its independent history. It is a matter of dispute among liturgists whether Prime and Compline were added to the Roman secular office through the influence of the Benedictines (Baudot, *The Roman Breviary*, pp. 19-26).

The period following the death of St. Benedict in 543 is a period of which little is known. "We repeat with Dom Baumer (vol. i., pp. 299-300) that the fifth century, at Rome as elsewhere, was a period of great liturgical activity, while the seventh and eighth centuries were, viewed from this point of view, a period of decline" (Baudot, *op. cit.* , p. 53). The labours of St. Benedict probably were continued and perfected by St. Gregory the Great (590-604). His labours are summed up by Dom Baumer (*Histoire du Breviare*, vol. i., pp. 289, 301-303): "It is he who collected together the prayers and liturgical usages of his predecessors and assigned to each its proper place, and thus the liturgy owes its present form to him. The liturgical chant also bears his name, because through his means it reached its highest state of development. The canonical hours and the formulary of the Mass now in use were also carefully arranged by him. " "The whole history of the Western liturgy supports us in maintaining that these books received from the great Pope or from one of his contemporaries a form which never afterwards underwent any radical or essential alteration. " The Roman office spread quickly through Europe. The enthusiasm of Gregory became rooted in the monasteries, where the monks learned and taught, with knowledge and with zeal, his liturgical reforms. Two important reforms of monastic practice are interesting as showing further progress in the evolution of the Roman Breviary. St. Benedict of Aniane (751-821), the friend and adviser of Louis the Pious, became a reformer of Benedictine rule and practice. His rule aimed at a rigid uniformity, even in detail. And the Council of Aix-la-Chapelle (817) helped him to establish his reforms. As a result of the saint's exertions the Penitential Psalms and Office of the Dead were made part of the daily monastic office. The Abbey of Cluny, founded in 910, supplied a further reform tending to guard the office from further accretions.

Did Hildebrand, Pope Gregory VII. (1073-1086), labour for liturgical reform? Liturgical writers give very different replies. Monsignor Battifol (*History of the Roman Breviary*, English edition, p. 158) maintains that Gregory made no reform, and that "the Roman office such as we have seen it to be in the times of Charlemagne held its ground at Rome itself, in the customs of the basilicas, without any sensible modification, throughout the tenth and eleventh centuries and even down to the close of the twelfth. " Dom Gueranger holds that Gregory abridged the order of prayers and simplified the liturgy for the use of the Roman curia. It would be difficult at the present time to ascertain accurately the complete form of the office before this revision, but since then it has remained almost identical with what it was at the end of the eleventh century. Dom Baumer agrees with his Benedictine brother that Gregory wrought for liturgical reform. Probably Pope Gregory VII., knowing the decadence which was manifest in liturgical exercises in Rome during the tenth and eleventh centuries, decided to revise the old Roman office which, although it had decayed in Rome, flourished in Germany, France, and other countries. Hence, in his Lenten Synod, 1074, he promulgated the rules he had already drawn up for the Regular Canons of Rome, ordering them to return to the old Roman rite. Thus he may be counted as a reformer, but not as an innovater nor an abridger. But his reform fell on evil days. The great struggle between Church and State about lay investitures had a baneful influence on liturgy, even in Rome itself. The times seemed to call for a modernised (i. e., a shortened) office. The "modernisers" respected the psalter, the curtailment was in the Lectionary. The modernising spirit showed itself in the arrangement and bulk of the office books. The Psalter, Antiphonary, Responsorial, Bible and Book of Homilies were gradually codified. Even then, a very large volume was the result. After a time the chant, which absorbed much space, was removed from the volume, but the resulting volume, noticeably smaller, was not yet small enough. In time, only the opening words of the antiphons, responsories and versicles were printed, and to the volume thus turned out was given the name *Breviary*. The Curial Breviary was drawn up in this way to make it suitable for persons engaged in outdoor pursuits and journeys. It gradually displaced the choir office in Rome, and Rome's example was universally followed.

This Curial Breviary was adopted by the Franciscans in their active lives. They changed the text of the Psalter only, *Psalterium Romanum*, to the more approved text, the *Psalterium Gallicanum*. The improved Curial Breviary was imposed on the churches of Rome by the Franciscan Pope, Nicholas III. (1277-1280), and henceforth it is called the Roman Breviary. Thus we see that the book used daily by priests got its name in the thirteenth century, although the divine office is almost from Apostolic times.

But liturgy is a progressive study, a progressive practice capable and worthy of perfecting. And the friars strove for the greater perfection and beauty of the new Breviary. They added variety to the unity already achieved and yet did not reach liturgical perfection nor liturgical beauty. They loaded the Breviary by introducing saints' days with nine lessons, thus avoiding offices of three lessons. And by keeping octave days and days within the octave as feasts of nine lessons, they almost entirely destroyed the weekly recitation of the psalter; and a large portion of the Breviary ceased to be used at all. The Franciscan book became very popular owing to its handy form. Indeed its use was almost universal in the Western Church. But the multiplication of saints' offices, universal and local, no fixed standard to guide the recital, and the wars of liturgists, made chaos and turmoil.

Liturgical reform became an urgent need. Everyone reciting the canonical hours longed for a great and drastic change. The Humanists, Cardinal Bembo (1470-1549), Ferreri, Bessarion, and Pope Leo X. (1513-1521) considered the big faults of the Breviary to lie in its barbarous Latinity. They wished the Lessons to be written In Ciceronian style and the hymns to be modelled on the Odes of Horace. Ferreri's attempt at reforming the Breviary dealt with the hymns, some of which he re-wrote in very noble language, but he was so steeped in pagan mythology that he even introduced heathen expressions and allusions, His work was a failure. The traditional school represented by Raoul of Tongres, Burchard, Caraffa, and John De Arze loved the past with so great a love that they refused to countenance any notable reforms, A third school, the moderate school, was represented by Cardinal Pole, Contarini, Sadolet and Quignonez, a Spanish cardinal who had been General of the Franciscans. The work of reform of the Breviary was undertaken by Cardinal Quignonez (1482-1540). He was a man of great personal piety and possessed a love for liturgy and an accurate knowledge of its history, its essentials, and its acquired defects. After seven years' labour at the matter and form of the Breviary, his work, Quignonez's Breviary (*Brevarium Romanum a Francisco Cardinali Quignonio*) appeared in 1535. It was for private use only, and was not intended as a choir manual. Yet so popular was his work that, in 1536, six editions had appeared, and in thirty-three years (until its suppression by St. Pius V,) it went through no less than a hundred editions. Its immense success shows how much the need of Breviary change and reform was felt by the clergy. The book, too, had an important influence on shaping the Breviary produced by Pius V. (1566-1572). Quignonez's book was reproduced with the variations of the four earliest editions, by the Cambridge University Press in 1888. It is an interesting study in itself and in comparison with later breviaries.

But it was felt by scholars that Quignonez's reforms were too drastic. Tradition was ignored. The labour for brevity, simplicity and uniformity led to the removal from this Breviary of antiphons, responses, little chapters and versicles, and to the reduction of lessons at matins to three, and the number of psalms in each hour was usually only three. His work had as a set principle the grand old liturgical idea of the weekly recitation of the whole psalter. The quick and almost universal demand for Quignonez's Breviary indicated the need of a reform and the outline of such a reform. The Pope, who commissioned Quignonez to take up breviary reform, requested the Theatines to take up similar work. The Council of Trent (1545-1563) took up the work of reform. But the Council rose before the work had made headway, and the matter of reform was finally effected by St. Pius V. (1566-1572), by his Constitution, *Quod a nobis* (1568).

The Reformed Breviary of 1568 is, in outline, the Breviary in our hands to-day. The great idea in the reform was to restore the weekly recitation of the whole psalter. Theoretically, the Breviary made such provision, but practically the great number of saints' offices introduced into the Breviary made the weekly recitation of the psalter an impossibility. The clergy were constantly reading only a few psalms out of the 150 in the psalter. The rubrics, too, were in a confused state. Changes were made in the calendar by suppression of feasts, by restoring to simple feasts the ferial office psalms, and by reducing the number of double and semi-double feasts. But in the body of the Breviary the changes were few and slight. The lives of some saints drawn from Quignonez's work were used, St. Gregory's canon of scripture lessons was adopted and the antiphons, verses, responses, collects and prayers were taken from the old Roman liturgy. The antiphons and responses were given in the older translation of St. Jerome owing to their suitability for musical settings. And the text of the psalms was the *Psalterium Gallicanum*, which had been in use in the Roman Curial Breviary,

But the Pian reform was soon to be followed by a reform of the Breviary text, in accordance with the Sixtine Vulgate, the Clementine Vulgate, and the Vatican text. Clement VIII. (1592-1605) published his edition of the revised Breviary in 1602; and thirty years afterwards Urban VIII, (1623-1644) issued a new and further revised edition, which is substantially the Breviary we read to-day. He caused careful correction of errors which had crept in through careless printing; he printed the psalms and canticles with the Vulgate punctuation, and he revised the lessons and made additions. He established uniformity in texts of Missal and Breviary. But the greatest change made in this new edition was in the Breviary hymns, which were corrected on classical lines by Urban himself aided by four learned Jesuits (see Note, Hymns, p. 259).

"The result (of their labours) has always given rise to very different judgments and for the most part unfavourable. It seemed to be exceedingly rash to regard as barbarous the hymns of men like Prudentius, Sedulius, Sidonius, Apollinaris, Venantius, St. Ambrose, St. Paulinus of Aquileia and Rabanus Maurus and to desire to remodel them after the pattern of Horace's Odes.... It is only fair to give them the credit, that out of respect for the wishes of Urban VIII. they treated these compositions with extreme reserve, and while they made some expressions clearer they maintained the primitive unction in a large number of passages" (Baudot, The Roman Breviary, part iii., chap. ii.).

The commission appointed by Clement VIII. in his work of revision and reform included Baronius, Bellarmine and Gavantus. The commission of Urban VIII. included, amongst other famous men, the famous Irish friar minor, Luke Wadding (1588-1657).

The need of revision, rearrangement and reform of the Breviary was in the mind of every Pope, and nearly every one of them took some step to perfect the historic book. In the eighteenth century Benedict XIV. (1740-1758) contemplated Breviary reform in some details, particularly in improving the composition of some legends and of replacing some homilies of the Fathers. He entrusted this work to Father Danzetta, S.J., but when the learned Jesuit's labour was presented to the Pope, so grave and so contrary were the reasons there put forth, that the Pope thought it well to abandon the thought of reform. Father Danzetta's notes are marvels of research and learning. They are to be seen in Ruskovany's *Coelibatus et Breviarium*, vol. v. They show to the ignorant and the sceptical, the dangers and difficulties which all Breviary reformers have to contend with.

Pope Pius VI. (1775-1799) returned to the project of Breviary reform. Dom Gueranger tells us that the plan of reform was drawn up and presented to the Congregation of Rites, but the actual reform was not entered on. Pope Pius IX. (1846-1878), at the request of Monsignor Sibour, Archbishop of Paris, appointed a commission to revise the Breviary, but their report caused the work to be abandoned. Petitions for reform were sent to the Vatican Council, but very little resulted. Leo XIII. (1878-1903) enriched the calendar by adding the names of many saints; he added votive offices, corrected the Breviary lessons for the feasts of a number of Popes, and, in 1902, he appointed a commission to deal with the hagiography of the Breviary and with its liturgy; but his death in the following year ended the work of the commission,

The unsatisfactory condition of the rules for the recitation of the Divine Office were apparent to everyone. Scholars feared to face Breviary reform, the difficulties were so innumerable and so immense. However, with wonderful courage and prudence, Pope Pius X. (1903-1914) tackled the work. He resolved not to adopt a series of minor changes in the Breviary, but to appoint an active commission of reform, whose first work should be a rearrangement of the psalter which must bring back the recitation of the Divine Office to its early ideal—the weekly recitation of the whole psalter. The problem which faced Pope Pius X. in 1906 was the very same problem which faced his predecessor St, Pius V. (1566-1572), more than three hundred years ago. St. Pius tried to solve the problem by a reform of the calendar, but the solution produced no permanent effect. Pius X. and his commission went to the root of the difficulty, and by a redistribution of the psalms have made the ferial and the festive offices almost equal in length, and have so arranged matters that the frequent recitation of every psalm, and the possible and probable recitation of every psalm, once every week, is now an accomplished fact; and the old and much-sought-after ideal—the weekly recitation of the whole Psalter—is of world-wide practice.

On the publication of the new Psalter, Pope Pius announced that a commission would undertake a complete revision of the Breviary, a matter of great importance and one which must demand long years of care and study to accomplish. A member of the committee which re-arranged the Psalter, Monsignor Piacenza, tells us that such revision must embrace: —

1. A reform of the calendar and the drafting of rules for the admission of feasts into the calendar of the universal Church;

2. The critical revision and correction of the historic and patristic texts;

3. The removal of spurious patristic texts;

4. The remodelling of the rubrics;

5. The institution of a new form of common office for confessors and for virgins to facilitate the lessening of the number of feasts of saints, without diminishing the honour due to them (Burton and Myers, *op. cit.* , p. 144).

We may sum up, then, all that has been said in this long section by stating that from Apostolic times there was public prayer, thrice daily. The Jewish converts, having the psalms committed to memory needed not, nor could they have in those bookless days, a psalter script. In the third century, morning, evening, and night offices are mentioned. Compline was in existence in the time of St. Benedict. "From the seventh century onwards, ecclesiastical writers, papal decrees and conciliar decrees recognise the eight parts of the office, which we have seen took shape during the sixth century, and regard their recitation by priests and monks as enjoined by positive law.

During this period, or at least at its commencement, Lauds and Vespers alone had a clearly defined structure and followed a definite arrangement. As far as we can see, St. Gregory arranged the little hours for Sunday only, and their arrangement for week days was left to the care of the bishops and metropolitans, or even of abbots. This was also the case, in many instances, with regard to Matins, for the number of psalms to be recited thereat was not definitely fixed. As regards the little hours—Prime, Terce, Sext, None and Compline—the freedom of the competent ecclesiastical authorities was as yet unconfined by canonical restrictions. Chrodegang (766) was first to follow the usages of the Benedictines of the Roman Basilica, in prescribing for secular clergy the celebration at Prime of the *officium Capituli* (*i. e.*, the reunion in the chapter for reading the rule or, on certain days, the writings and homilies of the Fathers). The rest of the chapter—*i. e.*, all that follows the *confiteor* in Prime as a preparation for the work of the day, seems to have been composed in the ninth century.... Under Charlemagne and his successors variations in the canonical hours completely disappeared" (Baudot, *op. cit.* , pp. 63-65).

On this foundation was built up the Office, to which additions were made, and of which reforms were effected, up to our own time.

"For us, traditional liturgy is represented by the Roman Breviary of Urban VIII., a book which constitutes for us a Vulgate of the Roman Office.... The thing which renders this Vulgate of 1632 precious to us is that, thanks to the wisdom of Paul IV., Pius V., and Clement VIII., the differences between it and the Breviary of the Roman Curia of the thirteenth century are mere differences of detail: the substantial identity of the two is beyond dispute. The Breviary of Urban VIII. is the lineal descendant of the Breviary of Innocent III. And the latter in its turn is the legitimate descendant of the Roman canonical Office, as it was celebrated in the basilica of St. Peter at the end of the eighth century, such as it had gradually come to be in the course of the seventh and eighth centuries, a genuinely Roman combination of various elements, some of them Roman and some not, but of which some, at all events, go back to the very beginnings of the Catholic religion" (Battifol, *op. cit.* , p. 353).

CHAPTER III.

EXCELLENCE OF THE ROMAN BREVIARY—THE ESTEEM WHICH WE SHOULD HAVE FOR THE BOOK ITSELF.

The Roman Breviary is excellent, firstly, in itself; and, secondly, in comparison with all other breviaries.

It is excellent in itself, in its antiquity, for in substance it goes back to the first ages of Christianity. It is excellent, in its author, for it has been constructed and imposed as an obligation by the supreme pontiffs, the vicars of Jesus Christ, the supreme pastors of the whole Church. It is excellent, in its perpetuity, for it has come down to us through all the ages without fundamental change. It is excellent in its universality, in its doctrine, in the efficacy of its prayer, the official prayer of the Church. It is excellent in the matter of which it is built up, being composed of Sacred Scripture, the words of the Fathers and the lives of God's saints. It is excellent in its style and in its form for the parts of each hour; the antiphons, psalms, canticles, hymns, versicles, follow one another in splendid harmony.

The opinions and praises of the saints who dwelt on this matter of the Breviary would fill a volume. Every priest has met with many such eulogies in his reading. Newman's words are very striking. "There is, " he wrote, "so much of excellence and beauty in the services of the Breviary, that were it skilfully set before the Protestants, by Romanistic controversialists, as the book of devotions received by their communion, it would undoubtedly raise a prejudice in their favour, if he were ignorant of the case and but ordinarily candid and unprejudiced.... In a word, it will be attempted to wrest a weapon out of our adversaries' hands, who have in this, as in many other instances, appropriated to themselves a treasure" (Newman, *Tracts for the Times*, No. 275, *The Roman Breviary*). This tract raised a storm amongst Newman's fellow Protestants. All the old Protestant objections against the Breviary and its recitation (See Bellarmine, *Controv.* iii., *de bonis operibus de oratione* i., i. clx.) were re-published in a revised and embittered form. What a change has come amongst non-Catholics! Hundreds of Anglican clergymen are reading daily with attention and devotion the once hated and despised prayer book, the Roman Breviary. How old Bellarmine would wonder if he saw modern England with its hundreds of parsons reading their *Hours*! How he would wonder to read "The

Band of Hope" (1915), an address delivered by an Anglican clergyman to a society of London clergymen. It includes a rule of life beginning, "Every day we say our Mass and our Office. " (*Cf.* R. Knox's *Spiritual Aeneid*, p. 102.)

The Roman Breviary is excellent, too, in comparison with every other breviary (e. g., Aberdeen, Sarum, Gallican). For none of these can show the antiquity, the authority, the doctrine, the sublime matter, the beautiful order, which the Roman Breviary presents. It was for these reasons that the emperors, Pepin (714-768), Charlemagne (742-814), Charles the Bald (823-888), adapted the Roman rite (Gueranger, *Institutiones Liturgiques*, tom. i.). And Grandicolas (1772), an erudite liturgist, but a prominent Gallican with no love for Roman rites, declared that the Roman Breviary stands in relation to other breviaries as the Roman Church stands in relation to all other Christian bodies, first and superior in every way (*Com. Hist. in Brev. Rom.* , cap. 2). St. Francis De Sales applied to his Breviary the words of St. Augustine on the Psalter, "*Psalterium meum, gaudium meum.* "

CHAPTER IV.

THE CONTENTS OF THE BREVIARY.

SECTION I.

The title of the Breviary is, BREVIARIUM ROMANUM EX
DECRETO SACROSANCTI CONCILII TRIDENTINI RESTITUTUM
S. PII V. PONTIFICIS MAXIMI JUSSU EDITUM, ALIORUMQUE
PONTIFICIUM, CURA RECOGNITUM PII PAPAE X.,
AUCTORITATE REFORMATUM. This work is divided into four
parts, the first part being called *Pars Hiemalis*, the winter part; the
second part, *Pars Verna*, the spring part; the third part, *Pars Aestiva*,
the summer part; and the fourth part, the *Pars Autumnalis*, the
autumn part.

The Church, guided by the Holy Ghost, has drawn up these volumes
of liturgical prayer, so that for each season, even for each day, her
official prayer may be suited to the time, to different degrees of
solemnity and of rite, and so that it may be fixed and determined, yet
having great beauty in its wonderful unity and variety. Hence,
nothing in her official prayer is left to chance, nothing is left to the
selection or caprice of the individual who recites this prayer; all is
foreseen, everything is in order, every tittle has a reason for its
existence and its place in the liturgy, and represents the end and the
intentions of the Church. For, every part of the Roman Breviary is
stamped with the wisdom, the zeal and the piety of the Church,
which presents it, as an offering all suitable for and worthy of God's
honour and glory.

Considering, then, the Breviary as a liturgical book, we find that the
Divine Office has four general divisions, corresponding to the
divisions of our Lord's life. First, from Advent to Septuagesima;
second, from Septuagesima to Easter; third, from Easter to Pentecost;
fourth, from Pentecost to Advent. These divisions correspond also to
the divisions of the year, winter, spring, summer and autumn.

The end and object of the Office are to invite us to join in the infinite
praise which the Son of God rendered to His Father during His life,
and which He renders still in Heaven and in the Tabernacle. *"Domine
in unione illius divinae intentionis qua ipse in terris laudes Deo persolvisti,
has tibi Horas persolvo, "* "O Lord, in union with that divine intention

17

wherewith Thou whilst here on earth Thyself didst praise God, I offer these Hours to Thee. " The life of Christ is divided into four principal divisions: first, His birth, circumcision, epiphany, presentation; second, His public life and His death; third, His resurrection, ascension, and descent of the Holy Ghost; fourth, His mystic life in the Church and in Heaven. Hence arise the four general divisions of the Divine Office: —

First General Division which begins the Church's year. From Advent to Septuagesima: —The birth of the Saviour preceded by His life in Mary's womb, and by the four weeks of Advent, representing (it is said) the passing of the four thousand years, and embracing the mysteries of the Holy Infancy, Circumcision, Epiphany, Holy Name of Jesus, and the Presentation.

Second General Division, from Septuagesima till Easter: —The death of Christ preceded by the events of His public life, His fasting, temptation, preaching, miracles, passion and death.

Third General Division, from Easter to Pentecost: —The Resurrection, the Ascension, Pentecost.

Fourth General Division, from Pentecost till Advent, the termination of the Church's year. The mystic life of Christ in the Church, which will end on the Judgment Day.

These divisions make up the four parts of the Roman Breviary.

The first part, *Pars Prima,* contains the Pontifical Bull, *Quod a nobis,* of Pope Pius V. (1568). It states: —1. That the cause of the new edition was to remove the regrettable variety in the public liturgy. 2. It recalls the labours of Pope Paul IV., Pius IV., and Pius V. for the same end. 3. It announces the abolition of the too-abbreviated Breviary of Quignonez and of all those which have not, for two hundred years preceding 1568, an authentic approbation or a lawful custom. 4. It gives permission to those using such breviaries to adopt the Roman Breviary. 5. It withdraws all privileges in respect to other breviaries. 6. It declares the Roman Breviary obligatory on all except those mentioned (*vide 3, supra*). 7. Even bishops are forbidden to make the smallest change in the new Breviary. 8. The recitation of offices from other breviaries does not fulfil the obligation of those bound to breviary recitation. 9. Bishops are requested to introduce the new Breviary. 10. The Pope suppressed the obligation of reciting on certain days the little Office of the Blessed Virgin, the Office of the Dead, the Penitential and the Gradual Psalms, 11. But he recommends their recitation on certain fixed days and grants an indulgence for the practice. 12. Where the custom of reciting the little Office, in choir, exists, it should be retained. 13. The appointment of the time for the adoption of the Breviary is obligatory. 14. Prohibition, under pain of excommunication, is made against those who print, distribute or receive copies of this Breviary without lawful authority. 15. The authentic publication and obligation of the Bull.

The second document in the *Pars Prima* of the Roman Breviary is the Bull *Divino Afflatu*, issued by Pope Pius X, on 1st November, 1911. It tells us: —

1. That the psalms were composed under divine inspiration, and that it is well known that from the beginning of the Church they were used not only to foster the piety of the faithful, who offered "the sacrifice of praise to God, that is to say, the fruit of lips confessing to His name" (Heb. xiii. 15), but—that retaining the custom of the Old Law—they held a conspicuous place in both the liturgy and Divine Office of the New Law. He quotes St. Basil, who calls psalmody the voice of the infant Church, and Urban VIII., who calls psalmody the daughter of hymnody which is chanted before the throne of God in Heaven. Two quotations from St. Athanasius and St. Augustine, in praise of psalmody, are added.

2. In the Psalms there is a certain wonderful power which arouses in souls a zeal for all virtues. Two quotations from St. Augustine are added. One says that as it is written that all Scriptures both of the Old and the New Testaments are divinely inspired and useful for our instruction.... Nevertheless, the book of the Psalms is, as it were, a very Paradise containing in itself the fruits of all the other books and expressing them in hymns; and moreover it joins its own hymns to them and merges them in the general song of praise. Two further quotations from St. Augustine, in similar strain, follow. For who will be, asks the saint, unmoved by those frequent passages in the Psalms in which are proclaimed the immensity, the omnipotence, the infallible justice, the goodness, the clemency of God? Or who is not moved by the prayers and thanksgivings for benefits received by the humble and trustful petitions, by the cries of souls sorrowing for sin, found in the Psalms? Whom will the Psalmist not fill with admiration when he recounts the gifts of the Divine loving kindness

towards the people of Israel and all mankind, and when he sets forth the truths of heavenly wisdom? Who, finally, will not be inflamed with love by the carefully foreshadowed figure of Christ, our Redeemer, whose voice St. Augustine heard in the Psalms, either singing or sighing or rejoicing in Hope or mourning in present sorrow?

3. In, former ages it was decreed by Popes and Councils and by monastic laws that the whole Psaltery should be recited weekly. Pope St. Pius V., Pope Clement VIII., and Pope Urban VIII. in their revisions of the Breviary ordered this weekly recitation. And even at the present time, such would be the recitation of the Psalter had not the condition of things changed.

4. This arose from the multiplication of saints' offices (*officia de sanctis*), which after the canonization of saints gradually grew to such a huge number that very often the Dominical and Ferial Office remained unread, and hence not a few psalms were neglected, which yet are as the rest, as St. Ambrose says, "the benediction of the people, the praise of God, the praise offering of the multitude, the acclamation of all, the expression of the community, the voice of the Church, the resounding confession of faith, the truly official devotion, the joy of liberty, the shout of gladness, the re-echoing of joy. "

Many complaints from prudent and pious men reached the Pope about the omission of psalms, which took away from those bound to recite the Office not only helps, well suited for God's praises and for the expression of their inmost souls, but also diminished that desirable variety in prayers which is so appreciated and which so well accords with and aids our worthy, attentive, and devout praise of God. For St. Basil says that "in smooth uniformity the soul often grows weary and while present is yet away, but when in psalmody and chant are changed and varied in every hour, the fervour is renewed and its attention is restored. "

5. This matter of the reform of the order of the psalter was brought before the Holy See by many bishops and chiefly in the Vatican Council, where the demand for the old custom of reciting the whole psalter weekly was renewed, with the provision that any new arrangement should not impose a greater onus on the clergy, now labouring more arduously in the vineyard of the sacred ministry on account of the diminution of toilers. These requests and wishes were

repeated to Pope Pius X., and he took up the matter cautiously, so that the honour due to the cult of the saints should not be diminished, nor the onus on the clergy increased by the weekly recitation of the full Psalter. Begging the help of God, the pontiff formed a commission of learned and industrious men, who with judgment and care carried out his wishes. The results of their labours were submitted to the Sacred Congregation of Rites, and after careful consideration by the members of the Congregation the matter was submitted to the Pope, who sanctioned the new arrangement, that is, as regards the order and the division of the Psalms, Antiphons, Versicles and Hymns, with the rubrics and rules pertaining to the same. And the Pope ordered an authentic edition of these new arrangements to be prepared and issued from the Vatican Press.

6. The arrangement of the Psalter has an intimate connection with the Divine Office and the Liturgy; and by these new decrees regarding the Office and the Psalms a first step in the improvement of the Breviary and the Missal has been taken. These matters will be dealt with by a commission of learned men which is soon to be formed. Amongst other things that this first step established was that the recitation of the Scripture lessons with the proper responses according to the rubrics should receive due honour and more frequent recitation, and that in the Liturgy the most ancient Masses of the Sundays throughout the year, especially those of Lent, should be restored to their places.

7. The use of the old order of Psalms found in the Roman Breviary is abolished and interdicted from 1st January, 1913, and the use of the new Psalter for all clergy, secular and regular, who used the Roman Breviary as revised by Pius V., Clement VIII., Urban VIII., and Leo XIII., and those who continue to use the old order do not satisfy their obligation.

8. Ecclesiastical superiors are to introduce the new order of the Psalter, and chapters are permitted to use it if the majority of the members agree to its introduction.

9. Establishment and declaration of the validity and efficacy of the Bull, notwithstanding all previous apostolic constitutions and rulings, whether general or particular. Any person infringing these papal abolitions, revocations, etc., sins and merits God's anger.

10. Date and place of promulgation.

SECTION II.

THE YEAR AND ITS PARTS.

The Council of Trent, Sess. XXIII., c. 18, orders *"ut in disciplina ecclesiastica clerici commodius instituantur grammaticas, cantus, computi ecclesiastici, aliarumque bonarum artium disciplinam discant. "* The minute study of the ecclesiastical calendar is not now so necessary for each priest, as it was centuries ago. The *Ordo Divini Officii recitandi,* issued yearly, and prepared with great accuracy, relieves priests of much labour and secures them from many doubts. And the decision of the Congregation of Rites (13th January, 1899) regarding the authority of the *ordo* gives greater security. *"Qui probabilius judicat errare Calendarium tenetur eidem Calend. stare, nec potest proprio inhaerere judicio quoad officium, Missam vel colorem Paramentorum. "* Of course this decision does not apply to errors which are *openly* and *plainly* at variance with the rubrics of the Missal and Breviary. However, it may be well to revise and to recall the student days' lessons on the Church's Calendar. The study is not an easy one, and in labouring to be brief, probably, I may be obscure and incomplete.

"Annus menses habet duodecim... " says the Breviary. The year has twelve months, fifty-two weeks plus one day, or 365 days and almost six hours. But these six hours make up a day every four years, and this fourth year is called bisextile.

In making calculations the six hours were taken as six complete hours, and not six hours wanting some minutes. And the aggregate miscalculation continued until the minutes added yearly, amounted to ten days and changed the date of the spring equinox. Pope Gregory XIII. (1572-1585) sought to remedy the error. He re-established the spring equinox to the place fixed by the Council of Nice (787). The year had fallen ten days in arrear from the holding of the Council until the year of the Gregorian correction, 1582. He again fixed it to the day arranged by the Council, the 14th of the Paschal moon. And he arranged, that such a time-derangement should not occur again. He omitted ten full days in October, 1582, so that the fourth day of the month was followed immediately by the fifteenth. He determined that the secular year must begin on 1st January, that three leap years should be omitted in every four centuries, e.g., 1700, 1800, 1900, 2100, and his arrangement has been observed throughout nearly the whole world.

Quarter Tenses fall on the Wednesdays, Fridays, and Saturdays after the third Sunday of Advent, after the first Sunday of Lent; after Pentecost Sunday, and after the feast of the exaltation of the Cross.

The Nineteen Years' Course of the Golden Number. This course or cycle was invented by an Athenian astronomer about 433 B. C. It was not exact, but was hailed with delight by the Greeks, who adorned their temples with the key number, done in gold figures; hence the name. The cycle of course is the revolution of nineteen years, from 1 to 19. When this revolution or course of years is run there is a new beginning in marking, No. 1, e. g., in the year 1577 the nineteenth number, the golden number, was 1; the following year it was 2, and so on until in 1597 the golden number again is 2. A table given in the Breviary shows how the golden number may be found and a short rule for the finding of it in any year is given. To the number of the year (e. g., 1833) add 1; then divide the sum thus resulting by 19 and the remainder is the golden number; if there be no remainder the golden number is 19.

EPACTS AND NEW MOONS.

The Epact (Greek [Greek: epaktos] from [Greek: eapgo] I add) is nothing more than the number of days by which the common solar year of 365 days exceeds the common lunar year of 354 days. So that the epact of the first year is 11, because the common solar year exceeds the common lunar year by 11 days, and these added to the 11 days of the first, produce 22 as the epact. At the end of the second year the new moon falls 22 days sooner than in the first year. The epact of the third year is three, because if 11 be added to the 22, the result is 33, and from this 33 we subtract 30 days which make up a lunar embolism and the remainder gives us 3, the epact for the year, and so on.

In the Breviary there is a table (*alia Tabella epactarum*) corresponding to the golden numbers from the year 1901 to the year 2000 inclusive. To take away all doubt in the use of this table, a new table of epacts, an example may be quoted. In the year 1901 the epact was X, which is placed under the golden number 2; and new moons appear on the 21st January, 19th February, and 21st March.... Again, in 1911 the epact is not marked by a number, but by an asterisk (see Table in Breviary) which is placed under the golden number 12, and in the calendar for the whole year will indicate the new moon on January 1st, January 31st (for in February there is no new moon indicated in the Table; the sign [*] is not found), on March 1st, March 31st, and on April 29th. In the year 1916 the golden number is 17 and the epact is 25 (written not in Roman numerals but in ordinary figures), the new moons occur on 6th January, 4th February, 6th March, 4th April, etc. For when the epact is 25, corresponding with golden numbers greater than the number 11 in the calendar, we must take in computation the epact 25 (written in modern figures) but where the epact corresponds with numbers less than the number 11, in the *tabella, the epact* XXV. in Roman numerals must be taken in calendar countings. This change takes place with epact 25 only, so that the computation of the lunar years may more closely respond to the solar year. It is for this cause, too, that in six places in the calendar two epacts, XXV. and XXIV., are given.

The new Breviary contains a *tabella* of Dominical letters, up to the year 2000 A. D. It needs no comment.

Indiction. Indiction was a cycle of fifteen years, the first of which dated from the third year of the Christian era. It was usual to indicate the number of the year in a cycle and no mention was made of the cycles already completed. Thus, the *indictio sexta* meant the sixth year of a cycle and not the sixth cycle or period of fifteen years. Hence, to know the year of indiction is useless for determining the date in old documents of State. Indiction was instituted by Constantine in 313 for fiscal purposes. In papal and imperial documents the name of Pope or emperor was generally given and the regnal years noted.

Movable Feasts. In virtue of the decree of the Council of Nice, in 325, Easter, on which all other movable feasts depend, must be celebrated on the Sunday which follows immediately the fourteenth day of the moon of the first month (in the Hebrew year), our March. Easter, then, is the first Sunday after the Paschal full moon (i. e., the full moon which happens upon or next after March 21st). If full moon happens on a Sunday, Easter Sunday is the Sunday after the full moon. The matter of the arrangement of Easter was for long a subject of very bitter contention in the Irish and in the English Church. The Irish, clinging tenaciously to the calendar of St. Patrick, carried it everywhere in their missionary labours, so that the controversy was not confined to Ireland and England. It was long and bitter, until at last the Irish Church agreed to follow the reform. (See Healy, *Ireland's Schools and Scholars*, p. 592; Moran, *Irish Saints in Great Britain*, "The Conference at Whitby in 664, " pp. 255-261).

Calendar study is interesting, and many valuable contributions on this matter have been given to us by Father Thurston, S.J., and other English and Irish scholars.

GENERAL RUBRICS OF THE BREVIARY.

The next document in the Breviary, Part I., has the title "Rubricae Generates Breviarii, " the general rubrics of the Breviary. They are called *general*, as they apply to every part of the Breviary and are to be distinguished from the rubrics dealing with the proper (*proprium*) of the Breviary, the proper of time or of the saints. The word "rubrics" was originally applied to the red marking lines used by carpenters on wood, later it referred to the titles used by jurisconsults in announcing laws, which were written in red colours. The word appears in Church literature to refer to signs and directions as early at least as the fourteenth century (*Cath. Encyclopedia*—word "rubrics").

The general rubrics are divided into thirty-seven Titles. Attention will be given to each; of these Titles, some of which must be modified by recent legislation. The order followed may not be the order followed in the general rubrics as given in the Breviary, as matters treated in the general rubrics found in the Breviary are treated under other headings here. However, a look at the table of contents or at the index shows the pages treating of these Titles.

TITLE I. THE DOUBLE OFFICE.

"Consequently, the civilised peoples already in remote antiquity have found a call to the worship of God in the changing seasons and times and so have introduced sacred seasons. Sacred times and places are common to all religions in general. The change of times bringing with them corresponding changes in nature made a religious impression upon mankind. In turn, man sanctified certain times and dedicated them to God, and these days, thus consecrated to God, became festivals. "

The entire number of ecclesiastical holydays and seasons is codified for us in the different Church calendars. Their contents fall into two essentially different divisions, each possessing an entirely different origin and history. The first division consists of festivals of our Lord, distributed over the year, regulated and co-ordinated in accordance with certain laws. The second division consists of commemorations of saints in no wise connected with festivals of our Lord or with one another. Occupying to some extent an intermediate position between these two chief divisions come the festivals of our Blessed Lady, which have this in common with the festivals of the saints, that they fall on fixed days; but, on the other hand, they are to a certain extent connected with each other and with some feasts of our Lord. This is carried out in such a way that they are distributed throughout the Church year and are included in each of the festal seasons (Kellner, *Heortology*, Part I.).

From Apostolic times the feasts of Easter, the Ascension and Pentecost were celebrated. In the second century feasts of the Apostles were celebrated and the cult of the Martyrs was of speedy and widespread development. But it was not, probably, till the fourth century, that the feasts of saints who were not martyrs were celebrated.

Origin of the different grades of feasts. To-day, we find Church festivals arranged in three grades, doubles, semi-doubles and simples, and it is very difficult, to determine clearly and accurately the origin and the nature of the arrangements. But from the works of scholars, who have studied this matter, the following may be considered as a fair and accurate summing up: —

In the first ages of the Church the Apostles and Martyrs only were commemorated in public prayers and, above all, in the Mass, perhaps, by a special prayer. Then, in time, followed the reading of a panegyric in their honour, and later still hymns and histories of martyrdom were added to the public recitation of the Office. Still later, there were added the feasts of the saints with an office resembling our simple office. Matins were entirely ferial, but had either a biography of the saint or a long extract from the Fathers added. The other hours were as in a Sunday office, save that these feasts had no Vesper matter.

In still later times, the Church added to the list of names on her saint roll, the names of saints who were honoured neither as Apostles nor as Martyrs. For these, special Masses, offices and feasts were established. St. Martin of Tours was the first confessor so honoured in the Western Church. For the more important feasts, an office of nine lessons was established and this came to be known as a semi-double office, and later such feasts were called doubles. Hence, before the thirteenth century, we find celebrations of simple feasts, of semi-doubles and of doubles. And Durandus, who wrote in the thirteenth century, tells us of the existence of doubles major and doubles minor. The Breviary of St. Pius V., published in 1568, gives three classes of doubles: doubles of the first class, doubles of the second class, and doubles per annum. But, in the revision by Clement VIII. the doubles per annum were again divided into doubles major and doubles minor. In the new Pian Breviary (1913) doubles are divided into Primary Doubles of the First Class, Secondary Doubles of the First Class; Primary Doubles of the Second Class, Secondary Doubles of the Second Class, Primary Doubles Major, Secondary Doubles Major. The list of feasts under each of these six headings may be seen in the Breviary.

Do double offices differ specifically from each other? No, the form is the same in all double offices. What then is the difference between doubles of different classes? The difference is chiefly in the preference which is given to them in cases of concurrence or occurrence of feasts of greater or of lesser rite.

The word "double" (*duplex*) is derived, some authors hold, from the ancient custom of reciting two offices or saying two Masses on the same day—one for the current feria and one for the feast (*festa*). Other authors say that the word is derived from the ancient practice of chanting twice or in repetition the complete responses and versicles. And, above all, the recitation of the full antiphons before and after each psalm, at Matins, Lauds and Vespers, was called "duplication, " and this name, it is said, was given to the office (double, duplex) in which the practice of duplication took place.

It is often asked why are there different grades of feasts. Three reasons are given by writers on liturgy. First, to mark the diversity of merit in God's saints, their sanctity and their different degrees of service to His Church. Second, to mark their different degrees of glory in Heaven. "One is as the sun; another, the glory of the moon; and another the glory of the stars. For star differs from star" (1 *Cor.*). Third, for some special national or local reasons—e. g., patron of a country.

The rules laid down in the general rubrics in the new Breviary, for doubles and semi-doubles, are left unchanged almost by the regulations laid down by the Commission and by the *Variationes*. Their numbers were reduced, so that there now stand in the new

Breviary only seventy-five doubles, sixty-three semi-doubles, and thirty-six movable feasts.

A reason for the new arrangement of double feasts in the Pian Breviary is the general one, that the Pope wished above all things the weekly recitation of the Psalter, and to bring about this weekly recitation and the restoration of the Sunday Office a mere rearrangement of the Psalms was quite insufficient, and a rearrangement of the gradation of feasts of concurrence and of occurrence was necessary.

TITLE II. —THE OFFICE OF A SEMI-DOUBLE.

Etymology, nature and synonyms. The word semi-double (*semi-duplex*) is derived from the Latin; and some writers hold that the word indicates feasts which are of lower rank and solemnity than double feasts. Others hold that it means simply, feasts holding a place between double feasts and simple feasts. Most writers on liturgy hold that on some days a double office—one of the feast and one of the feria—was held, and that in order to shorten this double recitation there was said a composite office, partly of the saint's office and partly of the feria; and they say that from this practice arose the term semi-double, or half-double.

Synonyms for the term "semi-duplex, " are "non-duplex, " "office of nine lessons. "

1. The antiphons are not doubled in a semi-double office.

2. The Sundays of the year, excepting Easter Sunday, Low Sunday, Pentecost and Trinity, are said according to the semi-double rite. In the new Breviaries the Psalms for Matins are only nine in number, instead of the eighteen of the older book.

3. The versicles, antiphons, responses, preces and suffrages of saints, which are recited in semi-double offices, are given below under their own titles.

TITLE III. —THE SIMPLE OFFICE.

Etymology, nature and *synonyms.* The word *simple* comes from the Latin *simplex*, to indicate the least solemn form of office and it is the direct opposite in meaning to the term "double. " It is synonymous with the term so often found in liturgical works, the office of three lessons.

This form of office is of great antiquity, going back to the fifth century. In the early ages of the Church and down to the fourteenth century the simple office consisted of the ferial office with lessons, antiphons and prayers. But in the end of the fourteenth century, simples came to be celebrated in the same manner as semi-doubles, with nine lessons and their nocturns, and in case of occurrence were transferred. As a result the offices of Sunday and the ferial offices were practically crushed out of the Breviary. The Commission of Reform applied an easy remedy, by restoring simple feasts to their ancient place and status. Now, they are not to be transferred; but in case of occurrence with a feast of higher rite they are merely commemorated.

These feasts have first Vespers only. At Matins, the nine psalms and three lessons are said as one nocturn. The psalms in semi-double feasts are from the Psalter under the day of the week on which the feast is celebrated. *"In quolibet alio Festo duplici etiam major, vel semi duplici vel simplici et in Feriis Tempore Paschali, semper dicantur Psalmi, cum antiphonis in omnibus Horis, et versibus ad matutinum, ut in Psalterio de occurrente hebdomadae die"* (Tit, I. sec, 3. *Additiones et Variationes*).

In commemorations in the Office, the versicle, response, antiphon and collect of a semi-double is made *after* the following commemorations (if they should have a place in the recitation of the day).

(1) Any Sunday, (2) a day within the privileged octave of the Epiphany or Corpus Christi, (3) an octave day, (4) a great double, (5) a lesser double. Of course the first commemoration is always of the concurring office except it be a day within a non-privileged octave, or a simple. In reckoning the order of precedence between feasts which occur on the same day, lists given in *The New Psalter and its Use*, p. 108, show that thirteen grades of feast stand before the feasts of semi-double rite. And in the order of precedence as to Vespers, between feasts which are in occurrence, these feasts stand in the eleventh place, being preceded by (1) doubles of the first class of the universal Church, (2) lesser doubles.

TITLE IV. —SUNDAY.

We translate the Latin *Dies Dominica* by our word Sunday, for in English the days of the week have retained the names given to them in Pagan times. In Irish, too, Deluain, Monday, moon's day, shows Pagan origin of names of week days.

The literal translation of the Latin *Dies Dominica*, the Lord's Day, is not found in the name given to the first day of the week in any European tongue, save Portuguese, where the days of the week hold the old Catholic names, *domingo, secunda feira, terca feira*, etc. It is said that the seven days of the week as they stand in numerical order were retained and confirmed by Pope Silvester I. (314-336): "*Sabbati et Dominici diei nomine retento, reliquos hebdomadae dies Feriarum nomine distinctos, ut jam ante in Ecclesia vocari coeperunt appellari voluit; quo significaretur quotidie clericos, abjecta caeterarum rerum cura, uni Deo prorsus vocare debere*" (*Brev. Rom.* in VI. lect. St. Silvester Pope; 31st Dec.).

There is no evidence of the abrogation of the Sabbath by Christ or by His Apostles, but St. Paul declared that its observance was not binding on Gentile converts. Accordingly, in the very early days of Christianity the Sabbath fell more and more into the background, yet not without leaving some traces behind it (see art. *Sonnabender* in Kraut's *Realenzyklop*). Among Christians the first day of the Jewish week, the *prima Sabbati*, the present Sunday, was held in honour as the day of our Lord's resurrection and was called the Lord's Day (Apoc. i. 10; I. Cor, xvi. 2), This name, *dies dominica*, took the place of *dies solis*, formerly used in Greece and in Rome. This day has many names in the works of Christian writers. St. Ignatius, M. calls it *Regina omnium dierum*; St. Chrysostom, *dies pacis*; *dies lucis*; Alcuin, *dies sanctus*; *feria prima*, Baronius tells us, was another name for our Sunday.

The subject of the liturgical celebration of the Lord's Day has been a great study and a problem to modern scholars. It appears that in the first ages of the Church, Sunday was a day of solemn reunion and of common prayer. St. Justin, in his second apology, writes that on the Lord's Day town and country met together at an appointed place for sacrifice, for the hearing of the word of God, for pious readings and for common prayer. This common, prayer consisted largely in the recitation of the Psalms, hymns and prayers, of what are called the Sunday Office. This office was nearly always the same in psalms, in hymns and in every part; so that Sunday after Sunday, for many years, there was very little change in the Sunday united-prayer part of the liturgy, although the preaching on the incidents of the life of our Lord (Beckel, *Messe und Pascha*, p, 91), the blessings and the thanksgivings relieved the service from monotonous sameness.

A nocturn, a round of Psalms, was said on Saturday night by the vigilants preparing for the Sunday services. Before the eighth century two other short nocturns were added. This addition, which was copied from the monastic practice, built up the three nocturn form of office and became the model and form of the office for saints. "There is good reason for believing that originally the Divine Office formed part of the Mass. The *synaxis*, for which the early Christians assembled by night, consisted of the 'breaking of bread, ' preceded by the singing of psalms and hymns, litanies and collects, readings, homilies, invocations and canticles. This was the whole official liturgical prayer, apart, of course, from private prayer" (Dom Cabrol, *Day Hours of the Church*, Introduction, p. xvi).

One of the chief objects of Pope Pius X. in his reform was the restoration of the liturgical importance of the Sunday office, the office of the Lord's Day, and, therefore, in its own right, superior to the saints' feasts by which it had been displaced from its special office, psalms and lessons. And this could only be effected by a change in the rules of occurrence, and in Title IV. (*De Festorum occurentia*, etc., section 2) we find the new rule for restoring Sunday offices to their proper liturgical rights.

In Title IV., sect, 1 (see Breviary, Additiones and Variationes) there is no change in the old rubric. The eight Sundays of the first class exclude every other feast. And the Sundays of the second class only give place to a double of the first class and then are commemorated at Lauds, Vespers and Mass, and have the ninth lesson in Matins.

But section 2 (*Dominicis minoribus*)... goes to the root of the matter of the new change in the rules for Sunday's liturgical office. The ordinary Sundays ranked as semi-doubles and hence their Mass and Office was superseded by the Mass and Office of some occurring feast. The length of the Sunday office, in the breviaries until lately in use, made many hearts rejoice over the occurring feast. But the almost total omission of the ancient and beautiful Sunday Masses was a misfortune and, in a sense, an unbecoming practice, which broke away from ancient liturgical rule and tradition. The abbreviation of the Sunday office in the new breviaries and the rule laid down in Title IV., sect. 2, restore Sunday's office and Sunday's Mass to their old and proper dignity.

The general rule laid down is that on Sundays throughout the year the proper office of the Sunday shall always be said. The exceptions are (1) Feasts of our Lord and their octaves, (2) Doubles of the first class, (3) Doubles of the second class. On these days the office will be the office of the feast, with commemoration in Lauds, Vespers and Mass. Henceforth Sundays are divided into:

(1) Sundays of the first class, which exclude all feasts;

(2) Sundays of the second class, which exclude all feasts save doubles of the first class;

(3) The ordinary Sundays, which exclude all but doubles of the first or second class, feasts of our Lord, and their octave days.

The date of Easter is the pivot of Calendar construction. Before Easter come the Sundays of Lent and Quinquagesima, Sexagesima, Septuagesima Sundays. Septuagesima cannot fall earlier than the eighteenth day of January, nor later than the twenty-second day of February. Hence, in some years there are fewer "Sundays after the Epiphany" than in others, owing to the dates of Easter and Septuagesima. The smaller the number of Sundays after Epiphany the greater is the number of Sundays after Pentecost. If the number of Sundays after Pentecost be twenty-five, the twenty-fourth Sunday will have the office of the sixth Sunday after Epiphany. If there be twenty-six Sundays after Pentecost, the twenty-fourth Sunday will have the office of the fifth after Epiphany, and the twenty-fifth will have that of the fifth Sunday; the twenty-sixth will be the sixth Sunday's office. It should be remembered that the Sunday called the twenty-fourth after Pentecost is *always* celebrated immediately before the first Sunday of Advent, even though it should not be even the twenty-third Sunday after Pentecost.

TITLE V. —FERIAL OFFICE.

Etymology and different signification of the word *Feria*. The word is derived probably from the Latin *feriari* (to rest). Among the Romans, the idea of a day of rest and a holy day was intimately united and received the name of *feria*. But it was amongst the Hebrews that the day set apart for the worship of God received the most distinctive character as day of rest (*Heortology*, p. 2). Hence the early Christians called the days of the week *feriae*.

Why did the Church adopt the word *feriae*? She wished to mark the day of the week and not to name them by their pagan name (*e. g.*, *dies lunae*) nor by their Jewish names (*e. g.*, *prima sabbati*), which should be a sort of recognition of the dead and dying synagogue. Hence she adopted the word *feria*, to denote the Christian rest in the Lord, the Christian peace and the abstinence from all sin, and that each and every day should be consecrated to God. The Christian use of the word is found in Origen (185-254) and was fully established in the time of Tertullian.

In the time of Amalare (circa 830) the ferial office had taken a well-defined form, Matins having twelve psalms and six antiphons. In Lauds of every *feria* were recited the psalms, *Miserere; Deus, Deus meus; Deus misereatur nostri*; a canticle drawn from a prophet and varying each day of the week (*e. g.*, *Confitebor*, Isaias xii., for Monday's Lauds; *Ego dixi*, Isaias xxxviii., for Tuesday's Lauds, etc., and the two psalms *Laudate* (148, 150) and the *Cantate*, psalm 149). In the small hours the Sunday psalms without antiphons were recited. Vespers had daily, fixed psalms. At each hour the *Kyrie Eleison* and ferial *prayers* were said on bended knees and the hours terminated — as do the hours of Holy Week still — with *Pater Noster and Miserere*.

Ferias are divided into three classes, major ferias, privileged ferias and non-privileged. Ash Wednesday and the three last days of Holy Week are the major ferias which are privileged and exclude all feasts (*vide* Tit. II., sec. 2). Non-privileged feriae are the feriae of Lent and Advent, Quarter Tense or Ember days and Rogation Monday. They take precedence of simple feasts only.

In the ferial office nine psalms are said, and not twelve, as in the old order of the Breviary. The psalms found arranged in the new Breviary for three nocturns are to be said with nine antiphons up to the versicle of third nocturn — the versicle of the first and second being omitted (Tit. I., sec. 7). Hence the psalms are to be said straight through (*sine interuptione*) omitting in the first two nocturns, the versicle and response, Pater Noster, absolutions and all pertaining to the lessons. This simplifies things and makes the ferial office shorter than the office of feasts.

TITLE VI. —THE OFFICE OF VIGILS.

Etymology, nature and synonyms. The word *vigil* is from the Latin *vigilare, to keep awake, to watch,* because in old times the night before any great event, religious or worldly, was spent in watching. Thus, the night prior to ordination to the priesthood, the night prior to a great battle, was spent in watching before the altar. Hence, the word vigil came to mean the prayers said during the time of watching or waking, preparatory to the great event. It signified, too, the fast accompanying the watching, and lastly it came to mean the liturgical office of Mass and Breviary fixed for the time of vigilance. In the Roman Church it was sometimes called the nocturn or night office. The Greeks call the vigil *profesta,* the time before the feast.

The custom existed among the pagans, almost universally, before the time of Christ. The Jews practised this ancient night prayer, as the scripture in several places shows, *"in noctibus extollite manus vestras in sancta"* (Psalm 133). Our Saviour sanctified this use by His example, and the early Christians were, on account of these night assemblies, the objects of fear and dread, of admiration and of hatred. Organised vigils lasted till the thirteenth century in some countries, but owing to abuses and discord they became not a source of edification, but the occasion and cause of grave scandals, and were forbidden gradually and universally. The Church now retains for the faithful one congregational vigil, the vigil of Christmas. Formerly, it was customary to observe a fast on a day or night of a vigil, but that custom was suppressed sometimes, or fell into disuse. Vigil fasts are now few. Almost the only relic of the vigil now remaining is the Mass and Office.

When were vigils held? In the early ages they were held only on Saturday nights and on nights preceding great solemnities or the festivals of the Martyrs. The early converts, if they had been pagans, knew few or no prayer formulae, and very little of the psalms was learned by them even in their Christian practice. But Jews who became Christians knew psalms and hymns and prayers. So that in the early Christian vigils, there was no attempt made at reciting the Divine Office, and the custom of such recitation was not introduced until about 220 A. D. and was not obligatory (Duchesne, *Christian Worship,* Chap. VIII.).

It is difficult to speak with certainty about the hour of beginning or the hour of ending these vigil services. Some think that the first nocturn was said about 9 p. m. Lauds was said before sunrise and hence was called *Laudes-matutinae*. But "after the middle of the ninth century, we gather from contemporary documents, that the office of vigils was, as a whole, regularly constituted and well known" (Baudot, p. 64). These vigils were held in cenacles or upper rooms of houses. During the days of persecution these meetings were not infrequent and were held secretly in crypts, catacombs, private houses and at martyrs' tombs. In times of peace they were held everywhere, in churches, monasteries, castles.

Vigils are divided into two classes, major and minor; major vigils are the vigils of Christmas, Epiphany and Pentecost, and they are called privileged vigils and are celebrated as semi-doubles. The vigils of Christmas and Pentecost are privileged vigils of the first class. The vigil of Epiphany is a privileged vigil of the second class. All others are minor or non-privileged vigils.

TITLE VII. -OCTAVES.

Etymology and nature. The word "octave" is from the Latin *octavus* (eighth) because, in the early ages of Christianity, the Church celebrated the eighth day only after the celebration of the feast itself; not until the twelfth century was the custom of a commemoration on each of the eight days introduced. We have, probably, an example of this still in our Breviaries. The feast of St. Agnes is celebrated on 21st January and on 28th it is mentioned at Vespers and Lauds only, and the name in old Roman service books is *Octavo, S. Agnetis*. The origin of the octave is Jewish. We read in the Old Testament that God ordered that the Feasts of Pasch and Pentecost should be celebrated for eight days. So, too, the Feast of Tabernacles lasted for eight days, the first and eighth days being days of special celebration and devotion. The Christian Church adopted the method of showing great honour and glory to the principal festivals of the Christian year, to the great saints, the patrons of countries, dioceses, etc. But just as the calendar became overcrowded with saints' offices, which excluded almost entirely the Sunday and ferial offices, so, too, the additions of octaves created confusion and further tended to the exclusion of the old liturgical use of the Psalter and the supplanting of the Sunday and ferial offices. Hence, in the *Motu Proprio Abhinc duos annos*, the octaves of the calendar are divided into three great classes, privileged, common and simple. Privileged octaves are further divided into three *orders*. Those of the first order are the octaves of Easter and Pentecost; the octaves of Epiphany and Corpus

Christi belong to the second order, and the octaves of the Nativity and Ascension belong to the third. The Christmas octave admits feasts of saints, but the octaves of Epiphany, Easter and Pentecost do not admit any feasts (Tit. V., sec, 3). A day within an octave has a right to first Vespers, and the antiphon and response should be from first Vespers (S. C.R., June, 1905). But the feast of the day falling within octave has a right to first and second Vespers. The exceptions are, when at second Vespers of St. Thomas, the office of the octave of the Nativity to be observed on 30th December has to be commemorated again, in octaves like octaves of Epiphany when each day has its proper antiphon at the *Magnificat*, and again on and July in second Vespers of Visitation the office of St. Peter and Paul is to be commemorated. In octaves the suffrages of saints and the Athanasian Creed are not said. When feasts of the Universal Church, which are celebrated with an octave are perpetually transferred to the next day, because of a perpetual impediment, according to the rubrics, the octave day is not therefore perpetually transferred but ought to be kept as in the Universal Church on its own day.

TITLE VIII. —OFFICE OF THE BLESSED VIRGIN FOR SATURDAY.

"In omnibus Sabbatis per annum entra Adventum et Quadragesimam, ac nisi Quatuor Tempora aut Vigiliae ocurrant, " etc. In all Saturdays throughout the year, except on the Saturdays of Advent, Lent, Ember Days or occurring Vigils, or unless a feast of nine lessons has to be said on the Saturday, then it is laid down in the rubrics that the Office of the Blessed Virgin should always be said with the rite of a simple office. The rubrics of the New Psalter (Title I., sec. 6) direct, *"In officio Sanctae Mariae in Sabbato et in festis simplicibus sic officium persolvendum est; ad matutinum, Invitatorium et hymnus dicuntur de eodem officio vel de iisdem Festis; Psalmi cum suis antiphonis et versu de Feria occurente I. et II. Lectis de Feria cum Responsoriis Propriis vel de Communi. III. vero lectio de officio vel Festo duabus lectionibus in unum junctis si quando duae pro Festo habeatur, ad reliquas autem Horas omnia dicuntur, prouti supra num. 5 in Festis Duplicibus expositum est. "* In the Office of the Blessed Virgin for Saturdays (Decree S. C.R., 26th January. 1916) the antiphons and Psalms at Matins, Lauds and small Hours are to be said from the Saturday and from the *capitulum* onwards all is to be taken from the office of the Blessed Virgin.

This office is not to be confounded with the *officium parvum Beatae Mariae.* The office *de Sabbato* is obligatory throughout the Church. The *officium parvum* was only for choir use, an addition to the office of the day. Saturday, dedicated to the Blessed Virgin, is of great antiquity, as the mention of it in the works of St. Peter Damien, St. Bernard and Pope Benedict XIII. shows, but as to the time of its origin or a history of its growth, little seems to be known. At first the cult consisted in various and voluntary prayers and practices. About the middle of the fourteenth century an office was composed for recital on Saturdays as dedicated to the Mother of God. The office in our Breviaries was composed by St. Pius V, (1566-1572).

TITLE IX, —COMMEMORATIONS.

The rules laid down in the general rubrics of the Breviary for commemorations were never very simple, and when we read the changes brought about in *De ratione Divini officii recitandi juxta novum Psalteri ordinem*, Titles II., III., IV., V., VI., with' the decrees of the Congregation (January, 1912), and subsequently (*Abhinc duos Annos*) everyone must fear to tread the maze with certainty and must often fall back gratefully on the labours of the compilers of the *Ordo* which he follows. Or, perhaps, doubts may be dispelled by *The New Psalter* (Burton and Myers) published in 1912. The chapter on the Calendar in that book is worth study, but needs now additions and corrections, owing to the issue of more recent decrees.

In the study of commemorations and translations of feasts there are two words which have a special meaning and which, being often used in calendar working, deserve a special note. They are "occurrence" and "concurrence. " *Occurrence* is the conjunction of two or more offices, which fall on the same day. It may be accidental when two movable feasts are concerned or when a movable feast falls on a day which has a fixed office; or it may be perpetual, when a fixed office falls on a day which already has a fixed office. The Church does not ask the recitation of a double or a triple office. She, by her fixed rules, prefers one out of the two of the "occurring" offices, transfers if possible the others, or at least commemorates them by an antiphon, versicle and prayer, and sometimes by a ninth lesson at Matins.

Concurrence is the conjunction of two offices, which succeed one another, so that a question arises as to which feast the Vespers belong to; whether to the feast of the day or to the feast of the following day, or whether the psalms should be of the feast and the remaining part of the Vespers should be as the *Ordo* so often notes (*a cap. de seq.*), from the *capitulum* the office is taken from the following feast.

The new rubrics contain five titles which make certain modifications in the rules hitherto observed. We thus obtain a ready made division of the subject: —

(1) Of the precedence of Feasts (Title II.). (2) Of the accidental occurrence of feasts and their translation (Title III.). (3) Of the perpetual occurrence of feasts and their transfer (Title V.). (4) Of the occurrence of feasts (Title V.). (5) Of the commemorations (Title VI.) (Myers and Burton, *op. cit.*).

The new rubrics without the aid of any commentator give pretty clear notions of the laws of precedence, occurrence and commemoration. For students in college these rules are expounded in detail with additions, changes, exceptions. But for priests, long past the student stage, it is difficult to undo the fixed liturgy lore of their student and early priest life; and the need of such a book as *The New Psalter and its Uses* is, for those interested, a necessity. Even since the publication of that book, changes have been made. For example, doubles, major or minor and semi-doubles, which were perpetually excluded on their own day were transferred to some fixed day. This is given in *The New Psalter and its Uses*. But this has now been changed. In the case of feasts of the universal Church, no translation is allowed now. But feasts proper to a nation, diocese, order, institute or particular church may still be transferred to a fixed day, if perpetually impeded on their own day. Another example of necessary changes in that excellent book is in the last paragraph of page 136 (see Decree S. C.R., June, 1912). The works of compilers and liturgists need constant revision to keep pace with new decisions and decrees.

In making commemorations, the order of the commemoration as laid down in the *Ordo* should be followed. Elements of a commemoration are the Antiphon of the *Benedictus* or the *Magnificat* with versicle and response. These antiphons are considered most excellent, preceding as they do the Gospel canticles (St. Luke I.). The antiphon, versicle and prayer of the commemoration at an hour should never be repetitions of others said in the same hour. Thus, if in the office of a confessor pontiff having the prayer *Da quaesumus*, another confessor pontiff's feast, commemorated in the same hour, should not have the same prayer. About the prayer, or, as it is called, the collect, the following should be noted: first, the commemoration is omitted if the prayer of the office which is being recited and the prayer of the feast to be commemorated have the same object. Thus, a feast of the Blessed Virgin, falling within the octave of the Assumption, should not be commemorated. Second, where a commemoration for a saint or saints of title similar to that of the saints whose office is being said, is to be made, the Congregation of Rites (5th May, 1736) arranged that not even the versicles and response be repeated and that the following order be observed: —

IN VESPERS—

1st Com. made by Antiphon and Versicle of Lauds. 2nd Com. made by Antiphon of second Vesper and Ver. of II. Nocturn. 3rd Com. made by Antiphon of I. Noct. and Vers. of III. Nocturn.

IN LAUDS—

1st Com. made by Antiphon and Vers. from first Vesp. 2nd Com. made by Antiphon I. Noct., and Ver., III. Noct. 3rd Com. made by Antiphon II. Vesp., Vers., II. Noct.

If it should happen in commemorating a day within an octave that the versicle from the common had already been taken for the office, then the rule is "*Sumenda est in laudibus antiphona de secundis Vesperis; et pro secundis Vesperis antiphona de laudibus in utroque tamen casu cum v. de primis Vesperis*" (S. C.R., 18th Dec., 1779). In the above given form of making commemorations it may be noted that the second commemoration in Lauds is made up from the versicles and response of Matins and not from second Vespers, so as to avoid repeating in Lauds what was said at Vespers (Cavalieri).

As regards prayers in the office the reminder that the same formula must not be repeated in the same hour may be supplemented. Because, prayers having all words identical, save one single word, are not considered in liturgy as different prayers (*e. g.*, *Accendamur exemplis; instruamur exemplis*, Feast of St. Philip and St. James, Feasts of several martyrs). So, too, prayers which have the same form of petition (e. g., the prayers on feast of St. Joseph and on feast of St. Mathew), are not considered as different and must not be repeated in the same hour. But where the petition is different, even though all the remainder of the prayers are similar in wording, they may be repeated in the same hour.

But what is to be done in offices where a commemoration prayer and the prayer of the office is from the common? What must be done where the feast is the feast of a Doctor and a commemoration of a Doctor is to be made? What is to be done when the office of the feast is of a virgin not a martyr, and a commemoration of a virgin not a martyr is to be made? In the first case the prayer from the office of a confessor or Pontiff should be said, adding to it the title of Doctor. In the other case, the prayer *Indulgentiam*, omitting the word *martyr*, is to be said.

The origin of these commemorations was, that the Popes in removing the solemn celebrations of certain feasts of Apostles and Martyrs, which were formerly of precept, provided that their *cultus* should not be forgotten, and that their commemoration in the office should remind priests and the faithful of those servants of God, whom the Church wishes ever to honour. I have said the order given for commemoration in the *Ordo* should be followed; but not to follow this order does not exceed a venial sin. Even the deliberate omission of a commemoration in Lauds or Vespers is not a violation of a grave precept.

TITLE X. — THE TRANSLATION OF FEASTS.

When several offices fall on the same day, only one office, the one of highest rank or most important, is said. The others are transferred or commemorated. The last section dealt with commemorations, and now we come to the difficult question of the translation of feasts. Title X. of the general rubrics must be read in connection with the Apostolic Constitution, *Divino Afflatu* (1911) and with the *Abhinc duos Annos* (1913).

Translation of a feast may mean the removal of a feast from an impeded day to a day which is free. Thus a feast of higher rank may fall on a feast day of a saint whose feast is of lower rank; the latter may then be transferred. Transference is either perpetual or accidental and temporary. The former applies to feasts which are always impeded by the meeting with a feast of higher rite on their fixed days. A feast which would fall on 6th January would suffer perpetual translation. This translation bears different names in rubrics, decrees and liturgical writings—*translatio ad diem, fixam, translatio ad diem assignatam, mutatio, etc.* Accidental translation means occasional transference, a transfer in one year and not in another.

Title II., section i, of the *Divino Afflatu* gives the characters of preferential rank which are to be considered in occurrence, concurrence or translation of feasts, *Ritus altior, ratio primarii aut secundarii, Dignitas Personalis, solemnitas externa.*

Although in the General Rubrics of the Breviary, the title *De Festorum praestantia* is not found, the four principles, (1)gradation of rite, (2)classification as a primary or secondary feast, (3)personal dignity, (4)external solemnity, are mentioned in the sixth section of Title X., *De Translatione Festorum*, and the degrees of personal dignity are added in the second section of Title XL, *de commemorationibus*. Before 1897 precedence, and hence transference, was settled first by the rank of the rite (Double major, etc.); then, too, between two feasts of the same rite, transference was settled by dignity and finally by solemnity. But in 1897 the Sacred Congregation of Rites indicated two further notes to be observed in the weighing of claims for transference, (1)the classification into primary and secondary feasts, (2)the distinction between fixed and movable feasts. This latter distinction—between fixed and movable feasts—has been suppressed by the new legislation and some changes made in the others.

I. *Gradation of Feasts* makes a distinction between doubles, semi-doubles and simples, and distinguishes the various kinds of doubles. The order of procedure will be—(1)Doubles of the first class, (2)doubles of the second class, (3)greater doubles, (4)doubles, (5)semi-doubles, (6)simples. But as the section shows (Tit. II., sec. i) this is subject to the privileges of certain Sundays, ferias, and octave days or even days within an octave. And hence, an ordinary Sunday, though! only a semi-double, will take precedence of a double; and an octave day, though only a double, takes precedence of a greater double.

II. Classification as a primary or a secondary feast. Tables of classification are to be found in the prefatory part of the new Breviary, under the headings *Tres Tabellae*. They give a revised list of feasts with their rank and rites. Some feasts are reduced from primary to secondary rank (e. g., Feast of the Dolours); and the tables give a new division of primary and secondary doubles and semi-doubles.

III. Thirdly, the order of precedence among feasts will be determined by the dignity of the person who is the special object of the office that is to be recited. Hence, in the order set down in General Rubrics (Title XI, *De Concurrentia officii*, sec. 2) all feasts of our Lord, other things being equal, take precedence of the feasts of our Lady. And then, in order, come the festivals of the angels, of St. John the Baptist, of St. Joseph, of the Apostles and other saints. Amongst the saints who are honoured as martyrs, confessors or virgins there is no precedence as to personal dignity.

IV. Lastly, there is the note of "external solemnity, " which may give precedence to one or two feasts, which are equal in the above-mentioned matters—i. e., in Gradation I., Classification II., Precedence III. But the main point is that only doubles of first and second class have the right, as a rule, of transference. Transference is now rather rare.

"From these rules it will be seen that in cases of concurrence, occurrence, perpetual transfer or translation, precedence between two feasts will first be decided by gradation of rite, a double of the first class being preferred to one of the second, and so on. If the feasts are of equal rank recourse must be had to the second test, the distinction between primary and secondary feasts. If both happen to be primary, or both are secondary, then precedence will be granted to the feast which has the greater personal dignity. And if both feasts should have the same dignity, then the fact of external solemnity would confer precedence" (*The New Psalter and its Uses*, p. 79). For practical help, a look at the first of the *Duae Tabellae* is a guide to find out which office is to be said, if more than one feast occur on the same day.

Before discussing new offices it may be well to remember that votive offices of all kinds, including the votive offices conceded by the decree of July, 1883, are abolished. These offices were drastic innovations, introduced to get rid of the very long psalm arrangement of the ferial office. The new distribution of the psalms got rid of the onus, and votive offices are no longer given in the Breviary.

TITLE XL—CONCURRENCE.

Concurrence is the conjunction of two offices which succeed each other, so that the question arises to which of the two are the Vespers of the day to be assigned. The origin of this conjunction of feasts was by some old writers traced to the Mosaic law in which the festivals, began in the evening, and they quote "from evening until evening you shall celebrate your sabbaths" (*Leviticus*, xxii. 32). The effect of concurrence may be that the whole vespers may belong to the feast of the day or may be said entirely from, the feast of the following day; or it may be that the psalms and antiphons belong to the preceding festival and the rest of the office be from the succeeding feast. The General Rubrics, Title XI, must be read now in conjunction with Titles IV., V., and VI. of the *Additiones et Variationes ad norman Bullae "Divino Afflatu"*. The rules for concurrence are given in Table III. of the *Tres Tabellae* inserted in the new Breviary (S. C.R., 23 January, 1912). These tables supersede the tables given in the old editions of the Breviary. The first of these two tables shows which office is to be said, if more than one feast occur on the same day, whether perpetually or accidentally. The second table is a guide to concurrence—*i. e.*, whether the first vespers of the following feast is to be said entirely without reference to the preceding feast, or if second vespers of the preceding feast is to be said entire, without reference to the following; or, again, first vespers of the following with commemoration of the preceding, or second vespers of the preceding with commemoration of the following, or vespers of the more noble feast with commemoration of the other—any of these may be the liturgical order to follow, and the *Tabella* makes things clear.

The "tables" are to be used thus: —Opening the Breviary at the *I Tabella, "Si occurrat eodem die, "* first find the number marked in that square in which the two feasts in question meet, and then read the direction printed, in column on same page to left-hand side, bearing the same number. For example: the question is about the occurrence of a Sunday of the first class and a Double of the first class. *Double of the first class* stands first word of page, and *Sunday of first class* will be found in column beneath the rows of figures. Now the square in which straight lines drawn from *double of first class* and *Sunday of first class* meet bears the number 6, and reference to number 6 in column of directions found on same page gives the rule, *"Officium de 2, Translatio de I, "* that is, the office must be of the Sunday of first class and the double of the first class must be transferred according to the rubrics. When in these brief directive notes, (1-8), mention is made of the "first or the preceding, " the reference is made to feast or office printed in the upper part of the Table, e.g., Double of first class. Reference to "the second" or "following" refers to feast printed in the lower section of the Table. Where *O* stands in a square in the *Tabella* it signifies that there can be no occurrence or concurrence between feasts whose "lines" meet in that square. These two tables are very ingeniously arranged. The lists, given in the Breviary following these tables, give the lists of greater Sundays and Ferias, privileged vigils, doubles of first and second class and greater doubles, and tell whether feasts are primary or secondary.

TITLE XII. —THE ARRANGEMENT OF THE OFFICE ACCORDING TO THE RUBRICS GIVEN ABOVE.

If any one wish from the rubrics given in the Breviary to arrange the office, he can see in the calendar and in the tables of movable feasts which office he is to say on the following day. And when he has found out the feast he determines, from the rules given, the vespers and the other hours.

If the office be the office of an excepted feast, the whole office is said from the feast as it is in the Proper or Common of saints; but the psalms of Lauds and the hours are taken from the Sunday psalms, as they stand in the new Psaltery, At Prime the psalm *Deus in nomine* is said in place of *Confitemini*. Compline is said from the Sunday psalms. If the office be the ordinary non-excepted office it is recited according to the rule laid down in the new rubrics. Tit. I., n. 5, : —

"Ad matut, invit. Hymnus, Lectiones II. et III. nocturni ac responsoria 2 et 3 nocturnorum propria vel de communi; antiphonae vero, psalmi et versus trium nocturnorum necnon Lestiones I. Nocturni cum suis Responsoriis de feria occurrente.... "

"Ad Laudes et ad Vesperas ant. cum Psalm. de Feria; Capit. Hym. Vers. et Antiph. ad Benedictus vel ad magnificat cum oratione aut in Proprio aut de Communi ad Horas minores et Complet. aut cum Psalm semper dicitur de occurrente Feria. Ad Primam pro Lectione breve legitur capit. Nonae ex Proprio, vel de Communi. Ad Tertiam, sextam et Nonam, capit. Respons. breve et orat. pariter sumuntur vel ex Proprio vel de Communi. "

(Matins and the other hours are treated of in another section.)

PART II.

RULES FROM MORAL AND ASCETIC THEOLOGY FOR THE RECITATION OF THE BREVIARY.

MORAL THEOLOGY GIVES THE RULES AND LAWS, WHICH MUST BE FOLLOWED FOR THE VALID AND LICIT RECITATION OF THE HOURS. ASCETIC THEOLOGY EXPLAINS THE MEANS, WHICH ARE TO BE USED IN THEIR FERVENT RECITATION.

CHAPTER I.

MORAL AND ASCETIC THEOLOGY.

Q. Who are bound to recite the Divine Office?

R. 1. Religious, that is, all those who have made Religious Profession, in the Canonical sense, and who are bound to Choir recitation (Canon 610, Juris Canonici).

2. Clerics in Holy Orders (Canon 135, Codex).

3. Beneficed Clergy.

Who are Beneficed Clergy?

Beneficed Clergy are those who hold a Canonically erected benefice. Canon 1409 of the *Codex Juris Canonici* defines an ecclesiastical benefice to be a "Juridical entity constituted or erected by competent ecclesiastical authority, consisting of a sacred office and the right of receiving revenues from endowments attached to the office. " Hence under this Canon, as previously three conditions are required for a benefice, first, a sacred office, second, the right of receiving revenues from endowment attached to that office, third, erection by ecclesiastical authority. There never was any doubt in the many discussions on this subject, that the work and care of a parish is a sacred office, and that parish priests hold such an office. But the second condition mentioned above received different interpretations. Some held that it implied a certain amount of ecclesiastical property set aside, from the revenues of which the holder of the benefice would derive his income. Hence the revenues of parish priests in these Kingdoms, arising from certain and voluntary offerings of the faithful, were not fixed revenues, did not fulfil the conditions of "endowment, " and parishes must not be regarded as benefices. This opinion is no longer tenable. Canon 1410 says: —"The endowment of a Benefice is constituted either by property, the ownership of which pertains to the Juridical entity itself, or by certain and obligatory payments of any family or moral personality, or by certain and voluntary offerings of the faithful which appertain to the rector of the benefice, or, as they are called stole fees, within the limits of diocesan taxation or legitimate custom, or choral distributions, exclusive of a third part of the same, if all the revenues of the benefice consist of choral distributions. "

This Canon seems to make it clear that the second condition is fulfilled in all the parishes of these Kingdoms, since to the sacred office is attached the right of receiving revenue from the certain and voluntary offerings of the faithful or from stole fees or from both.

The third condition, erection by ecclesiastical authority, is qualified by Canon 1418 which prescribes that benefices should be erected by a legitimate document defining the place of the benefice, its endowment and the duties and rights of the person appointed.

This law has not an invalidating clause, hence it is not now necessary nor ever was it necessary to have such a written document. A valid appointment was and can be made without any writing.

Where these three conditions are fulfilled there is a benefice, true, real, and canonical. Normally parishes are benefices. (See *Irish Ecclesiastical Record*, Vol. XIV., No. 623; and *Irish Theological Quarterly*, October, 1917, p. 209.)

Every cleric in holy orders is bound under pain of mortal sin to recite daily the Divine Office. No General Council, no Pope, has made such a law, but the old-established custom has grown, until it has the force of a law (Bened. XIV., *Instructio Coptharum*). Authors are not agreed as to the date of the first traces of this old custom. Billuart quotes the text of the fourth Council of Carthage to prove that it existed in the fourth century, *Clericus, qui absque corpusculi sui inequalitate vigiliis deest, stipendiis privatus, excommunicatur*. Gavantus can find traces of it only as late as the sixth century. Several decrees of provincial councils regarding this custom are quoted by writers on liturgy. However, the matter is clearly and definitely dealt with by the General Council of Lateran (1213) and by the Bulls, *Quod a nobis* and *Ex proximo*, of Pope Pius V. (1571). This Pope expressly states that wilful omission of the Divine Office is a grave sin—*"grave peccatum intelligat se commississe. "*

The obligation of reciting the office binds those in Holy Orders, even though they may be excommunicated, suspended, degraded or imprisoned. The obligation binds for the first time when subdeaconship has been conferred. Subdeacons are bound to recite "the hour" in the office of the day, corresponding to the time of their ordination. If the ordination is finished before nine o'clock, the sub-deacon is bound to begin his recitation with Terce. If the ordination is held between nine o'clock and mid-day the recitation begins with Sext. The question is discussed by theologians if the recitation of Terce or Sext may be lawfully and validly made before the ordination. Some authors deny that it may be justly and lawfully done, while others, with some probability, affirm that before ordination the debt may be paid in advance.

Are priests bound to follow the Proper in their own diocese?

They are, if it has been approved by the Sacred Congregation of Rites (S. R.C., 4597-4746). But a priest travelling (*peregrinus*) should recite the office according to the calendar of the church to which he is attached regularly, but the obligation of following the calendar of his home church was not binding by a grave precept. A reply of the Sacred Congregation of Rites (Nov., 1831) arranged (1) that beneficed clergy are always bound to recite the office of their own proper church or diocese; (2) that simple priests may read either the office as arranged for the place they tarry in or travel in, or the office of their own home diocese; (3) for unattached priests (*vagi*) it is the wiser order to follow the office as laid down in their own diocese.

Must every holder of a benefice read the Divine Office?

Every holder is bound, under pain of mortal sin, to recite the Divine Office daily, if the benefice be an ecclesiastical benefice fulfilling the conditions named above. The omission of the recital of the Divine Office by a beneficed person is a grave sin against the virtue of religion and a grave sin against the virtue of justice. For the Church imposes on the beneficiary the duty of the Office recital, on condition that he may not take the fruits of his benefice if he do not recite the Office.

What sin is committed by the omission of a notable part of the daily office?

He who wilfully omits a notable part of the daily Divine Office commits a mortal sin. A notable part of the Divine Office for any day is held by some theologians to be the omission of one psalm in one of the small hours, or a corresponding quantity of matter in lessons, responses, etc. They hold that such wilful omission is a grave sin. Other theologians hold — and their opinion is the more common and the more probable one — that, although one psalm is a notable part of a small hour, in relation to the whole office it is not a notable part, and its omission is not a grave matter. These theologians hold that the wilful omission of an entire small hour or equivalent matter (e. g., Sext, or the third nocturn of Matins) is an omission of a notable part and cannot be excused from grave sin.

The omission of the entire office of a day, the seven canonical hours, is held by some theologians to carry the guilt of seven mortal sins. Because, there is a different precept for each hour and the omission of each hour violates a precept. The Salamenticenses think this opinion probable. The more common and the more correct opinion is that by such omission only one sin is committed. And the theologians who hold this opinion say that the recitation of the canonical hours is imposed under one precept only, and hence there is only one obligation embracing the seven hours. This is the opinion of St. Alphonsus (n. 148) who quotes several authors (including Lessius, Sanchez and St. Antoninus) in support. If a person in Holy Orders omit several hours with a retractation, or a moral interruption in his sinful intentions, he may commit several mortal sins, because all the omissions, which in themselves are grave matter, may become independent of each other by the interruption and renewal of the intention (St. Alphonsus, n. 148).

What must a person do who has a doubt that he has omitted something in his recitation of the office? Is he bound to make assurance doubly sure by reciting the part of which he doubts?

If the doubt be a positive doubt, that is, if he have good reason to believe that he has recited it, he is not bound to anything further regarding the part in question. For instance, if a priest remembers having started the recitation of a lesson, and in a short time finds himself at the end of it, and cannot be sure if he have recited it, the presumption is in favour of the priest and of the recitation, because it is his custom to recite completely whatever part he commences. He has, thus, moral certainty that he has satisfied the precept, and it is not necessary to repeat it; if the necessity for repetition be admitted in such a case, a fruitful source of scruples is opened up.

On the other hand, if the doubt be negative—that is to say, if a person has no reasonable motive for believing that he has recited the full office or the full hour, he is bound to recite the part omitted, because in such a doubt, the precept of recitation is, as the theologians say, "in possession. " (St. Alphonsus, n. 150).

It is not allowed to change anything nor to add anything to the daily office without permission. The Sacred Congregation of Rites (10 June, 1690, n. 3222) replied to a query, that in saints' offices nothing is to be added and nothing is to be changed, and this reply applies to all sorts of offices, old and new.

THE ORDER TO BE OBSERVED IN RECITING THE DIVINE OFFICE.

In reciting the Divine Office two points of order are to be noted: (1) the order or arrangement of offices, (2) the order or arrangement of Hours. The order of offices indicates which office is to be said on each day as laid down in the calendar. The order of the Hours points out which of the seven hours should be recited, firstly, secondly, etc., Matins, Lauds, Prime, Terce, etc. It is of obligation to observe both orders. But is it a sin to change wilfully the order of the office? It is not, if there be a reasonable cause for the change. For instance, if a priest cannot say the office proper to his diocese on a certain day, but says some other approved office, the change is not a sin. But if a priest, *ex industria*, substitute one office for another, it is *per se* a venial sin; but if an office be said which is very much shorter than the calendar office, or if this changing or substituting be so frequent as to disturb gravely the good order of the year's offices, the sin may be (and, according to some authors, is) a mortal sin.

It is asked whether a person fulfils his debt to the Church if he has recited by mistake an office other than the one assigned in the calendar of the day. Theologians teach that such a recitation fulfils the debt. The Church does not wish to impose a second recitation, and her axiom *"officium pro officio valet"* holds, provided always that the order of the psalms as laid down in the new psaltery is followed. This order is necessary always for validity. However, if the substituted office be very much shorter than the omitted office, it is advised to equalise them by reciting the psalms of Matins, This is a counsel and was not laid down by theologians as an obligation.

An office thus omitted is not to be transferred to another day (S. C.R., June 17th, 1673). The office may be omitted altogether for that year. If there be leisure the omitted office should be recited. This practice is in conformity with the spirit of the liturgy and with the right order of the calendar. The Sacred Congregation of Rites, questioned on this matter, replied *sic debere fieri*, such should be done. If a priest recites by mistake one day's office for another (e. g., the Tuesday office on a Monday) he is bound to recite Tuesday's office on Tuesday (St. Alphonsus). If, however, after a portion of the office has been read, it is noticed that a mistake has been made in reading the calendar or the *Ordo*, and that the office partly recited is not the office of the current day, what is to be done? If the priest has without fault made the mistake of reciting some office not ascribed to the current day, he is not bound to repeat the part already recited (e. g., Matins); it is sufficient, valid and lawful to follow the correct office in the following Hours. The priest reciting is not bound to repeat even part of an hour, if he finds out his mistake during the recitation of even a small hour. And he may finish the psalm or hymn or prayer which he was reciting when he discovered his mistake, and he may then take up the correct office at the part or hour at which he leaves off, or he may finish the Hour at which he was engaged. The former solution of the difficulty seems the better, as it more accurately agrees with the maxim, *error corrigatur ubi apprehenditur*. If the error in the selecting of the office has been wilful, say, through gross carelessness, and is the fault of the priest who changes a notable part of a canonical Hour, he is obliged—the more probable opinion teaches—to repeat the full Hour, and this obligation binds under pain of venial sin—*i. e.*, the obligation to recite the office in the prescribed manner.

What is a person bound to do who forgets part of an Hour—is he obliged to repeat the full Hour?

He is bound to recite the part forgotten only, unless the mistake be made through gross carelessness, and unless it be a considerable part (e. g., two nocturns); in that case he is bound under pain of venial sin to repeat the full Hour. If a person say the same Hour (e. g., Terce) twice, may he compensate for extra labour by the omission of an equivalent part (e. g., None)? Such omission is unlawful; he must recite all the Hours without omission (Scavini, 391).

Is there an obligation to repeat the Hours in the order fixed in the Breviary? Yes, there is such an obligation. And a person may sin venially by the inversion of the Hours, The obligation binds *sub veniali* only. The inversion does not mean any grave breach of order, which is fixed by a secondary precept and as a circumstance of light importance. If the whole office be recited, the substance of the office—which is the main and primary matter—is safeguarded. Several authors argued that any inversion of the Canonical Hours, if frequent, is a mortal sin, but the opinion which says that the inversion of the Hours is only a venial sin is the more probable (St. Alph. 169; Gury, 77; Lehmkuhl II., 621).

Which causes justify an inversion of the Hours? Any reasonable cause justifies this inversion. Thus, if a friend invite a priest to joint recitation of an Hour, and the priest have not the preceding canonical Hours recited, he is justified in accepting the invitation and in inverting the order of the Hours. Or if a person have a Diurnal only at hand, he may read the day Hours, although he have not Matins for the day read. Again, a priest may not have the lessons for Matins at hand, but he may recite the psalms for Matins, Lauds, and add the lessons at Matins when they are to hand (Gury, n. 78; St. Alph., n. 170).

Is it a sin to say Matins for following day before finishing office of current day? Some theologians answer affirmatively, because the office of the current day should be complete before another office is begun. Others hold that such recitation is both valid and licit, as the office of one day and its obligation have no bond with the office of another day, and that any reasonable cause exempts from all sin or fault (Gury, n. 79). Not to recite the commemorations in the prescribed order set out in the *Ordo* is held by some theologians to be a venial sin, as they hold that the rubric is preceptive; others hold that it is not any sin, as they say that the rubric is directive.

ARTICLE III. —TIME OF RECITATION.

The time fixed for the recitation of the entire office of the day is from midnight to the midnight following, and anyone bound to recite the Divine Office does not sin gravely if he has recited carefully the entire office of the day between these limits of time; because, within these limits, the substance of the obligation binding to time is fulfilled. Of course, it is lawful in virtue of a privilege granted by the Church to recite on the previous evening Matins and Lauds for the following day. In the recitation the times fixed by the Church for each hour should be observed. But the non-recital at those fixed times is never a mortal sin and is rarely a venial sin, unless their postponement or anticipation is without cause.

When may a priest begin the recitation of Matins and Lauds for the following day? There were two different replies given to this question. One opinion stated that it was lawful to begin Matins and Lauds after 2 o'clock, p.m., and this could be lawfully done every day in the year, and in every land. Another opinion—and St. Alphonsus calls it *sententia verior*—denies that such a course is lawful. The old French Breviaries gave a *horarium* arranging the hour of anticipation of Matins and Lauds, so that no one should, through temerity or ignorance, begin the anticipation before the sun had passed half way in its course between mid-day and sunset. On January 20th the time to begin the anticipation of hours was 2.15 p. m., but on June 8th the anticipation was not to begin till 4 p. m.

Nowadays, the first opinion is held almost universally. The principal *internal* argument for this opinion is the teaching that the anticipation may begin from the public hour of first vespers, and these may be recited publicly according to present-day custom at 2 p. m. Therefore, this time, 2 o'clock p. m., is the beginning of the ecclesiastical day, and can be taken as the time for private anticipation of Matins and Lauds. The *external* argument in favour of this opinion is the authority of theologians. In 1905, the Sacred Congregation of Rites was asked the question "*Utrum in privata recitatione Matutinum sequentis diei incipi possit, 2da pomeriddiane?* ". The reply was, "*Consulantur probati auctores*" (*Acta Sanctae Sedis* XXXVII., p. 712). Now many approved authors (e. g., Lehmkuhl, II., 793; Ballerini-Palmieri, IV. 515; Slater I., p. 609) hold that it is lawful, privately, to anticipate Matins and Lauds at 2 o'clock, p.m. Lehmkuhl, who previously favoured a stricter view, was compelled, in the latest editions of his *Moral Theology*, to say of this opinion which allows anticipation to begin at 2 o'clock, p.m. : "*Quae sententia hodie a multis usque gravissimis viris tenetur et observatur, ut, spectata consuetudine, extrinseca saltem probabilitas negari nequit.* " We conclude, accordingly, that always and everywhere the private anticipation of Matins and Lauds may begin at 2 p. m. (*cf. Irish Ecclesiastical Record, Fifth Series, Vol. I., No. 541*).

Doubts have arisen in connection with time changes made by various States in Europe. The various schemes of new time, of daylight saving, of co-ordinations of time, uniformity of time all through certain States, have given rise to doubts and queries regarding the time for fulfilling the precept of the office and also regarding the time for lawful anticipation of Matins and Lauds. These doubts were solved several years ago, and now there is no longer any difficulty or anxiety over "true time, " "new time, " "legal time, " in relation to matters ecclesiastical. In reply to queries, Dr. M. J. O'Donnell, in the *Irish Ecclesiastical Record* (Vol. III., p. 582), explains clearly this time difficulty and its solution by the Congregation of the Council on 22nd July, 1893. The Bishop of Trier explained to the Congregation of the Council that owing to the State legislation in the German Empire all public clocks should register the same time, and that this meant that in his diocese the legal computation differs by half an hour from the mean time. "May clerics follow the legal time in reciting the Divine Office? " was the bishop's question. The Congregation of the Council answered by a simple affirmative. In 1892, Greenwich time was introduced for State purposes into all railway, postal, and Government offices in Holland. The query was put to the Congregation of the Inquisition if the clergy and people might, for the purpose of fast and other ecclesiastical obligations, follow the new time, or were they obliged to retain the true time? The reply was *"affirmative ad primam: negative ad secundam partem. "* "In a word, the constant Roman answer has been 'Do as you please'; so far as the approval of the legal time is concerned it confirms the conclusion of the editor of the *Acta* (xxxii-251) that in computing time the Church follows the rule that regulates all business concerns in different localities....

"In the meantime, taking into account the conventional character of 'time' and the liberal principles of Rome in the past, we have no doubt that everyone, priest or layman, is fully justified in following the new time if he feels so inclined. " (See *Codex Juris. Canon. , Can. 33).

Are priests bound to recite Matins and Lauds before Mass?

The first sentence of the *Ritus servandus in celebratione Missae* in the Missal contains the clause *"saltem Malutino cum Laudibus absoluto, "* The word *saltem* indicates that the Church notifies the minimum and expects a further hour, Prime or even others of the small hours, to be finished before Mass. But theologians hold that there is no grave obligation for such prior-to-Mass recital, and that any reasonable cause excuses from the obligation (Lehmkuhl II., 628). In connection with this matter a very instructive and devotional essay in the *Irish Ecclesiastical Record* (Fourth Series XXXI., n. 533) by Father M. Russell, S.J., is well worth reading. It is entitled "A Neglected Adverb"; the adverb being *saltem*, from the clause quoted.

At what times should the small hours be recited? Prime may be, and, probably with more appropriateness, should be used as morning prayer and said before Mass. Terce and Sext may be said before mid-day, or Sext and None may be said after mid-day. Vespers should be said after mid-day. Compline was the night prayer of the monks, who probably instituted the hour. It should be borne in mind that the substance of the law of recitation is fulfilled if the whole office of the day be recited before midnight, and that the obligation for entire and complete recitation is grave; while the recitation of the hours at set hours of the day is a light obligation.

ARTICLE IV. -OF THE PLACE OF RECITATION AND THE ATTITUDE IN RECITING THE OFFICE.

Where should the Divine Office be recited? The Divine Office should be recited in the place intended and set apart by the Church for that purpose—viz., in the choir or in the Church (Con. Trid., sess. 24). Canons and religious are bound to recite their office in choir; of course, this refers to Canons in residence at a cathedral for daily service, and to religious in the strict application of the term. The Divine Office may be recited by priests anywhere, in the church, in a dwelling-house, walking, in the fields, etc.

In reciting the office a priest should observe an attitude in harmony with the great work in which he is engaged, prayer to God. Hence, his attitude should be becoming, on his knees, standing, sitting, walking, but not sprawling or lying. The rubrics which prescribe kneeling, sitting, standing, apply to choir recitation only. But writers recommend that in private recitation these directions should not be altogether omitted, and they say that the practice of these rubrics of kneeling, bowing, standing, etc., is laudable and an aid to devout recital.

ARTICLE V. — PRONUNCIATION OF THE WORDS.

What kind of pronunciation is to be attended to in the recitation of the Divine Office? The pronunciation should be vocal—that is, there should be some sound, *aliquis sonitus verborum*, as St. Alphonsus writes (n. 162). Hence, to read the Breviary merely mentally or with the eyes only, does not satisfy the obligation. [A] Although the reader may not hear the sound produced, he must be careful to form with his lips every syllable. This must be done, not necessarily in a throaty way. The formation of the words clearly with the lips suffices. But writers on this point emphasise the importance of audible recitation as a preventive of slurred, mutilated Latinity, which often leads to careless, or even invalid recitation. They note, too, that the reading with the eye merely, is a habit which readers bring from the reading of other books to their reading of the Breviary. German authors dwell at length on the fact that many priests, very early in their career, contract the habit of faulty vocalisation of liturgy, and that they never seem to notice their fault, or at least never seem to attempt an amendment. These authors attribute the defect to sub-voce recitation and recommend audible recitation, long and frequent audible recitation, to all priests reading their hours.

[Footnote A: The privilege of mental recitation was granted to the Friar Minor by Pope Leo X. and Pius V., but it is probable that the privilege was withdrawn by Pope Gregory XV. in 1622, in his letter *Romanus Pontifex*; and Urban VIII., 1635, withdrew all privileges granted *vivae vocis oraculo*. The text of the document granting the privilege is obscurely worded. Still, several theologians of repute maintain that the privilege still exists and extends to the whole office. This is taught by the Salaraenticenses, *De hor. can. cap.* 3, n. 55; Tamburini, Rodriguez, etc., others opposed this view of the privilege existing after Pope Urban's letter *Alias*. This privilege extends to secular priests who are Franciscan tertiaries, if it exists at all.]

Can a priest fulfil his obligation by reciting the office with a companion? Yes, he can, for such recitation is the Church's ideal; and the priest who says his part (alternate verses, etc.), as in choir, fulfils his obligation, even when his companion is a layman or an inattentive person. In such recitation a priest should be careful (1) that his recitation be of alternate verses, (2) that the verse recitation be successive and not simultaneous, (3) that the verses, etc., chanted by one companion (or by one choir) be heard by the other companion or choir. There is no necessity for a priest at such recitation to say one verse in a loud voice and to say his companion's verses in a low, inaudible voice. Some priests do this with distressing results. Imperfect vocal recitation often leads to doubts and scruples in old age when remedies either cannot be applied or prove useless.

Those who recite the office in choir are bound by the rubrics concerning kneeling, sitting, standing, etc. Secondly, they are bound to observe the rules of the liturgy, especially the rule as to the stop in each verse at the asterisk mark. Thirdly, they are bound to recite clearly and distinctly; but even if they cannot hear distinctly the alternate choir, or even if they recite in a low voice, they fulfil the obligation of recitation; and canons are bound at Cathedral offices to sing and chant or to lose their manual distributions and the fruits of their prebends. If a person reciting his office with a companion or in a choir does not understand the words recited by his companion or by the choir, he is not bound at the end to repeat the part which he did not understand, because such a person has the intention of offering prayer and praise to God, and that intention suffices. Moreover, the Church's precept of reciting the office should he interpreted benignly, otherwise it must give rise to many scruples; for, companions in recitation, then, always, should be anxious as to the duty of repetition or the non-fulfilled duty of complete recitation.

Pronunciation of the words of the office should be *integral*. That is, the words and syllables are to be repeated fully without mutilation or abbreviation. Hence, if mutilation of the words occur to such an extent that the sense or meaning of the words is notably changed, mortal sin may be committed. But if the mutilation be small in quantity there is only a venial sin committed, and often no sin at all may be committed, as the mutilation of words or syllables may be quite involuntary, or may be done inadvertently, or may arise from an inveterate habit very difficult to correct, and in the attempt to cure it time and patience may have been spent (St. Alph., 164-165). This bad habit, if it extend over a large portion of the recitation and destroy notably the sense of the words, may bind *sub gravi* to repetition, as this fault or habit affects the very substance of recitation. Priests seldom are bound to such a repetition, as the mutilation is not destructive to the sense of a notable part of the office and hence does not affect the substance of the obligation to vocal recital. St. Alphonsus holds (n. 165), that the obligation is fulfilled as long as the meaning is not destroyed, *quando servatur aliqua significatio verborum*.

Pronunciation should be *continuous*. That is, the recitation of each hour should be continuous, non-interrupted, and every notable stoppage or break in the recitation of a canonical hour is a venial sin, if there be no excusing cause for such an interruption. Any reasonable cause for interruption (e. g., to obey a bell call, to see a parishioner who calls, to hear a confession) excuses from all fault (St. Alph., n. 168).

If the recital of the office for any canonical hour be interrupted, should the whole hour be repeated? Some theologians say that it should be repeated. But the more probable opinion denies that there is any such obligation; it holds that the union of the prayers prescribed by the Church is not broken, as each psalm, each lesson, each prayer, has a complete signification and they are united sufficiently in one round of prayer by the intention formed of continuing the Hour, or even by the actual continuation. Gury states that a priest interrupting the office between the verses of a psalm is not bound to repeat the entire psalm on resuming the recitation, as he says each verse has its own signification.

May Matins be said separately from Lauds without any excusing cause? Yes, for it was the practice of the early Church to say these parts of the liturgy at times separated by intervals. But if Matins be said separately, without Lauds following immediately. *Pater Noster* with Dominus Vobiscum and the prayer of the day should be said at the end of the *Te Deum*, If Lauds follow Matins immediately the *Pater* and *Ave* should not be said, for the Congregation (same decree) says "*Laudes incohandas ut in Psalterio,* " but in the Psalter the *Pater* and *Ave* are not assigned for the beginning of Lauds.

A notable time may elapse between the nocturns of Matins without any excusing cause. In the early Church intervals occurred between each nocturn. Some authors state that an interval of three hours between two nocturns is quite lawful, even when there be no cause for the delay. With a reasonable cause the interval may last as long as the excusing cause requires.

ARTICLE VI. —INTENTION AND ATTENTION.

The valid recitation of the Divine Office requires that the priest should have in his mind an intention of praying, for the Divine Office is a true and real prayer, not a mere vocal exercise. Hence, a priest reading his office as a mere study or as a means of remembering the words of the psalms does not validly recite his office (St. Alph., n. 176). Now, what sort of intention is best and what sort of intention is necessary? An actual, explicit intention which states expressly when the Breviary is opened, "I intend to pray, " is the best intention. The devout recital of the prayer *"Aperi Domine"* expresses well the best form of the actual, explicit intentions of those reciting the office. But such an express, actual intention is not necessary; a virtual intention, which finds expression in the opening of the Breviary to recite the office, suffices. The mere opening of the book, the finding out of the office, the arrangement of the book markers, are ample evidence of the existence of a virtual intention quite sufficient for the valid recitation of the office. St. Alphonsus writes, *"Imo puto semper adesse exercite, intentionem actualem implendi officium"* (n. 176). This question of intention gives great trouble to the timid and scrupulous, whose doubts and difficulties seem hard to solve. The common sense and common practice in everyday affairs seem to desert some people when they prepare to read the canonical hours. For, who has not seen the nervous, pious, anxious cleric, stupidly labouring to acquire even a sufficient intention before beginning his hours?

Attention in reading the hours is a much more discussed and much more difficult mental effort. It means the application of the mind to the thing in which we are engaged. When we listen to a conversation or when we write a letter the mind is fixed and attentive to the matter spoken or written. Intention is an act of the will; attention is an act of the understanding.

Attention may be either external or internal. External attention is attention of such a kind that it excludes every exterior action physically incompatible with the recitation of the office—e. g., to write or type a letter, to listen attentively to those conversing, are acts incompatible with the simultaneous recitation of the office. But walking, poking a fire, looking for the lessons, whilst reciting from memory all the time, are not incompatible with the external attention required in office recital; because such acts do not require mental effort which could count as a serious disturbing element. However, in this matter of external attention no rule can be formulated for all Breviary readers; for what may lightly disturb and distract one reader may have no effect on another, and yet may seriously disturb the recitation of another (St. Alph., n. 176). External attention is necessary for the valid recitation of the office.

Internal attention is application or advertence of the mind. Is such internal attention, such deliberate application or mental advertence necessary for the valid recitation of the office?

There are two opinions on this matter, two replies to the question. According to one opinion, and this is the more common and the more probable one, internal attention is required for the valid recitation of the Hours. 1. Because the Divine Office is a prayer, but there can be no true or real prayer without internal attention, for prayer is defined as an elevation of the soul to God, but if there be no internal attention, there is no elevation of the soul to God, and no prayer. 2. Our Lord complained of those who had external attention at prayer, but lacked internal attention or advertence, "This people honour me with their lips, but their heart is far from me" (St. Matt. xv.). 3. The Church appears to demand internal attention at prayer, for although she has not given any positive precept dealing with this kind of attention, she does the same thing when she commands that the recitation of the Divine Office take the form of prayer for God's honour, and this recitation of words cannot be true prayer without internal attention. 4. The Council of Trent seems to exact this attention when it wishes that the Divine Office be said reverently, distinctly and devoutly, reverenter, distincte, devote. 5. If no internal attention be required in reciting the Hours, it is difficult to see how voluntary distractions are forbidden by Divine Law.

This is the opinion held by Cajetan (1496-1534), Sa (1530-1596), Azor (1539-1603), Sanchez (1550-1610), Roncaglai (1677-1737), Concina (1687-1756), and St. Alphonsus, the great Doctor of prayer (1696-1787).

According to the other opinion, external attention suffices always and ever to satisfy substantially the obligation of reading the office and for the avoidance of mortal sin which invalid recitation entails. For,

(1) To pray is to speak to God, to trust in Him, to manifest to Him the wishes and wants of the soul; but this can be done by a person who has voluntary distractions of mind, just as a man can read to his king an address, setting forth the thanks and requests of his subjects, although the reader's mind is far from dwelling on the words or the meaning of the sentences before his eyes. But he is careful to read all the words in a clear, intelligible manner. Now the theologians who maintain this opinion say that, *a fortiori*, this method of reading the

Hours should be valid; for, in the reading the priest acts principally in the name of the Church, as her minister, and offers up prayers to God in her name, and they say that the irreverence of the servant does not render the prayer of the Church unpleasing to Him,

(2) He who makes a vow, and resolves to do a certain act, fulfils his vow, even when fulfilling it he acts with voluntary distractions; so, a pari, with the recitation of the office,

(3) The administration of the sacraments—even the administration of Extreme Unction, the form of which is a prayer—with full voluntary distractions is valid; so, too, should be the recital of Breviary prayers.

(4) In the other opinion it is hard to see how, if voluntary distractions destroy the substance of prayer, involuntary distractions do not produce similar effect, and hence, there can be no prayer if there be distraction of any kind.

This opinion was held by Lugo (1583-1660), Gobat (1600-1679), Sporer (1609-1683), St. Antonnius (1389-1459), and other eminent men. It is quoted by St. Alphonsus, as *satis probabilis*. Of it, Lehmkuhl writes, "Quae ad substantiam divini officii dicamus satis probabiliter sufficere cum intentione orandi observasse attentionem externam" (II. 635).

What are the divisions or kinds of internal attention?

I. Objectively they are (1) spiritual attention, (2) literal attention, (3) superficial or material attention. Spiritual attention is that advertence of soul which tends towards God, the Term of all prayer, when the soul meditates on the power, wisdom, goodness of God, on the Passion, on the Mother of God, on God's saints. Literal attention is that which strives to lay hold of the meaning of the words said in the office. Superficial attention is that advertence of soul which applies itself to the correct recitation of the words, avoiding errors of pronunciation, mutilation, transposition, etc., etc.

II. Subjectively, virtual attention suffices; habitual is divided into actual and interpretative. Actual attention is that which exists at the moment—e. g., the attention paid by a pupil to a question put by a teacher. Virtual attention is attention which was once actual, but is not such at the time spoken of, but which lives virtually. Habitual is attention which once was actual, which does not remain in act, but which was not retracted. Interpretative attention is that which never existed at all, but which would have existed if the agent had adverted.

Which kind of internal attention is required in the reading of the Office? I. Objectively, material, or superficial attention is necessary, since the Breviary is a vocal prayer, and therefore it is necessary to pronounce distinctly all the words of the day's office and to observe the rubrics. But this suffices; it is not necessary that a priest reciting his Hours should carefully notice each word, it is sufficient to have general and moral attention to recite every part well, and with the intention of praying, "Sed sufficere moralem et generalem qua quis curet bene omnia dicere cum intentione orandi" (St. Alphonsus).

Hence, objectively, neither attention, which is called spiritual, because it is not easy to attain, nor the literal attention, which religious who do not understand Latin strive after, is needed for valid recitation. By this, it is not meant to convey that spiritual attention is not very excellent and very commendable and praiseworthy.

Subjectively, virtual attention suffices; habitual does not suffice, neither does interpretative. Best of all is actual attention, but it is not necessary, because it is not always within the power of mortals.

This want of internal attention is called mental distraction. Theologians distinguish two kinds of distractions, voluntary and involuntary. Voluntary distractions are thoughts which the mind freely and directly embraces to the exclusion of pious thoughts which should occupy it in prayer, of which the office is a high form; or they may be thoughts which arise from previous laziness, thoughtlessness, pre-occupation or some engrossing worldly affair. Involuntary distractions are those which come unbidden and unsought to the mind, are neither placed directly, nor by their causes, by the person at prayer.

Does a person reciting the Hours sin if he have distractions?

If the distractions be involuntary there is no sin. But if the distractions be voluntary there is sin, But, unless the mind be altogether filled with distractions, not thinking of God, of prayer, of the words or of the meaning, and unless the distractions are *fully voluntary* and *reflective* during a notable part of the office, there is no mortal sin. Hence, St. Alphonsus, the great Doctor of Prayer, wrote, *"ut dicatur aliquis officio non satisfacere, non solum requiritur ut voluntarie se distrahat, sed etiam ut plene advertat se distrahi, nam alias iste, licet sponte se divertat non tamen sponte se divertit a recitatione"* (St. Alphonsus, n. 177). Therefore, before a person accuse himself of not satisfying the precept of recitation, on account of inattention or distractions, he must be able to affirm positively (1)that he was wilfully distracted, (2)he must have noticed not only his distraction and mental occupation by vain thoughts, but he must have noticed *also* that he was distracted in his recitation; (3)he must be able to state positively that the intention, resolution or desire to recite piously, which he made at the beginning of his prayer, was revoked with full advertence and that it did not exist either actually or virtually during the time of distraction in his recitation. Seldom, indeed, are these conditions fulfilled, and seldom are there gravely sinful distractions.

This subject of attention in prayer, in the official prayer of the Church, is important. Long and learned disputes about its nature and requirements occupied great thinkers in times long gone by. To-day theologians argue on different sides; and anxiety, serious, painful and life-long, reigns in the souls of many who struggle to recite the office, *digne, attente ac devote.*

ARTICLE VII. -CAUSES WHICH EXCUSE FROM READING THE OFFICE.

Authors generally give six causes which excuse a person from saying the Hours: lawful dispensation, important work, grave illness, grave fear, blindness, want of a Breviary. They are recorded in the well-known lines: —

"Quem Papa dispenset multus labor opprimit aeger Qui timet aut occulus, officioque caret. "

1. The obligation of reading the Office is imposed by the Church and the Pope can dispense in it even without cause. Bishops can give temporary dispensations.

2. A grave occupation excuses from the whole or from a part of the Office. Thus, missioners giving missions or parish retreats are excused from the whole Office; so, too, are priest combatants in the battle line; but when in rest camps they are bound to say the Hours. A priest engaged in saying his Office, if he receive an urgent call to a

dying person may not have time to finish his Office before midnight. He is exempt from the part of the Office omitted and does not sin by the omission. The proposition claiming exemption from the Office for those engaged in great studies was condemned by Pope Alexander VII. The biographers of Lamennais trace the beginning of his downfall to his exemption from his daily Office.

A difficulty arises sometimes as regards the full or partial or non-exemption of those who foresee that serious occupation which cannot be neglected must arise to prevent the recitation of the Hours. In such cases priests are bound to recite the Office, or as much of it as possible, within the limits of the current day. In doing this they may anticipate the times fixed for the recitation of the small Hours, and they may anticipate Vespers and Compline by reciting them in the forenoon. If a priest foresees that he may not be able to recite Matins for next day he is not bound to anticipate, as there is no obligation to anticipation; the obligation is "recital between midnight and midnight. " It is becoming to anticipate, if possible, so that the Office may be full and entire. If before midnight there be a cessation from necessary professional work (e. g., hearing confessions), a priest is bound to finish his Office for the day or to say as much of it as time allows. If, however, there be time merely to take a necessary meal before midnight (e. g., to prepare for a late Mass on next day, Sunday), and not time to eat and to recite, the obligation of saying the Hours ceases.

A grave illness exempts from the saying of the canonical Hours. Hence, those seriously ill, those who fear the saying of the Office may upset them in their weak state, and convalescents from a serious illness, are excused from saying the Hours. In this matter the advice of a spiritual or a medical adviser should be faithfully carried out by patients. St. Alphonsus teaches that invalids and convalescents may be allowed to say Mass and yet not be bound to say the Office, as the saying of Mass does not fatigue them so much as the saying of the Office (St. Alphonsus, n. 155).

A grave fear exempts from the saying of the Office. A priest amongst furious persecutors of the Church should be excused from any recitation of his Hours which he fears may draw on him cruel or severe punishments.

Blindness makes the recitation of the Office a physical impossibility. Even very defective sight, although not total blindness, exempts from the obligation of saying the Office. In all such cases a formal declaration of exemption should be sought. Some theologians hold that such priests, if they have committed to memory a notable part of the psalms, should repeat that part from memory. The new psaltery makes such memorising an extremely difficult feat and no obligation for such a repetition from memory can be imposed.

Want of a Breviary excuses from the recitation of the Office. For example, if a priest setting out on a long journey forgets to take his Breviary or leaves it in a railway carriage, and cannot procure another, or cannot procure another without, great inconvenience, he is exempt from the obligation of his Office; and the omission being involuntary is sinless. The wilful casting away of a Breviary, as an excuse for not being able to read the Office, is gravely sinful; and unless the sinful desire be retracted there may be question of many mortal sins of wilful omission to fulfil the obligation, as the omissions are then wilful in cause. Priests travelling are unable sometimes to recite the proper Office of the day, as their Breviaries lack something (e. g., the proper prayer or the lessons of the second nocturn). The Sacred Congregation of Rites (December, 1854) decided "*Sacerdos peregre profectus cui molesti difficiliorque esset officii recitatio cui et pauca desunt in libro officii praesentis, nempe oratio et legenda, valet de communi absque obligatione propria deinde ad supplementum recitandi... atque ita servari mandavit.* " The psalms as arranged in the new psalter must always be said for a valid recitation of the Office (*v. Divino Afflatu*).

What is a priest bound to do, who from a grave cause cannot find time to recite the whole Office but only a part of it?

St. Alphonsus gives the rule, "If you can recite a part equivalent to a small Hour, you are bound to do so under pain of mortal sin. But if you cannot read or repeat a part equivalent to a small Hour, you are bound to nothing, as a part so small—less than a small Hour—taken separately, is considered inappreciable for the end the Church's law of recitation has in view. "

ARTICLE VIII. — THE DIRECTION OF THE SCRUPULOUS.

Persons who are scrupulous about the recitation of the Hours should have help from their confessors, who should deal specifically with any of the scruples which arise in the daily task. Scruples generally concern the necessary intention, the necessary attention, pronunciation, and the time necessary for a good and faithful recitation of the canonical Hours. How should a confessor deal with scruples about intention? A confessor should tell a cleric, scrupulous in this point, that his fear is groundless and that by the very act of taking up his Breviary he expresses his intention of praying, of saying his Hours; that it is not necessary that such intention be actual or reflexive, it is sufficient if it be virtual, and that such an intention *does* exist every time one opens the Breviary to say his Hours. The saying slowly and deliberately the prayer *"Aperi Domine"* is a great aid to the scrupulous in forming a right intention and in dispelling their vain fears.

Clerics troubled about attention are helped and comforted by their confessor repeating to them what they well know themselves, about voluntary and involuntary distractions, and the telling of the anxious ones that this very anxiety and anguish show that their fear of losing attention in their prayer is a true and real sign of its existence. In dealing with scruples about vocal and integral pronunciation a confessor should advise that no stopping should be made in the saying of the psalms, etc., but that the recitation should be continued quietly, without restraining the voice, without impatience, and without scrutiny of the pronunciation of the part said, "God is a father, full of goodness, not an exacting taskmaster, and He is more honoured by moderate care than by a disturbing solicitude. " Above all things, a confessor should remember that it is important to forbid scrupulous persons to repeat the whole or even the part of an Hour. An effort should be made by him to tranquilise the troubled soul with the principle that the precepts of the Church do not bind him to repeat the Hours with such inconvenience as leads to bodily and mental illness. The Church is our mother and does not wish her children to be troubled and solicitous, but to pray in peace.

CHAPTER IV.

SOME RULES OF ASCETIC THEOLOGY FOR THE PIOUS RECITATION OF THE BREVIARY.

There are many reasons why we should recite the Divine Office devoutly, for (1) the words which we read are holy; (2) He to Whom we speak is God; (3) we speak in the name of Holy Church; (4) we are the associates of thousands on earth and in heaven who sing God's praises; (5) the purpose of our prayer is sublime; (6) it gives glory to God and draws down His grace and mercy on His Church; (7) and, finally, the recitation of the Office brings help and strength to those who repeat it fervently.

And, firstly, let us see what are the words of the Office. They are the words of God or of His Church. In the psalms, scripture lessons, gospel extracts, responses and antiphons, we have God's inspired word. In the prayers, sermons, homilies, hymns, and often in the responses and antiphons, as the Church is guided and assisted by the Holy Ghost, it may be, in a sense, true to say that these her words are divine. For what is more worthy of respect than the word of God? St. Augustine says that it is no less worthy of respect than the body of Jesus Christ. *Non minus est verbum Dei quam corpus Christi* (Sermon 300). How very careful should we be to treat the word of God with respect, worthily, attentively, and devoutly (*digne, attente ac devote*).

(2) To whom do we speak in our daily service of prayer? We speak to our Master, Whose very special work we are doing in offering up the great prayer. His adorable eyes are fixed upon us at this sacred duty. He listens to us, He reads our thoughts. He judges our intentions, our efforts and their fulfilment. He is the King of kings, the Almighty God. Mindful of His presence and majesty should we not try earnestly to bless His Holy name and to free our hearts from vain, evil and wandering thoughts? We pray *ad benedicendum nomen sanctum tuum; munda quoque cor meum ab omnibus vanis perversis et alienis cogitationibus.*

(3) In whose name do we speak? It is a great honour to be an ambassador for a great king and a mighty kingdom, guarding the interests of the fatherland in a foreign land. The priest is always such an ambassador. "For Christ, we are ambassadors, " says St. Paul. In

this work of daily recitation of the Office, we are ambassadors, not of some petty king or tiny state, but we represent the entire Church, the well-beloved spouse of Christ, to whose prayer He ever hearkens. *Sonet vox tua in auribus meis; vox enim tua dulcis est* (Canticle of Canticles, ii. 14). And St. Bernard says *"Sacerdos publica persona et totius Ecclesie os. "* Hence, every priest is the ambassador of Christ and of His Church, the guardian of His interests. And as it is the duty of ambassadors to study carefully, to watch and further the interests of the kings whom they represent, it is a priest's duty to study carefully and further the interests of Christ's Church by the devout fulfilment of the great daily duty, the recitation of the Divine Office. History brands as traitors those ambassadors who through ignorance of the language of the foreign court, or through want of vigilant attention, allow the interests of their royal masters to suffer. What a punishment awaits the days and years of ignorant, careless or inattentive fulfilment of the great official work of a priest—the Divine Office.

Who are a priest's associates in this work? They are the thousands of priests and religious throughout the world who say the Hours, and who send up daily and nightly the great prayer of praise and thanksgiving to God. *Secundum nomen tuum, sic et laus tua in fines terrae* (ps. 47, v. ii). *Dies diei eructat verbum et nox nocti indicat scientiam* (ps. 18, v. 3). In this holy work of reciting the Hours, we are united with the angels and saints in heaven in honouring our common Creator; for, the Church herself reminds us of this ineffable honour in the hymn for the dedication of the Church: —

> "Sed ilia sedes Coelitum
> Semper resultat laudibus
> Dumque trinum el unicum
> Jugi canore jungimur
> Almae Sionis aemuli."

> "That house on high—it ever rings
> With praises of the King of kings;
> For ever there, on harps divine,
> They hymn th' eternal One and Trine
> We, here below, the strain prolong;,
> And faintly echo Sion's song."

What are the ends for which the Office is said? (a) To glorify God, (b) to help holy Church, and (c) to sanctify ourselves.

(a) "To glorify God, " that is, to adore His infinite majesty, to thank Him for his innumerable and constant blessings, to satisfy His justice in expiating the sins of the world and to beg His grace and mercy. The ends for which the Office are said are the same as those for which Mass is offered, for the Office is the supplement of the Mass (Tronson).

(b) "To help holy Church. " The Church militant has many and great needs. It is her mission to extend the Kingdom of Christ, and to do this great work she needs freedom from hostile laws, strength and courage to withstand tyrants and persecution, unity and peace amongst her children and pastors, zeal in her ministers and recruits for her militant forces. To obtain these results the Church relies very much on the devout recitation of the Office. Doubtless, it is for these purposes that the Church has confided to the care of her chosen ministers this public official prayer and has laid no such obligation on the laity. St. Alphonsus did not hesitate to say that if priests and religious said the Office as they should say it, the Church should not be in the deplorable state that it then was in. This Doctor of the Church adds "that by devout saying of the Office many sinners could be drawn from the slavery of the devil and many souls would love God with more fervour. " The wants of the Church are greater now than they were ever before. Each devoutly-said Hour draws down God's blessing on His Church. What a vast number of blessings come from a life of daily recitation offered worthily, attentively and devoutly (*digne, attente, ac devote*).

(c) "The benefit of the person who recites the Hours. " The third end for which the canonical Hours are offered is for the benefit of the person who recites them. St. Alphonsus wrote, "If they said the Office as they ought, priests themselves should not be always the same, always imperfect, prone to anger, greedy, attached to self-interest and to vanities.... But if they recited the Office, not as they say it with distractions and irreverences, but with devotion and recollection, uniting the affections of the heart with so many petitions which they present to God, they should certainly not be so weak as they are, but would acquire fervour and strength to resist all temptations and to lead a life worthy of priests. "

Another blessing springs from the attentive recitation of the Breviary—viz., the daily withdrawal from the world and its cares which must be banished from the soul which speaks with God. For, as St. Alphonsus writes, the saying of the Hours devoutly, gives occasion to pious souls to elicit many acts of virtue, acts of faith, of hope, of charity, of humility, etc. For one psalm, says the saint, moves all the powers of the soul and causes us to elicit a hundred acts. And in the Breviary are found the most beautiful formulae of adoration and praise, the psalms above all other parts of the Office being wonderfully rich in magnificent praise of God's attributes. Where can such sublime forms of prayer and praise be found as in Psalms, 8, 9, 17, 18, 21, 23, 28, 29, 33, 45, 46, 49, 54—to name but a few?

Finally, the attentive recitation of the Breviary is a source of light and of grace and of merit. How many lights in prayer spring from these divine words; how many maxims enter the soul, how many beautiful prayers are said, and if they be well said, they would obtain for priests treasures of grace, according to Christ's infallible promise, "Ask and you shall receive"? A person can merit several degrees of glory by one devout recitation of the Office, what an abundance of merit may be gained by the devout recitations in a life of twenty, thirty or forty years! And it was this thought of lost opportunities and of the great treasures within the reach of priests, which caused St. Alphonsus when an old man, to study the Breviary psalms and to write his well-known work.

Nor was St. Alphonsus alone in his opinion of the great means of sanctification which the Breviary affords to priests. St. Joseph of Cupertino (1603-1663) was asked by Monsignor Claver, Bishop of Potenza, to point out a means for the greater sanctification of the priests of his diocese. The saint replied, "Monsignor, if you wish to sanctify your priests strive to procure two things for them, that they say the Office piously and that they say Mass with fervour. Nothing more is necessary to ensure their salvation" (*Life of St. Joseph Cupertino* by Bernini). The words of the wonderful Franciscan, whose life was a marvel of piety, were repeated a century later by St. Leonard of Port Maurice (1671-1751) and are often quoted as his own.

In every age of the Church earnest souls drew great sweetness and consolation from reading the psalms or from reading the canonical Hours. Writers dealing with this part of priestly work quote the words of eminent servants of God, They quote St. Augustine, St. Gregory Nazianzan, St. Bernard, St. Catherine of Bologna, St. Philip Neri, St. Francis De Sales and St. Alphonsus. It would make this section of this book too long to quote the words of these saints. But the words of St. Francis De Sales seem to have a special force. "Sometimes I am so low-spirited, " wrote the Saint, "by business and events, that I do not know where to turn nor at what end to begin: but during the Office nothing annoys me, I have not even distractions, I imagine that I am in heaven singing with the angels the praises of my Creator; and on leaving the choir I find often that the mighty problems which had given me trouble are cleared away and, solved in an Instant. " Biographies of God's servants record many great favours bestowed on priests who recite the Breviary piously. Cardinal Bona, recording a vision vouchsafed to St. Bernard, tells how the saint saw an angel beside each choir monk, recording his disposition of soul. Some angels wrote in letters of gold, others in letters of silver, others in ink, others in water, and others held their pens but wrote nothing. Our Lord explained to the saint the meaning of the vision; the writing in gold typified charity and the fervour of the recitation; the writing in silver denoted devotion but little charity or fervour; the words in ink-writing signified careful attention to the full verbal recitation but to little else; the words written in water meant distraction and little attention to the meaning or to the words; and the angels who wrote nothing watched the insolence of those who were voluntarily distracted. The vision has furnished the theme of much pious writing and a theme for Christian painters. It shows how God watches over the daily work of priests, while His angels record in golden or silvern letters the work of pious recitation, or perhaps hold their pens at rest.

What means should be used to promote pious recitation?

ARTICLE II. — THE MEANS TO ADOPT FOR THE PIOUS RECITATION OF THE BREVIARY.

A. — THE MEANS TO ADOPT BEFORE THE RECITATION.

Preparation is necessary before beginning every prayer, for the Holy Ghost says, "Before prayer prepare thy soul, and be not as a man that tempteth God" (Ecclesias. 18. 23). This preparation necessary before other prayers is above all necessary before the recitation of the Divine Office, which is the greatest of all prayers. Two kinds of preparation are necessary, the remote and the proximate.

The remote preparation demands the removal of all obstacles which impede prayer, and the greatest of all prayers, the Church's official prayer. The chief or capital obstacles which impede or prevent a pious recitation of the Breviary are: sin, the passions, the absorbing thoughts of creatures and the ignorance of the Divine Office. And the means to remove these obstacles are to purify the conscience, science, to mortify the passions, to guard the sense and to have an intelligent knowledge of the duty and requirements of a proper fulfilment of the daily task of the saying of the Canonical Hours.

The first means is to purify the conscience from sin, for sin hinders prayer. But what effect has sin on the recitation of the Office? The Office is a prayer, an elevation of the soul to God, and as all writers on ascetics teach, sin is a chain that binds us to earth; it is, says St. Francis, as birdlime which impedes the soul in its flight upwards. Prayer is a conversation with God, but a soul loving sin cannot converse with God; *"Peccatores Deus non audit"* (St. John, ix. 31). Prayer is an intimate union with God, but a soul resting in sin can have no intimate union with God; there can be no intimate union between light and darkness, between sanctity and sin, between good and evil; in a word, between Christ and Belial. *Quae participatio, quae societas lucis ad tenebras? Quae conventio Christi el Belial?*

The second means of procuring fervent prayer is the mortification of the passions. It is not enough to secure fervour in prayer that our souls should be free from sin; we must struggle to master our passions. This point is important—for a soul upset by its passions, anger, pride, etc., cannot with fervour recite the Hours, for it cannot converse with God, it cannot elevate itself to God, it can have no true union with God. It cannot converse with God, for God will not converse with an unmortified soul for three reasons. First, He will not speak if there be no one to listen, for the Holy Ghost tells us "Where there is no hearing, pour not out words" (Eccli. xxxii. 6). God wishes a soul in converse with Him to be calm and still, for God is not in the earthquake (3 Kings, xix. ii.). Again, even if God speaks to an unmortified soul, it cannot hear Him as the passions fix its attention on worldly matters. And even when such a soul tries to listen and to understand, the passions surging and warring drown all sound and sense of holy things. For, "the animal man perceiveth not these things that are of the spirit of God, for it is foolishness to him and he cannot understand, because it is spiritually examined" (I. Cor. ii. 14). The human soul cannot truly unite itself to God if the passions are not conquered, because by their very nature they are opposed to God and hence inspire estrangement from, and disgust for, holy things.

Thirdly, the senses must be guarded. Our five senses can impede the recitation of the Office because they present to our souls images of the things which occupy them, and they can draw our will towards the pleasures which correspond with these objects. It is necessary for the worthy, attentive and devout saying of the Office that each sense be guarded. The sense of sight should be guarded from gazing at objects at hand, persons, books, landscape, etc. The sense of hearing should be guarded in flying from the company of evil speakers, calumniators, detractors, those who speak of worldly affairs or who give evil counsel. It is necessary, too, to guard the tongue from evil speech. "I have set a guard to my mouth, when the sinner stood against me" (Psalm 38, 2); and it is well to guard against too frequent or too long conversations, which fill the soul with thoughts disturbing to a prayerful disposition. The sense of touch should likewise be guarded, for St. Thomas says that the sense of touch is the maintenance of the other senses (1 P. q. 76, a. 75). And when the foundations of a house commence to fall asunder, the walls, the frame and the roof totter and fall. So it is with the senses; when the sense of touch is disturbed the other senses quickly complete the ruin.

What knowledge is needed for the valid and for the licit recitation of the Hours? Must the person know the meaning of the words read? No such knowledge is necessary, for God hears the prayer of the ignorant and illiterate and of the babes. To the chief priests and scribes, who hearing the children crying out the Saviour's praise in the temple, Christ said "Yea, have you not read 'Out of the mouths of infants and sucklings thou hast perfected praise'" (St. Matth. xxi. 15-16), St. Augustine defended from the sneers of the learned, those who prayed to God in rude and barbarous words, or words which they did not understand. "*Noverint non esse vocem ad aures Dei nisi animi affectum*" (*De Catech.* Rud. C.I.). The Church has bound religious, both men and women, to say the Office in choir, even though they may not understand Latin. Nevertheless, it is highly desirable that those who understand Latin should understand what they read daily in the Breviary. God, the Church, the practice of the saints, our own intelligence, our spiritual advantage, demand that every priest should read with knowledge so that with more certainty he may read attentively and devoutly.

For (1) the Holy Ghost warns us to sing wisely, *Psallite sapienter* (Ps. 46.8); (2) that priests may sing wisely, may say the daily Office piously is the reason and end of liturgical studies of the psalms and of the Breviary in theological colleges; (3) the saints who wrote so piously and so learnedly on the psalms and on psalmody are for ever impressing this matter of intelligent recitation. St. Augustine wrote, *"Et quare dicta sunt, nisi ut sciantur? Quare sonuerunt nisi ut audiantur? Quare audita sunt nisi ut intelligantur"* (Tract xxxi. in Joan). Again, commenting on psalm 146, he writes, "David teaches that we sing wisely; let us not seek the mere sound for the ear, but a light for the soul. " St. Thomas Aquinas commenting on "For I pray in a tongue, my spirit prayeth, but my understanding is without fruit" (I. Cor. xiv. 14) wrote *"Constat quod plus lucratur qui orat. Nam, ille qui intelligit reficitur quantum ad intellectum et quantum ad affectum; sed mens ejus qui non intelligit est sine fructu refectionis. "* And (4) our own intellect tells us that the Breviary should be read intelligently and devoutly. One of the ends of the Church in imposing the Divine Office as an obligation is, that by honouring the holy mysteries, or the holy memories of the saints, we may raise our hearts and souls to God, as St. Paul wishes us, "May the God of patience and of comfort grant you to be of one mind towards one another according to Jesus Christ, that with one mind and one mouth you may glorify God" (Rom. xv. 5-6), an effect that cannot be produced by the recital of words which are not understood. It is almost impossible to avoid very grave distractions and to sustain attention if there be not a good knowledge of the matter and form of the Hours recited.

It seems irrational that, priests should spend daily more than an hour reading words that they understand not at all, or very imperfectly; and that the beautiful and sublime thought and language of the book of psalms, which are admired by all educated men, should be, to those who read them every day for years, nothing but a tinkling cymbal, *vox et praeterea nihil*. This is often the case even with priests who practise piously and methodically mental prayer. And yet nowhere are such beautiful acts of faith and confidence in God's power expressed as in the Psalms (e. g., 3, 4, 5, 6, 7, 10, 12, 16, 19, 25, 27, 30, 34, 43, 54, 55, 56, etc.); no more sublime expressions of praise exist than in the Psalms 8, 9, 17, 18, 20, 21, etc. Time spent in studying the history of the Breviary, the structure and the growth of the contents of each Hour, the meanings of the prayers and hymns, is time well spent.

B. — THE IMMEDIATE PREPARATION FOR THE RECITATION OF THE HOURS.

First. It is necessary to foresee from the reading of the *Ordo* what is to be said, and to mark all the psalms, lessons, responses, antiphons and prayers. By this practice, St. Bonaventure says, all is recited and recited in order. *Libri et alia necessaria ad officium praeparantur et legenda studiose ante praevisa, quando et quomodo sint dicenda dicuntur* (Intit. Novit, p. I., c. 4). Unless this matter be arranged before the prayer, *Aperi* is begun, a priest is certain to suffer from distractions, to run the risk of violating the rubrics and to lose some of the spiritual profit which arises from preparation. This point of preparation is attended to by all thoughtful priests and it was ever the practice of the great students and lovers of liturgy.

Second. It is necessary to recollect ourselves. This is simply to draw off from profane thoughts the mind and the heart, and to apply them to the sublime work of conversing with God, which we do in the Divine Office. This recollecting of our wandering thoughts before prayer is impressed on us by Holy Scripture, by the example of the saints, and by our own common sense. Holy Scripture warns us "Before prayer prepare thy soul and be not as a man that tempteth God" (Ecclus. 18. 23). And as typical of the preparation made by saintly priests, the example of St. Charles Borromeo may be mentioned. The saint always spent a quarter of an hour in preparatory prayer before beginning the Church's official prayer. The Venerable John D'Avila made the same practice general amongst his disciples. This holy man narrates, how one day he met a priest of the Society of Jesus, who asked him to recite the Hours with him, and that before beginning their prayer the Jesuit fell on his knees, saying, "There are some who speak of saying the Office as if it were a trifle. Come, they say, let us say our Hours together, and so immediately begin. This is showing very little appreciation for so holy a duty, for it well merits a few moments at least of recollection" (Bacquez). Our own common sense tells us not to rush heedlessly to begin any important work. To converse with God is a work of sublime importance which needs preparation, so that it may be done attentively.

Third. We must invoke God's aid by prayer. No prayer is more suitable than the prayer given as a preparatory prayer in the Breviary, "*Aperi, Domine, os meum...* Open Thou, O Lord, my mouth to bless Thy holy name; cleanse my heart from vain, evil and wandering thoughts; enlighten my understanding, inflame my will, that so I may worthily, attentively and devoutly recite this Office and deserve to be heard in the presence of Thy Divine Majesty. Through Christ our Lord. Amen. O Lord, in union with that divine intention wherewith Thou whilst here on earth didst Thyself praise God, I offer these Hours to Thee. "

Fourth. To unite ourselves with Jesus Christ. In the prefatory prayer *"Aperi, Domine, "* we say *"Domine, in unione, "* etc. In Baptism, Christians are united to Jesus, to His life, to His spirit. He is the Head of the Church and we are its members. And this union should be a real, explicit, vivifying union when we fulfil our ministry of social prayer. This union with Christ is sought for by Himself, by the Apostles, by the Church, and is practised ever by God's saints. The words of the prayer should be reduced to action.

1. Christ our model in all things is our model in prayer, and so He teaches us that when we pray we must say "Our Father, Who art in Heaven, " that is, to use His very words and sentiments. And this desire of our Lord, that souls should be united to Him in prayer, has often been manifested by Him to His saints. To St. Gertrude He said, "My daughter, behold My Heart; look upon It in future as supplying your own defects. When you would pray, ask It to help you to give My Father the homage you owe Him. I shall be ever ready to second you as soon as you call Me to your aid. " St. Bernard, schooled in this practice by the Holy Ghost, knew all its sweetness: "David, " he says, "rejoiced of old to have found his heart to pray to his Master and his God—*Invenit servus tuus cor tuum ut oraret te oratione hac* (II. Kings viii. 27). And I, that I may pray, have found the heart of my King and my Brother, of my sweet Saviour; shall I not then also pray? Yes, certainly, for I am, too, happy, as I have, if not the Heart of Jesus in place of mine, at least have I mine in that of Jesus" (Bacquez, p. 191).

2. St. Paul recommends us to offer our prayers through Jesus Christ. "By him, therefore, let us offer the sacrifice of praise always to God, that is to say, the fruit of lips confessing to His name" (Heb. xiii. 15).

3. The Church wishes this union with Christ and mentions it several times in her prayers, *Per Dominum nostrum Jesum Christum.* She expresses her wish in the preparatory prayer, *Aperi, Domine;* she wishes the words and sentiments of the psalms to be applied to Jesus, the Saviour, whom David typified, and to whom the psalms in

great number relate. And in the frequent repetition of the *Pater Noster*, we speak Christ's sentiments and words.

4. The lives of the saints furnish many examples and precepts of this union with Christ in our prayer. To the examples of St. Gertrude and St. Bernard many others can be added. Several such examples are quoted by Bacquez in his work on the Office.

5. The remembrance of the sublime work of the Office should aid in its fervent recitation. Priests should remember the words of St. Alphonsus: "After the sacrifice of the Mass the Church possesses no treasure so great as the Divine Office. " "It is God's Church, the Spouse of Christ, who has done me the honour of choosing me for this great work—me, in preference to a hundred others. She puts into my hand her holy book of heavenly language, and asks me to read its words before God, to unite with the angels and saints in honouring God. "

6. To propose some particular intention before the recitation of the Hours begins, and to renew it during the recitation is an excellent means of guarding against distractions and mechanical routine. It sustains during the prayer the fervour with which it was begun. St. Bonaventure said to priests "Give *great* attention to the signs (*i. e.*, to the directions, about kneeling, standing, sign of cross, etc.), *greater* attention to the words, and the *greatest* attention to the (particular) intention. "

But what intention ought we to have?

We should have general intentions and particular intentions. We must have the general intentions of the Church, whose ambassadors we are. We must pray that God be known and adored, loved and thanked and praised. We must pray that the Church have freedom, that she may be exalted, that the kingdom of Christ may spread and flourish, that the Pope and clergy of the world may be blessed and guided by God, that holy souls may be confirmed in virtue and that sinners may be converted.

We should have also some particular intentions in reading our Hours. Thus, we may pray to obtain a more lively faith, a greater hope, a more ardent charity, greater meekness and humility, greater patience, detachment from the world, greater fraternal charity, help in keeping vows—in a word, an increase of virtues, especially those in which we may have great wants. Again, a priest may and should beg God to help him and guide him by his light and grace, in doubts, in trouble, in crosses, in his daily work as a priest, in his parish, in his schools, in his college. Particularly and fervently should a priest pray for success in his religious instruction in school, in church, in the pulpit. For St. Augustine tells us that success in this matter depends more on prayer than on preaching (*De Doc. Christ., Lib.* 4, chap. 15). And at every Hour a priest should pray for a happy death.

Before saying his Hours, a priest may form a special intention of praying for others, his superiors, his parents, his brothers and sisters, his benefactors, his friends, his enemies, for those who have asked for prayers, for some one in sorrow, for some one in sin, for a soul in purgatory. Of course, these prayers benefit the priest who offers them, for as St. Gregory the Great said so well, *"Plus enim pro se valere preces suas efficit qui has et pro aliis impendit"* (Moral II. 25).

AIDS DURING THE RECITATION.

I. A suitable place should be selected. The Psalmist sang *"In omni loco dominationis ejus, benedic, anima mea, Domino"* (Ps. 102, 22). Our Lord wishes us to pray always; St. Paul says (I. Tim. ii.) that we should pray in every place, and theologians teach that a priest may validly and licitly say his Hours walking in the fields, in his room, or in any suitable place. The most suitable place is the church. For it is a house of prayer (St. Matt. xxi. 43), and the Holy Ghost asks us to go there to pray, *"in templo ejus omnes dicent gloriam"* (Ps. 28, 9). The Apostles, going to the temple to pray at the sixth and at the ninth hour, show us how suitable is the place holier than the temple—the church. The practice of the saints impresses on us the suitability of the church for the Church's official prayer. In the life of every modern saint we find recommended and practised the saying of the Hours at the altar. Perhaps, the example which is best known to missionary priests, is the example of the Cure d'Ars, who in the early days of his priestly life always said his Breviary kneeling in the sanctuary. His parishioners liked from time to time to slip into the church to watch him. "Often, " says an eye-witness, "he paused while praying, his looks fixed on the Tabernacle, with eyes in which were painted so lively a faith that one might suppose our Lord was visible to his gaze. Later, his church being continually filled with an attentive crowd following his least movements, he took pains to avoid everything that might excite their admiration. Yet still, he might be frequently found, after a long day passed in the sacred tribunal, reciting his Hours on his knees, either in the sacristy or in a corner of the choir, a few steps from the altar; so strong was the attraction that drew him to unite his prayer to that of our Lord, so great was the love and respect inspired by the presence and infinite majesty of his Divine Master" (*Life of Cure d'Ars*, by Monnin).

Every priest must feel that the church benches, or the sanctuary, with their silence, their every part awakening and reminding the soul that this is the house of God, this is the gate of Heaven, are places most suitable for prayer and are great aids to fervent prayer. The thought of the presence of Christ with His adoring angels, to whose songs of praise the priest should unite himself, should help wonderfully in the devout recitation of the Hours. St. Alphonsus recommends that priests saying the Breviary should say it before a crucifix or before a statue or picture of the Blessed Virgin, so that gazing from time to time on these holy objects may foster or renew pious thoughts.

II. A great aid to pious recitation of the Hours is to take up a respectful position. The Office is a prayer, an elevation of the soul to God, and should be treated as such; and as everyone knows, the union of soul and body is such that in vocal prayer both are employed. If the body take up a lazy or unbecoming position in prayer, it is an insult to God to Whom prayer is offered, and is a certain source of distraction and faulty prayer. Habit does much in this matter, and where a priest labours to correct an inclination to take up a too comfortable position in saying his Hours, he is striving to pray well.

Priests, young and old, say writers on this point, should be vigilant in this aid to fervent prayer. The well-known words of St. Teresa recommending a comfortable attitude in prayer do not clash with this doctrine. In the *Selva*, St. Alphonsus writes: "It is related that while two religious recited Matins a devil appeared, caused an intolerable stench, and through mockery said, 'To the prayer which you offer such incense is suited'—*ad talem orationem tale debetur incensum.* "

Which attitude is the best? Seeing the examples of the saints, St. Charles Borromeo, St. Vincent de Paul, St. Francis de Sales, St. John de la Salle, the Cure d'Ars, and of many other saintly men, the best attitude in reciting the Hours is kneeling. Other saints accustomed themselves to recite their Hours standing, with head uncovered. Others followed, in private recitation, all the positions—sitting, kneeling, standing—required in choir. The practice is said to aid in banishing distractions, and contributes greatly to attention and devotion. Of course, in private recitation no one is bound to any of these practices. But they have proved useful to many in practising devout prayer. Everyone is bound to pray with fervour, and a respectful attitude is a big help towards that end.

Slow, deliberate pronunciation is another aid to the fervent saying of the Hours of the Breviary. The lives of saintly men show their practice in this matter. Knowing that they were the ambassadors of the Church in presenting her praise, thanks and wants to God, they read with care and attention. From their slow and deliberate reading of the holy words, their souls drew out the sublime thoughts and sentiments which their lips expressed. In rapid reading, the mind and heart have not time to think well on the meaning of the words and of the sentiments, and hence, no holy thoughts fill the soul, no acts of virtue are elicited, no prayer of petition is offered, no holy resolutions are formed. Indeed, very often—to quote the words of a venerable author—priests seem to say with their lips and to express by their rapid reading, not *Deus in adjutorium meum intende*, O God, make haste to help me! but *Domine ad festinandum me adjuva*—"O God, help me to hasten? " Wise old Rodriguez advises readers of spiritual books to observe a hen drinking and to imitate her slow and deliberate sipping, by reading in small quantities, with pauses. Sometimes priests acquire the habit of hurried reading, quite unconsciously, and afterwards labour hard, and in vain, too, to correct it. It is important for beginners in the Breviary to go at a slow pace, as the trot and the gallop are fatal to good and pious recitation. Sometimes priests excuse this hurried reading, as they wish to save time! Why do priests wish to save time? "For study, " some may say; but the obligation of the Divine Office precedes all obligations of study, and its devout recitation is of far greater importance to the priest and to the Church than is any other or every other study. Some priests gallop through the Hours, to gain time for other ministerial work, they say. But they forget that the primary work— after the celebration of Mass—and the *most important work* of a priest, is the great official prayer of the Church. Who amongst priests leads the life of ceaseless toil which the Cure d'Ars led? And we have read how he said his Hours. St. Francis Xavier found time to preach to his many neophytes, to teach them, to baptize them, and yet he did not use the permission given him to shorten his Breviary prayer. He read the whole Office daily and added to it prayers to obtain the grace of better attention and devotion.

Sometimes the reading of the Hours is hurried for a motive less praiseworthy than the motives of study or of priestly work. *Producitur somnus, producitur mensa, produncuntur confabulationes, lusus, nugae nugarum; solius supremae Magestratis, cultus summa qua potest celeritate deproperatur* (Kugler, *De Spiritu Eccles.*), "On this, God complained one day to St. Bridget, saying that some priests lose so much time every day in conversing with friends on worldly affairs; and afterwards, in conversing with Him, while they recite the Office, they are so hurried that they dishonour Him more than they glorify Him" (St. Alphonsus, *Selva*). In the hurried reading of the Office, time, a few minutes perhaps, is gained, but what is lost? Does the loss of all the lights and graces and blessings of the Office compensate for the time gained? It is important that all who read the Breviary hurriedly, or who may be tempted to acquire the habit, should weigh well the words read therein (Friday's Vespers) "*Labor labiorum ipsorum operiet eos; cadent super eos carbones*" (Ps. 139). "The labour of their lips shall overwhelm them; burning coals shall fall upon them. "

To acquire this important habit, the practice of reading at a slow pace the words of the Breviary, authors suggest several little hints. One is, never to start reading the Hours unless there be *ample* time for finishing the Hour or Hours intended to be then and there read. The practice of squeezing the small Hours into scraps of time (e. g., in the intervals between hearing confessions in the confessional, at a session) is fatal to careful and pious reading. Another hint is, to read everything, every word (*e. g., Pater Noster, Ave, Credo*), and to repeat nothing from memory, because the printed words meeting the eyes and the spoken words reaching the ears help to fix the attention and there is less risk of their passing unnoticed. This was the practice of St. Charles Borromeo. St. Philip Neri never recited from memory even in saying the small Hours. St. Vincent de Paul always spent a great time in saying his Breviary. His intense fervour was helped by his careful reading of every word, and this practice of keeping his eyes fixed steadily on the printed matter of the book he recommended to his congregation of priests. Some holy priests maintained that they could recite from memory with greater fervour than from the reading of the pages of the Breviary; but the practice is not one for the many. Another hint to help pious recitation is to *earnestly wish* to say the Office worthily, attentively and devoutly. This wish must bring up before the mind the thought of how displeasing to God and how great is the daily loss—not to speak of a lifetime's loss-to the soul of a priest who prays carelessly, tepidly and mechanically. But in spite of all precautions, it may be noticed during the recitation of the Hours that, without our own fault, the words are said too quickly. It is advised, then, to pause and to say mentally what the Venerable Boudon was wont to say to his soul in similar circumstances: "To punish and mortify thee, I will go more slowly; I will devote to my office to-day a longer time" (Bacquez).

IV. To prevent distractions and to banish them are no easy matters. It is impossible to avoid all distractions. Involuntary distractions do not hinder merit; still it is important that an effort be made to diminish and repress the quality of such disturbing elements in prayer.

First of all, we can never totally avoid all distractions, nor can we entirely and completely remove them when they enter our souls. The human soul cannot pray for any notable time without distraction. The greatest saints knew this well. St. Augustine wrote, *"Vult se tenere ut stet, et quodammodo fugit a se nec invenit cancellos quibus se includat"* (in Psalm 95). St. Thomas wrote *"Vix unum Pater noster potest homo dicere quin mens ad alia fertur. "* The author of the *Imitation of Christ* wrote, "For I confess truly that I am accustomed to be very much distracted. For oftentimes I am not there where I am bodily standing or sitting, but am rather there where my thoughts carry me" (Bk. iii. c. 48). The same writer wrote, "And I, a wretch and the vilest of men.... I can hardly spend one half hour as I ought. " St. Teresa wrote, "I am not less distracted than you are during Office, and try to think that it arises from weakness of head. Do not fear to think so, too. Does not our Lord know, that when we perform this duty we would wish to do it with the greatest possible attention? "

After reading these words we can understand how prayer offered up with involuntary distractions is true, holy prayer. St. Thomas tells us *"Dicendum quod in spiritu et veritate orat, qui ex instinctu spiritus ad orandum accedit, etiamsi ex aliqua infirmitate mens postmodum evagetur.... Evagatio vero mentis quae fit praeter propositum orationis fructum non tollat"* (2.2. q. 83, a. 13).

Nevertheless, every effort should be made to avoid and to banish distractions. The ways of doing this are given in all treatises on prayer. Every priest knows them well. There are negative means and positive means. The negative means consist in withdrawing the senses and the powers of the soul from everything disturbing the soul's converse with God; in guarding against any too absorbing interest in worldly affairs, so that the mind is unmanageable and cannot be fixed on sacred things. St. Francis of Assisi, working at a piece of furniture before saying Terce, was, during the saying of that hour disturbed by the thought of his manual work. When he re-entered his cell he took the bit of work and threw it in the fire saying, "I wish to sacrifice to the Lord the thing which hindered my prayer to Him. "

The positive means of avoiding and of banishing distractions are given above; they are to read slowly, to read every word, to read in a becoming position, to observe choir directions, to give ample time to each Hour. Another rule given by writers on the pious recitation of the Office, is to pause at certain places in the psalms to renew attention and elicit affections. Some authors recommend such pauses at the end of the invitatory, at the end of each hymn, or after each *Gloria*. "Study well the *Gloria Patri*, " said St. Francis of Assisi, "for in it you find the substance of the scriptures. "

V. To apply the mind to what is read is another help to pious recitation. It seems to be a useless repetition of an obvious fact that to apply the mind to the prayers read, helps to ward off and to drive away distractions. Such a practice is natural for a person of intelligence, and the Church wishes and expects such intelligent and heartfelt prayer. God said to the Jewish priests what applies to the Christian priesthood, too: "And now, O ye priests, this commandment is to you, if you will not hear, if you will not lay it to heart to give glory to My name, saith the Lord of Hosts, I will curse your blessings, because you have not laid it to heart" (Mal. ii. 1-2). Christ complained about the Jewish people who honoured Him with their lips, but had their hearts far from Him. And God's great servants realized this fully. St. Paul said, "And he that speaketh by a tongue (the gift of speaking strange tongues) let him pray that he may interpret. For if I pray in a tongue my spirit prayeth, *but my understanding is without fruit*. What is it then? I will pray with the spirit. I will pray also with the understanding. I will sing with the spirit, I will sing also with the understanding" (I. Cor. xiv. 13-15). St. Gregory the Great said that true prayer consists not only in the articulation of the words, but also in the attention of the heart; for to obtain the divine graces our good desires have greater efficacy than mere words (*Moral, lib.* 22. *cap.* 13). Peter de Blois wrote of the priests of his time, "*Labia sunt in canticis et animus in patinis*! Their lips are in the psalms, but their heart is in the dishes! " (*Selva*). "*Age quod agis*, " says the *Imitation of Christ*.

VI. It is advisable not to dwell on the literary excellence of the Breviary during the recitation of the Office. It is a useful thing that priests should recognise the authorship of the psalms recited, their probable dates, the circumstances of their composition, the sublimity of their thought, the peculiarity of their Hebrew style, the rhythm and poetry of the Hebrews. But the *dwelling* on these thoughts leads to distractions. Again, some priests, like the clerics of the Renaissance and post-Renaissance times, despise and dislike the Breviary for its alleged barbarous style. These unworthy and foolish sentiments are met with, very rarely. They are opposed to the priestly spirit, which should love and respect the Scripture extracts, God's inspired words. The homilies from the Fathers are well chosen, and suitable for the greatest prayer and for the greatest prayerbook the world has ever known. The hymns are the wonder and study of scholars of every religion. St. Augustine, after his conversion even, felt a repugnance for the holy Scriptures as unequal to Cicero in form. But in his mature age and considered judgment, the saint reversed his judgment; "*non habent,* " he wrote of the Pagan classics, "*illae paginae vultum pietatis, lacrymas confessionis spiritum contribulatum cor contritum et humiliatum*" (Confess. Bk. 7, c. 21).

VII. To think of Christ's Passion is another aid to good Breviary recitation. We have seen in the theological part of this book (page 4) the seven principal stages of the Passion which correspond with the seven principal parts of the Office. And this devout thought on some scene of the Passion is recommended by all writers on the Divine Office, as an easy and very profitable means and aid to attentive and devout saying of the Hours. It is a means practised by thousands of priests.

St. Bonaventure recommended that at each Hour some thought of the mysteries of the life and death of Christ should be held in mind. Thus, Matins, the night Office, might be offered up in honour of the birth and infancy of Christ; Lauds, in honour of His resurrection; Terce, in honour of the coming of the Holy Ghost; None, in memory of Christ's death; Vespers, in thanksgiving for the Eucharist.

VIII. To remember the presence of God, of our angel guardian, and of the demons, is a practice recommended by writers on recitation of the Office in or out of choir. This thought of the presence of God was one of the aids recommended by St. Benedict to his religious, to aid their devout fulfilment of the great work of reciting their Hours worthily, attentively, and devoutly. Centuries after St. Benedict's death we find St. Bonaventure repeating this advice to his novices. Blessed Peter Faber, S.J., to make his Breviary prayer more fervent, used to picture to himself the presence of his guardian angel at his side recording his pious and holy thoughts, and the demon recording his distractions. "Dearly beloved priest, " wrote St. Alphonsus, "when you take the Breviary in your hand, imagine that an angel stands on one side to register your merits in the Book of Life if you say the Office with devotion, and on the other a devil who, if you recite it with distraction, writes your faults in the book of death. With this thought excite yourself to say the Office with the greatest possible devotion. Endeavour, then, not only at the beginning of the Office, but also at the beginning of each psalm, to renew your attention, that you may be able to excite in your heart all the sentiments that you shall read" (*Selva*).

ARTICLE IV. — AFTER SAYING THE DIVINE OFFICE.

1. Give God thanks for His goodness in permitting us to join in the great work, for hearing our prayer, and for His helps and graces during its duration.

2. Ask God's pardon for faults committed in the course of this prayer of His Church.

3. Devoutly recite the "*Sacro-sanctae et Individuae Trinitati...* Amen. V. *Beata viscera....* R. *Et beata ubera....* " This prayer, which is generally printed in Breviaries immediately before the Psalter, is to be said kneeling, where this is physically possible. This is necessary in order to gain the indulgence granted by Pope Pius X. to all persons obliged to recite the Divine Office. It is not of obligation and its omission is not sinful. It forms no part of the obligatory Office. "It must be said kneeling, but at the request of Cardinal Asquini, Prefect of the Congregation of Indulgences, Pope Pius IX. was pleased to make one exception (July 12, 1865) in favour of persons who were not able to say it kneeling — *infirmitatis tantum causa*. Hence, travellers or persons on a journey are not exempted, for they can say it kneeling at the end of the journey. It is sufficient to say the '*Sacro-sanctae*' once only, that is, at the end of Compline, with the intention of obtaining pardon of all the defects a person may have been guilty of in saying the entire Office. Yet it may be repeated after each Hour, e.g., after Matins, and Lauds, after the small Hours and after Compline; in each case one would thereby get forgiveness for the faults committed during the part of the Office recited. This explanation has been given by the

Holy Father (Pius IX.) himself. The usage amongst the chapters at Rome, as at St. Peter's, St. Mary's, etc., is to recite it every time they leave the choir" (Maurel, S.J., *Le chretien e claire sur la nature et l'usage des Indulgences*). The beauty and sublimity of this prayer is not always appreciated. Its translation here may inspire fresh thoughts of fervour. "To the most holy and undivided Trinity, to the humanity of our Lord Jesus Christ crucified, to the fruitful virginity of the most glorious Mary ever a Virgin, and to the company of all the saints, be given by every creature eternal praise, honour, power and glory, and to us the remission of all our sins. Amen. Blessed be the womb of the Virgin Mary, which bore the Son of the Eternal Father. And blessed be the breasts which gave suck to Christ, our Lord. "

In connection with this prayer an interesting question is discussed in the *Irish Ecclesiastical Record* (No. 540. December, 1912). Is this prayer merely a sacramental? Has it an indulgence attached to it at all? The querist quotes *The new Raccolta*, in answering the second part of his query but wishes to know if it be an indulgence how it produces its effects. "For either the defects committed in reading the Divine Office are voluntary or involuntary. If voluntary they are sins and consequently cannot be touched by an indulgence; if involuntary they are not sinful and therefore stand in no need of an indulgence. " In a very long reply Dr. John M. Harty sums up, "For our part we adhere to the view which says that the efficacy of the privilege annexed by Leo X. and Pius X. to the *Sacro-sanctae* is derived from an indulgence. At the same time we think that these prayers are also sacramentals, since they are official prayers of the Church. Under this aspect, they obtain the ordinary benefits which are attached to sacramentals, and, accordingly lead to a remission of sin and temporal punishment by means of sorrow and satisfaction, which are elicited under the influence of the abundant graces given by God, through the intercession of the Church. They also placate God, so as to render Him willing to grant His favours even though defects exist in the recitation of the Office.... Though these defects are not produced *ex opere operato*, they nevertheless are real, and are an encouragement to priests, whose human frailty prevents the perfect performance even of the most sacred functions of their priestly office. "

PART III

THE CANONICAL HOURS.

CHAPTER I.

MATINS.

Etymology. The word *Matins* is derived from *Matuta*, the Latin name for the Greek goddess of morning. The word used in the Roman Breviary is *matutinum (i. e., tempus)*. It is the old name for Lauds, *Laudes matutinae*. The word was also used to denote the office of Vigils. Hence, the word was used in three senses, to denote the nocturns and lauds, to denote Lauds only and to denote the vigil office. In liturgical study the word was confusing, and sometimes it is the context only which gives the author's meaning. This, the principal Hour of the Church's public prayer, was, in the early days of Christianity, said at night, and was called *Nocturnum* and *Vigiliae*.

Origin. The night office of vigils dates from the very earliest days of Christianity. It derived its name from the vigils or night watches of the soldiers, who divided the night, from six o'clock in the evening to six o'clock in the morning, into four watches of three hours each. The nightly meetings of the Christians came to be called by the name *vigils*, but the meetings were not begun at the stated hours of military vigil and did not finish with them. Why these meetings of Christians were held at night, and in what their religious exercises consisted in, both in matter and form, is an unsolved problem. But it is certain that they resembled the services of the Jewish synagogue in the readings from Scripture, psalm-singing and prayers, and differed from those services by having readings from the Gospels, the Epistles, and from non-canonical books, such as the Epistle of St. Clement. The Eucharistic service always formed part of them. Indeed, the very name, Synagogue was given to these assemblies of Christians, as we see from the Pastor of Hermes. In their common prayer, they faced towards the East, as the Jews did towards Jerusalem. They had precentors and janitors as in the Jewish rites. Their services consisted of the readings from the Mosaic law, from Gospels and Epistles, exposition of Scripture, a set sermon, long and fervent "blessings" or thanksgiving and psalms. Before there were any written gospels to read, we gather that the reading of the Old Law, of the Prophets and the Psalms, was followed by a set sermon on the life and death of Christ (Bickel, *Messe und Pascha,* p, 91). From St. Basil (fourth century) it is concluded that two choirs sang the Psalms. Cassian writes that the monks of the fifth century celebrated the Night Office with twelve psalms and readings from the Old and the New Testaments. Hence, "we find the same elements repeated, the psalms generally chanted in the form of responses, that is to say, by one or more cantors, the choir repeating one verse which served as a response, alternately with the verses of the psalms, which were sung by the cantors, readings taken from the Old and the New Testaments and, later on, from the works of the Fathers and Doctors; litanies, supplications, prayers for divers members of the Church, clergy, faithful, neophytes and catechumens; for emperors, travellers; the sick; and generally for all the necessities of the Church, and even for Jews and for heretics. It is quite easy to find these essentials in our modern Matins" (Dom Cabrol, *Cath. Encyclopedia*, art. "Matins").

Matins on account of its length and position in the Breviary is the most important part of the daily Office. And, on account of the variety and beauty of its elements, is considered the most remarkable.

The prayer *Pater Noster* begins the Office. It is the Lord's prayer, *divina institutions formata*, when Christ told His Apostles "*Sic vos orabitis*" (St. Matt. vi. 9). It is the most excellent of all prayers, being most excellent in its author, its form, its depth of meaning, its effects. The prayer consists of a preface, "Our Father, Who art in heaven, hallowed be Thy name, Thy Kingdom come, Thy will be done on earth as it is in heaven. " And in the body of the prayer are seven petitions—three for the honour and glory of God, in and by ourselves, and four for our own wants, spiritual and temporal. Very excellent matter on the greatest of prayers is to be found in the *Catechism of the Council of Trent* (translation, Duffy, Dublin) and in *A Lapide* (St. Matt. vi.). Writers on liturgy say that the recitation of the *Pater Noster* as the opening prayer of Matins was *not obligatory* until the beginning of the twelfth century. It is said that the monks were wont to say a *Pater Noster* at each altar in the church before entering their stalls for Office recitation. This practice delayed the beginning of the Office in choir, and a rule was made that those who wished to say this prayer must say it in their stalls, in a low tone. Of course, in the Breviary of Pius V. (1568) this practice became obligatory on each person bound to read the Hours.

Ave Maria. This is a leading prayer amongst the great prayers of the Mass and the Office. It, too, is excellent in its authors, its form (clear, short devotional), in motive (in honouring Mary, Mother of God, and in begging her intercession). It is divided into three parts, the words of the angel, of St. Elizabeth and of the Church, Devout thoughts on this prayer have been penned by countless clients of Mary in every age. Priests are familiar with many such writings, great and small, but *A Lapide* (St. Luke I.) bears reading and re-reading. The prayer, as it stands in the Breviary to-day, is not of very ancient date. "In point of fact there is little or no trace of the Hail Mary as an accepted devotional formula before 1050.... To understand the developments of the devotion, it is important to grasp the fact that the *Ave Maria* was merely a form of greeting. It was, therefore, long customary to accompany the words with some external gesture of homage, a genuflexion, or at least an inclination of the head.... In the time of St. Louis the *Ave Maria* ended with the words *benedictus fructus ventris tui*: it has since been extended by the introduction both of the Holy Name and of a clause of petition.... We meet the *Ave* as we know it now, printed in the Breviary of the Camaldolese monks and in that of the Order de Mercede C. 1514.... The official recognition of the *Ave Maria* in its complete form, though foreshadowed in the Catechism of the Council of Trent, was finally given in the Roman Breviary of 1568" (Father Thurston, S.J., *Cath. Encyclopedia*, art. "Hail Mary. ")

Credo. The Apostles' Creed is placed at the beginning of Matins, because Matins is the beginning of the whole Office, and faith is the beginning, the *principium* of every supernatural work. St. Paul teaches us that it is necessary for us to stir up our faith when we approach God, "For he that cometh to God must believe that He is. " In reciting the Creed we should think of the sublime truths of our faith, and our hearts should feel, what our lips say, "For with the heart we believe unto justice; but with the mouth confession is made unto salvation" (Rom. x. 10). We should remember too, that this formula of faith comes to us from Apostolic times and that it has been repeated millions of times by saints and martyrs; their sentiments of belief, of confidence in God and love of God should be ours.

Domine labia mea aperies. The practice of this beautiful invocation dates from the time of St. Benedict (480-553). In his Office it stood after the words *Deus in adjutorium*. These words *Domine labia mea aperies*, taken from the Psalm *Miserere*, remind us of God purifying the lips of Isaias His prophet with a burning coal, of how God opened the lips of Zachary to bless God and to prophesy. "And immediately his mouth was opened and his tongue loosed, and he spoke blessing God" (St. Luke, i. 64). Very appropriately, does the priest reciting the Divine Office ask God to open his lips, to fortify his conscience, to touch his heart.

Deus in adjutorium. These words, the opening words of Psalm 69, were always and everywhere used by the monks of old, says Cassian, who called this short prayer the formula of piety, the continual prayer. The Church repeats it often in her Office. St. John Climacus says it is the great cry of petition for help to triumph over our invisible enemy, who wishes to distract us and to mar our prayer. It should be said with humility and with confidence in God. In repeating these holy words we make the sign of the Cross; for, all grace comes from the sacrifice of the Cross; and besides, it is a holy and an ancient practice to begin all good works with the sacred sign.

Gloria Patri. This little prayer indicates the purpose and end of the recitation of the Office, the glory of the Holy Trinity. "Bring to the Lord glory and honour; bring to the Lord glory to His name" (Psalm 28). The many repetitions of this formula in the Church liturgy shows the great honour which she pays to it, and the trust she places in its efficacy. It was especially loved by St. Francis of Assisi, who said that it contained all wisdom.

This form of doxology, "Glory be to the Father, to the Son, and to the Holy Ghost, " was adopted to repel Arianism, by giving to the faithful a compact theological formula by which they could end every dispute. Some authors quote St. Ephrem (circa 363) as the originator of this much-used prayer. The form would seem to be of Syrian origin, translated into Greek and later into Latin (Dom Cambrol, *Dictionnaire d' Archeologie Chretienne*, I., 2282, *et seq.*, word Antienne, Liturgie; *Month*, May, 1910).

Invitatory. Venite Adoremus.... The cry of the Church calling on all to adore and praise God, Who has done all for us, Who is the Great Shepherd, and we, the sheep of His fold, should not harden our hearts as did the ungrateful Jews. We should pray for all, Catholics, infidels and sinners.

"A message from the saints. Let us imagine, like St. Stephen at his martyrdom, we are privileged to see the heavens opened, and before our eyes the City of God, with its twelve gates all of pearl, and its streets of pure gold, as it were transparent glass, is laid bare, and that we see the angels in their legions, and the redeemed of the Lord around the throne of God. Thousands of thousands are ministering to Him, " as St. John tells us, "and ten thousand times a hundred thousand stand before Him, " and we hear the voice of God, as the noise of many waters in company with that great multitude which no man can number, out of every tribe and nation, clothed in white robes, with palms in their hands, coming into Sion with praise, with everlasting joy upon their heads, for from their eyes God has wiped away all tears, and sorrow and mourning have fled away.

"There are the white-robed army of Martyrs, holy Confessors, too, men of renown in their generation, and Virgins, the Spouses of Christ: there are those who have come through great tribulation, who once, perchance, were far from God, but have washed their robes in the blood of the Lamb and are now numbered among the people of God, sitting in the beauty of peace and in the tabernacle of confidence and in wealthy rest. Let us bring them all before us in vision. They have overcome the beast and are standing by the sea of glass, having the harps of God; the Prince of Pastors has appeared to them and they have received a never-failing crown of glory and by the Lamb of God they have been led to fountains of the waters of life. " Let us listen as they sing their canticle to God, "Holy, Holy, Holy, Lord God of Hosts, who is and who was and who is to come"; let us listen as they sing to us, for we are fellow citizens with them, and where they are we also must be if we remain faithful to the end. What do they sing, "O come let us praise the Lord with joy; let us joyfully sing to God, our Saviour" (*Sing ye to the Lord*, pp. 94-95— Rev. R. Eaton).

The authorship of this psalm—which is said daily in Matins—is attributed to David in the Septuagint and Vulgate. Its Latin form in the invitatory differs slightly from the Vulgate text. The Breviary retains here the text of St. Jerome's revision and the Vulgate contains the second and more correct revision.

Hymns. The hymn is an answer to the invitation given to us in the invitatory, to praise God and to rejoice with Him. It is a song of joy and praise. Hymns were introduced into the Divine Office in the Eastern Church before the time of St. Ambrose (340-397). To combat the Arians, who spread their errors by verse set to popular airs, St. Ambrose, it is said, introduced public liturgical hymn-singing in his church in Milan, and his example was followed gradually through the Western Church. (See Note A, *infra.*)

The final stanza of a Breviary hymn is called the doxology ([Greek: doxa] praise, [Greek: logos] speech), a speaking of praise. Hymns which have the final stanza proper, the *Ave Maris stella*, Lauds hymn of the Blessed Sacrament, Matins hymn for several Martyrs, the first Vesper hymn of the Office of Holy Cross, and the Vesper hymns of St. Venantius and St. John Cantius, never change the wording of the stanza.

But, *where the metre of the hymn* admits such a change as possible in the last stanza.

(a) From Christmas to Epiphany *Jesu tibi sit gloria, Qui natus es de Virgine* is inserted in all hymns, even on saints' offices.

(b) From Epiphany till end of its octave, *Jesu tibi sit gloria, Qui apparuisti gentibus.*

(c) From Low Sunday till Ascension Thursday, on Pentecost Sunday and its octave, all hymns end in *Deo Patri sit gloria, Et Filio qui a mortuis.*

This is the ending for all hymns of saints' feasts in Paschal times, excepting those hymns mentioned above.

(d) From Ascension to Pentecost (except in the hymn *Salutis humanae Sator*) the doxology is *Jesu tibi sit gloria, Qui victor in coelum redis.*

(e) Feast of Transfiguration has *Jesu, tibi sit gloria, Qui te revelas parvulis.*

In all other hymns the doxology is read as it is printed in the Breviary.

Antiphons. Antiphon, coming from Greek words meaning a re-echoing of the sound, is a chant performed alternately by two choirs, and was used in pagan drama, long before the Christian era. At what date it was introduced into Church liturgy it is difficult to determine. Some say it was introduced by St. Ignatius, second Bishop of Antioch. It is certain that it was used by bishops and priests to attract, retain and teach the faithful during the Arian heresy. In church music, the lector ceased to recite the psalm as a solo and the faithful divided into two choirs, united in the refrain *Gloria Patri.*

With us, the antiphon generally is a verse or verses from Scripture, recited before and after each psalm. "The verse which serves as the antiphon text contains the fundamental thought of the psalm to which it is sung and indicates the point of view from which it is to be understood. In other words, it gives the key to the liturgical and mystical meaning of the psalm, with regard to the feast on which it occurs" (*Cath. Encycl.*, art. "Antiphon").

Psalms. In the Breviary, before the recent reform, twelve psalms were recited in the first nocturn of Sundays and on ferias. This recitation of twelve psalms was, Cassian tells us, caused by the apparition of an angel, who appeared to the monks and sang at one session twelve psalms, terminating with *Alleluia.* The event was mentioned at the Council of Tours, In the new reform, nine psalms are recited at Matins; they should, the old writers on liturgy tell us, remind us of the nine choirs of angels who without ceasing sing God's praise.

In the new Psalter, the Psalms have been divided into two large divisions, Psalms I. —CVIII. being assigned to the night Office, Matins; and Psalms CIX. —CL. for the day Offices, Lauds to Compline. From this latter division has been made: —

(1) a selection of psalms suitable by their character and meaning to Lauds (*vide infra*, psalms at Lauds);

(2) a selection of psalms suitable to Compline;

(3) the psalms long used in the small Hours of Sunday's Office;

(4) the first psalms assigned by Pope Pius V. to Prime on Monday, Tuesday, Wednesday, Thursday and Friday.

The remaining psalms are divided into seven groups, in simple numerical order. The psalms of Matins generally come first, and are followed immediately by the groups of psalms for the day Hours.

In the new Breviary, seven new canticles are added to the ten, which stood in the older book. The ten taken from the old and from the new Testament are *Audite coeli* (Deut., chap. 32) in Lauds for Saturday;

Benedicite (Daniel, chap. 3) Sunday's Lauds; *Cantemus* (Exod., chap. 15) Thursday's Lauds; *Confitebor* (Isaias, chap. 12) Monday's Lauds; *Domine audivi* (Habacuc, chap. 3) Friday's Lauds; *Ego dixi* (Isaias, chap. 38) Tuesday's Lauds; *Exultavit* (I. Kings, chap 2) Wednesday's Lauds. From the new Testament we have *Benedictus, Magnificat, Nunc dimittis.* To these are now added *Audite verbum* (Jeremias, chap. 31), *Benedictus es* (I. Paralip., chap. 29), *Benedictus es* (Daniel, chap. 3), *Hymnum cantemus* (Judith, chap. 16), *Magnus es* (Tobias, chap. 13), *Miserere nostri* (Ecclus. 36), *Vere tu es Deus* (Isaias, chap. 45). (*Cf. The New Psalter*, Burton and Myers, pp. 51-52).

"The psalms retain the accentuation of the Latin words, which was inserted at the request of Pius V. in the Reformed Breviary of 1568; and also the asterisk, which was introduced to mark the division of the verses of the Psalms in Urban VIII. 's Reform in 1632. " The verse division of the psalms do not, in the Breviary, always coincide with those of the Vulgate—e. g., Psalm X. : —

PSALTER   VULGATE

Dominus in templo sancto suo   Dominus in templo sancto
suo Dominus in coelo sedes ejus   Dominus in coela sedes
ejus: (v. 4).   Oculi ejus in pauperem
                                   palpebrae ejus interrogant
                                   respsiciunt;
                                   filios hominum (verse 5).

The present verse divisions of the Vulgate were introduced by a Calvinistic printer of Geneva, who used them in an edition of the Greek new Testament published in 1561. Formerly, biblical chapters were, for sake of reference, divided into seven sections denoted by letters of the alphabet a, b, c, etc. In the older breviaries, the reference to the little lesson at Compline stood, I. Pet. v.c. The new Breviary has adopted the modern form of reference, and we now read I. Pet. v. 8-9. It is sometimes confusing to find reference made to the psalms by non-Catholic writers. This arises from the different method of numbering which is used by them. In the Greek version of the old Testament—the septuagent—the Psalter is arranged differently from the Hebrew. Psalms 9 and 10 are counted as one and so are Psalms 114 and 115, but 116 and 117 are divided into two, leaving the complete number 150, as in the Hebrew version. The Vulgate and the Douay version follow the Greek, and Psalm 9 contains 21 verses, not

38 as in the English Authorised Version. The English revised version follows the numbering of the Vulgate.

"Our Latin version of the Psalms is that of the old Itala; it was not made directly on the Hebrew original... it is then a translation (the Greek). By the time of St. Jerome, it had become very faulty, owing to the very many transcriptions which had been made of it; and this great scholar revised it, about 383 A. D., on the request of Pope Damascus. His corrections were not very numerous, because, he feared to upset, by too many changes, the habits of the faithful, most of whom knew the psalms by heart. This first version is known as the Roman Psalter. It was soon deemed insufficient. St. Jerome once more set to work between 387 and 391, and published a second edition, more carefully and more extensively corrected, of the Italic version of the Psalms; it is called the *Gallican Psalter*, because it was adopted by the churches of Gaul. When he, later on, translated the Old Testament from the Hebrew, he published his third edition of the Psalms, the *Hebraic Psalter*. This version was a good one, but the faithful were so familiar with the old Itala psalter that the Church, in her wisdom, thought best to keep it in the editions of the Vulgate according to the Gallican form.... Our official version of the psalms is then in many ways defective. It is frequently incorrect and barbarous in style, obscure in places, and even fails at times to give the exact sense of the original. Although our Vulgate is not perfect, it possesses admirable strength and conciseness, joined to an agreeable savour which gives it the greatest value and causes the words of the sacred singers, under this form of the Latin spoken by the people, to strike the mind and become engraved upon the memory much better than if they were clothed in all the elegance of a modern tongue" (Vigouroux; *Manuel Biblique*, tom. ii., 663-664).

The following replies by the Biblical Commission (May, 1910) may not be deemed out of place: —

I. Whether the appellations, Psalms of David, Hymns of David, Davidical Psaltery, employed in the old collections and in the Councils themselves to designate the Book of the one hundred and fifty Psalms of the Old Testament, as well as the opinion of many Fathers and Doctors who held that absolutely all the psalms of the Psaltery are to be ascribed to David alone, have so much force that David must be regarded as the sole author of the entire Psaltery?

ANSWER: In the negative.

II. Whether it may rightly be argued from the concordance of the Hebrew text with the Alexandrine Greek text and other ancient versions, that the titles prefixed to the Hebrew text are older than the version known as the Septuagint, and that therefore they have been derived if not from the authors themselves of the Psalms at least from the ancient Judaic tradition?

ANSWER: In the affirmative.

III. Whether the said titles of the Psalms, as witnesses of Judaic tradition, may be prudently called into question when there is no grave argument against their genuineness?

ANSWER: In the negative.

IV. Whether, considering the not unfrequent testimonies of the Sacred Scripture concerning the natural skill of David, illumined by the gift of the Holy Ghost, in the composition of religious canticles, the institutions laid down by him for the liturgical chant of the Psalms, the attribution to him of Psalms made both in the Old and New Testament and in the very inscriptions which have been prefixed to the Psalms from antiquity, and in addition to all this the agreement of the Jews and the Fathers and Doctors of the Church, it can be prudently denied that David is the principal author of the canticles of the Psaltery, or that it can be affirmed that only a few of the canticles are to be attributed to the Royal Psalmist?

ANSWER: In the negative to both parts.

V. Whether, specifically, the Davidical origin can be denied of those psalms which both in the Old and the New Testament are cited expressly under the name of David, among which are specially to be reckoned Psalm II., "Quare fremuerunt gentes"; Psalm XV., "Conserva me Domine"; Psalm XVII., "Diligam te, Domine fortitudo mea"; Psalm XXXI., "Beati quorum remissae sunt iniquitates"; Psalm LXVIII., "Salvum me fac, Deus"; Psalm CIX., "Dixit Dominus Domino meo"?

ANSWER: In the negative.

VI. Whether it is possible to admit the opinion of those who hold that among the Psalms of the Psaltery there are some, either of David or of other authors which on account of liturgical or musical reasons, the carelessness of amanuenses or other unknown causes, have been divided or united; and also that there are other Psalms such as the "Miserere mei, Deus, " which in order that they might be better adapted to the historical circumstances or solemnities of the Jewish people have been slightly revised or modified, by the omission or addition of a versicle or two saving, however, the inspiration of the whole sacred text?

ANSWER: In the affirmative to both parts.

VII. Whether the opinion can with probability be maintained of those among more recent writers who have endeavoured to show from merely internal indications or an inaccurate interpretation of the sacred text that not a few of the psalms were composed after the time of Esdras and Nehemias, or even after the time of the Macchabees?

ANSWER: In the negative.

VIII. Whether from the manifold testimonies of the Sacred Books of the New Testament, and the unanimous agreement of the Fathers, as well as from the admission of the writers of the Jewish people, several prophetic and Messianic psalms are to be recognised, as prophesying concerning the coming kingdom, priesthood, passion, death and resurrection of the future Redeemer; and that therefore the opinion is to be absolutely rejected of those who, perverting the prophetic and Messianic character of the Psalms, twist these same prophecies regarding Christ into merely a prediction regarding the future lot of the chosen people?

ANSWER: In the affirmative to both parts.

On May 1, 1910, in an audience graciously granted to both Most Reverend Consultors Secretaries His Holiness approved the foregoing answers and ordered that they be published.

Rome, May 1, 1910.

PULCRANUS VIGOUROUX, P.S. S.

LAURENTIUS JANSSENS, O.S. B.

Consultors Secretaries.

The Psalms were always dear to the hearts of Christians. Our Lord died with the words of a psalm on His sacred lips: "Into thy hands I commend my spirit" (Psalm 30, v. 6). Millions of dying Christians have repeated His great prayer. On the Church's very birthday, when St. Peter preached the first Christian sermon, he had three texts and two of them were from the Psalms (Acts II.). To an educated and rigid Pharisee like St. Paul they were a treasure house of teaching. To the early Christians the Psalms were a prayer book, for there was no Christian literature. It was twenty-five years after the Ascension before the first books of the New Testament were written. Hence St. Paul and St. James tell their fellow Christians to use the Psalms in worship (Ephesians, v. 19; Colos. iii. 16; I. St. James 5-13). Some of the greatest of the early Christian writers and saints, Origen, St. Athanasius, Hilary of Poitiers, St. Ambrose, St. Chrysostom, Bede, and St. Augustine all studied the psalms deeply and wrote learned commentaries on them. The works of later saints abound in happy and beautiful quotations from these religious poems. With them, too, as with those holy people of whom St. Chrysostom wrote, "David is first, last and midst. " For many years no priest was ordained who could not recite the whole Psalter without the aid of a book, This veneration of the inspired words deserves respect and imitation. The learned Calmet (1672-1757) writing of the universal esteem and study of the Psalms, said that then there existed more than a thousand commentaries on them. Since then, the number has been doubled; so great and universal is the reverence and esteem in which this book of Scripture is held. To conclude this very long note on the Psalms I quote the quaint words of a mediaeval poet. It shows how the saints of old found their Master in the songs of His great ancestor: —

> Rithmis et sensu verborum consociatum
> Psalterium Jesu, sic est opus hoc vocitatum,
> Qui legit intente, quocunque dolore prematur,
> Sentiet inde bonum, dolor ejus et alleviatur;
> Ergo pius legat hoc ejus sub amore libenter,
> Cujus ibi Nomen scriptum videt esse frequenter.

Versicle and respond are placed after the psalms and before the lessons to rouse the attention which is necessary before all prayer, and the lessons are a noble form of prayer. These little prayers are of very ancient origin and were dealt with by Alcuin (735-804) in his recension of the Gregorian books for use in Gaul. His pupil, Amalare, also studied them, so that a meaning should be found in what was sung, and that the truncated repetitions should be avoided. He retained what was traditional and ancient, introduced versicles and responds taken from ancient Roman books and from books belonging to Metz, selected passages from the Gospels which seem to fit in with the antiphons and added them to what he found in the Roman books, made alterations in the order here and there and gave completion to the whole by adding some offices for saints' days proper to the Church of Metz (Baudot, *The Roman Breviary*, p. 88). Amalare had been administrator of the diocese of Lyons during the exile of Agobard the Archbishop. The latter, with learning and bitterness, attacked the reforms of Amalare, but, "in spite of all, the reform of Amalare held its ground in Metz, and then in the greater number of the churches north of the Alps" (Baudot, *op. cit.*). Much of the work of Amalare stands in our Breviary.

Pater Noster is said to beg from God, light and grace to understand the doctrine contained in the lessons. In choir, a part of the Pater Noster is said in common and in a loud voice to recall the Communion of saints.

Absolutions and Blessings. "The custom of giving a blessing before the lections was already in existence in the fourth century. The ruler of the choir, who gave it in the beginning, gave also the signal for the termination of the lesson by the words, 'Tu autem' (scil, desine or cessa), to which the reader responded 'Domine miserere nobis, ' while the choir answered *Deo gratias*. In the palace of Aix-la-Chapeile, it was by knocking, and not by the words *Tu autem*, that the Emperor Charlemagne gave the signal for the conclusion of the lections, while the lector recited himself, *Tu autem, Domine miserere nobis*. The *Rituale Ecclesiae Dunelmensis*, containing fragments of the Roman liturgy from the end of the seventh to the ninth and tenth centuries, includes forms of blessing for the different festivals, sometimes three, sometimes nine. In the latter case each lesson was provided with its own form of blessing, which correspond with the mystery commemorated by the festival. The absolutions, *Exaudi Domine* and *A vinculis peccatorum* did not appear until the succeeding period" (Baudot, *op. cit.* , p. 74).

In offices of three and of nine lessons, the lessons are preceded by the absolutions and blessings as they stand in the ordinarium, except in the Office for the Dead and Tenebrae Offices when they are not said. The Absolution is said immediately after the Pater Noster which follows the versicle and response under the third, sixth or ninth psalm. The first benediction is said immediately after it, and the second and third at the conclusion of the responses after each lesson and in reply to the words Jube Domine benedicere. The three words are to be said (when only one person recites the office) before the short Lesson at Prime and Compline.

In an office of nine lessons, the absolutions and benedictions in the first two nocturns do not vary; but in the third nocturns the eighth benediction may be, if the office is of a saint, Cujus festum, or if of two or more saints, Quorum (vel quarum) festum. The ninth may be *Ad societatem* or, if the ninth lesson be a gospel extract with homily, *Per evangelica*.

In offices of three lessons the Absolution Exaudi is said on Monday and Thursday; Ipsius, on Tuesday and Friday; A vinculis, on Wednesday and Saturday. But the benedictions vary. Thus, when a gospel extract and a homily are read, the three benedictions are Evangelica, Divinum, Ad societatem. When with the three lessons, no gospel extract is read, the benedictions are Benedictione, Unigenitus, Spiritus Sancti. In an office of a saint or saints, where the total number of lessons to be said is three (e. g., the Office of SS. Abdon et Sennen, 30 July), where first two lessons are from Scripture occurring and last lesson gives lives of these saints, the benedictions are, Ille nos, Cujus (vel Quorum aut Quarum) festum, Ad societatem.

Lessons. In the early days of Christendom, the Divine Office consisted in the singing of psalms, the reading of portions of Sacred Scripture and the saying of prayers. The principle of continuous reading of the books of the Bible bears an early date. Later were added readings from the acts of the martyrs, and later still, readings from the homilies of the Fathers. Till the seventh century the ferial Office had no lessons and the Sunday Office had only three, all taken from the Bible, which was read in its entirety, yearly. In the seventh century, ferial Offices received three lessons. About the time of St. Gregory, (died 604) the Office for Matins was divided into three parts or nocturns, each having lessons. The lessons for the second and third nocturns were not taken from the Bible, but from the works of the Fathers. These extracts were collected in book form—

the *homilaria*. The collection of extracts made by Paul the deacon (730-797) and used by Charles the Great (742-814) in his kingdom, form the foundation of the collected extracts in our Breviaries. The scripture lessons in our Breviaries are generally known as "the scripture occurring, " and are so arranged that each book of scripture is begun at least, except the books, Josue, Judges, Ruth, Paralipomenon and the Canticle of Canticles. Quignonez arranged in his reform that the whole Bible should be read yearly. But his book was withdrawn by Pope Paul IV. in 1558.

Although the ecclesiastical year begins with Advent, the beginnings of the Bible are not read till March. Hence, we begin the lessons from Genesis, after Septuagesima Sunday, and not, as we should naturally expect, at Advent, the beginning of the ecclesiastical year. The order in which the Scripture lessons are read does not follow the order in which the books of the Bible stand in the sacred volume. Thus, the Acts of the Apostles begin on the Monday after Low Sunday and are read for a fortnight; The Apocalypse begins on the third Sunday after Easter and is read for a week; then the Epistle of St. James begins, and so on, with special regard to the feasts of the time, rather than to the order of the books of the Bible.

The lessons of the second nocturn are generally commemorative of a saint or some episode of a saint's life. They have been much, and often ignorantly criticised, even by priests. The science of hagiology is a very wide and far-reaching one, which demands knowledge and reverence. Priests wishing to study its elements may read with pleasure and profit and wonder *The Legends of the Saints*, by Pere H. Delehaye, S.J., Bollandist (Longmans, 3s. 6d.). "Has Lectiones secundi Nocturni ex Historiis sanctorum, quas nunc habemus recognitas fuisse a doctissimis Cardinalibus Bellarmino et Baronio, qui rejecerunt ea omnia, quae jure merito in dubium revocari poterant et approbatus sub Clemente VIII. " (Gavantus). And Merati adds "quod aliqua qua controversia erant utpote alicujus aliquam haberent probabilitatem, ideo rejecta non fuerant sed retenta eo modo quo erant cum falsitatis argui non possent, quamvis fortasse opposita sententia sit a pluribus recepta" (Merati, *Obser. ad Gavant*, sec. v., chap. xii., nn. 10 and 16). The words of these learned men and the writings of the learned Bollandist mentioned above are worthy of consideration, as sometimes priests are puzzled about the truth and accuracy of the incidents recorded in those lessons of the second nocturn. They should be treated with reverence. The ignorant flippancy of a priest in an article (in a very secular periodical) on St.

Expeditus gave great pain to Catholics and gave material for years to come to scoffing bigots.

"Legends, *i. e.*, narratives, were based upon documents of the nature described above, and worked up by later writers, either for the purpose of edification or from the point of view of the historian. The writings, however, differ endlessly as to their value, according to the knowledge and authority possessed by the writers, and according to their nearness to the events described. There were many martyrs whose sufferings were recorded in no acta or passiones, but were imprinted on the memory of men and became part of the traditions handed down in the community, until they were finally committed to writing. The later this took place the worse for the authenticity. For it was then that anachronisms, alterations in titles, changes in the persons and other similar historical errors could more easily creep into the narrative, as we know in fact they have done in many instances. The historical sense was unfortunately lacking to the Franks and Byzantines, as well as all idea of sound criticism.

"A false kind of patriotism and national pride often go along with credulity, so that we find here and there in literature of this kind, even downright fabrication. After the introduction of printing, by which literature became more widely diffused, and comparative criticism was rendered possible, it at once became evident among Catholics that error was mixed with truth and that a sifting of the one from the other was necessary, and, in many cases, possible" (Kellner, *Heorlology*, pp. 209-210). "It was not the intention of the Church or of the compilers and authors of the service books to claim historical authority for their statements. And so, the Popes themselves have directed many emendations to be made in the legends of the Breviary, although many others still remain to be effected" (Dom Baumer, *Histoire Du Breviare Roman*). Cf. Dom Cabrol, *Le Reforme du Breviare*, pp. 61-63.

Responsories. (Title XXVII.). In the new Breviary the responsories to the lessons have been restored to their place of honour. They are of ancient origin, but "how they came to have a place in the Divine Office, who was responsible for their composition, what was the process of development until they reached their present form, are questions upon which liturgical writers are not quite agreed" (Rev. M. Eaton, *Irish Eccles. Record*, January, 1915). Amalare of Metz found them fully formed and placed. The rule of St. Benedict, written about 530 A. D., mentions them as a recognised part of Matins. In solemn vigils, in the early Church, the congregation took part in the psalm singing, and hence we find *psalmi responsorii* mentioned, and we still have a typical instance in the Invitatory Psalm of our Office. Probably, some similar practice existed in the readings from Sacred Scripture. "At those primitive vigils, then, after the reading of the Sacred Scripture, the responsory was given by the precentor and the assembled faithful took up the words and chanted them forth in the same simple melody. Next, a verse was sung frequently echoing the same sentiment, and the choir again, as in the *psalmi responsorii*, repeated the refrain or the responsorii proper. Frequently other verses were added according to the dignity of the festivals, and after each the faithful struck in with the original refrain.... At first those responsories would probably have been extempore... left to the genius or to the inspiration of the individual chanter, but gradually, by a survival of the fittest, the most beautiful ones became stereotyped and spread throughout several churches.... Later they were carefully collected, arranged and codified by St. Gregory or one of his predecessors and passed into all the books of liturgy" (Rev. M. Eaton, *loc. cit.*). Monsignor Battifol (*History of the Roman Breviary*, Eng, trans., p. 78) says that these parts of the liturgy, in beauty and eloquence rival the chorus dialogues of Greek drama, and quotes as an example the *Aspiciens a longe* from the first Sunday of Advent.

Rubrics. The responsories, as a rule, are said after each lesson of Matins. When the *Te Deum* is said after the ninth lesson, there are only eight responsories. At the end of the third, sixth and eighth lesson the *Gloria Patri* with a repetition of part of the responsory is said. It is said in the second responsory in offices of three lessons only. In Passiontide the *Gloria Patri* is not said, but the responsory is repeated *ab initio*. In the Requiem Office *Gloria Patri* is replaced by "*requiem aeternam.* " In the Sundays of Advent, Sundays after Septuagesima until Palm Sunday, and in the triduum before Easter, there are nine responsories recited.

Perhaps an explanation of the rubric may not be useless. The asterisk (*) indicates the part which should be repeated first after the verse and immediately after the *Gloria Patri*. The *Gloria Patri* should be said to include the word *sancto*, and *sicut erat* should not be said. Some responsories have two or three asterisks, and then the repetitions should be made from one asterisk to another and not as far as the verse ending. Examples may be seen in the responsories for the first Sunday of Advent and in the *Libera nos* of the Requiem Office. The responsories of the Requiem Office—which is almost the only Office which missionary priests have an opportunity of reciting in choir—are highly praised for their beauty of thought and expression. They were compiled by Maurice de Sully (circa 1196), Bishop of Paris.

Symbolism of the Rubric. The responsories are placed after the lessons, the old writers on liturgy say, to excite attention and devotion, to thank God for the instruction given in the lessons, to make us realise and practise what has been read and to teach us that "Blessed are they who hear the word of God and keep it. " Again, those writers knew why the chanter said only one verse and the worshippers replied in chorus—to show that all their souls were united and free from schism.

Te Deum (Title XXXI.). *Author.* In the Breviary prior to the reform of Pius X., this hymn was printed under the words "Hymnus SS. Ambrosii et Augustini. " However, "no one thinks now of attributing this canto to either St. Ambrose or St. Augustine" (Battifol, *op. cit.* , p. 110). Formerly, it was piously believed to have been composed and sung by these saints on the evening of Augustine's baptism. The question of the authorship of this hymn has led to much study and much controversy. Some scholars attribute it to St. Hilary, others to Sisebut, a Benedictine; others to Nicetas, Bishop of Treves, in the year 527. To-day, the opinion of the learned Benedictine, Dom. Morin—who follows the readings of the Irish manuscripts—that the hymn was written by Nicetas of Remesiana (circa 400 A. D.), is the most probable. This opinion has been criticised by several Continental scholars (V. *Cath. Encly.*, art. "Te Deum").

Rubrics. The Te Deum is always said at the end of Matins, unless in Matins of Feast of Holy Innocents, of Sundays of Advent, and from Septuagesima to Palm Sunday, and ferias outside Eastertide (from Low Sunday to Ascension Day).

The Structure of the Hymn. In this wonderful composition, there are probably two hymns connected, and followed by a set of versicles and. responses, which might be used with any similar hymn. It is probable that the first hymn (*Te Deum... Paraclitum Spiritum*), lines 1 to 13 of Te Deum are older than the second part, which was written probably as a sequel to the early hymn. The rhythm of the hymn is very beautiful, being free from abruptness and monotony. Students of poetry may note that seven lines have the exact hexameter ending, if scanned accentually, as voce proclamant; Deus sabbaoth, etc.

Seven have two dactyls, as laudabilis numerus, laudat exercitus; one ends with spondees, apostolorum chorus. The other six lines have a less regular ending.

This hymn of praise to the Blessed Trinity is divided into two parts and seems to be modelled on the lines of the Psalm 148, *Laudate Dominum de coelis* (see Sunday Lauds I.). The verses 1 to 6 of the hymn, like the opening verses of the psalm, record the worship and adoration of the angels. The second part of the hymn records the worship of human beings living or dead—Apostles, Prophets, Martyrs. The second hymn, *Tu Rex gloriae Christi*, etc., is a prayer to Christ, the God Incarnate, the Redeemer now in Glory, to aid His servants and to aid them to be of the number of His saints in everlasting glory.

The third part of the hymn, vv. 22-29 (*Salvum fac... in aeternum*) is considered by scholars to be simply versicles, responses and prayers; the verses 22-23 (Salvum fac... usque in aeternum). being the versicle, and verses 24-25 (Per singulos dies... saeculi), verse 2 of Psalm 144 being the response before the beautiful verses of prayer "Dignare Domine die isto sine peccato nos custodire, " etc. "Vouchsafe, O Lord, to keep us this day from sin; O Lord, have mercy on us, " etc., etc.

This hymn has a special interest for Irish priests, as the Irish recensions of it, found in the Bangor Antiphoner (to be seen in the Library of Trinity College, Dublin) are of the greatest value to scholars engaged in critical study. They date from the tenth century, and give Nicetas as the author. The wording in the old Irish Antiphoner differs in some verses from the text given in our Breviary. Thus, in verse 6, the Bangor text has, *universa* before the word *terra*; again, in verse 18, the Breviary reads "*Tu ad deteram Dei sedes*, " Bangor, and probably more correctly, reads *sedens*. Verses 26-29, "*Dignare Domine... confundar in aeternum*" are not found in the Irish book. Those who wish to study these old Irish MSS. may receive great help from Warren's *Bangor Antiphoner* (II., pp. 83-91) and light comes too from Julian's *Dictionary of Hymnology* (pp. 1120-1121).

SOME TEXTS AND INTENTIONS WHICH MAY HELP TOWARDS
THE WORTHY RECITATION OF MATINS (*vide* pages 4, 120).

"Matutina ligat Christum qui crimina purgat."
"Although I should die with Thee, I will not deny Thee."
"And in like manner also said they all."
"Pray, lest you enter into temptation,"
"And being in agony He prayed the longer."
"Friend, whereunto art thou come?—"
"And they holding Jesus led Him away"—the Garden.
"Art thou one of His disciples?"
"My kingdom is not of this world"—Before the High Priest.

General Intentions: -Exaltation of the Church; the Pope; the Mission to
the heathen; Christian nations; the conversion of the heretics, infidels
and sinners; the Catholic laity; the Catholic priesthood.

Personal Intentions: -Lively faith; a greater hope; ardent charity.

Special Intentions: -For parents; for benefactors; for those in sorrow;
dying sinners; deceased priests of Ireland; for the conversion of
England; for vocations to the priesthood.

CHAPTER II.

LAUDS.

Etymology, Definition, Symbolism. The word "Lauds" is derived from the Latin *laus*, praise. It is applied to this Hour, as it is *par excellence*, the hour in which God's praises are chanted by His Church. This Hour succeeds Matins and precedes Prime. The name is said to have been given to this Hour on account of the last three Psalms, which formerly formed part of the Office. In these Psalms, 148, 149, 150, the word *Laudate* recurs several times. Before the eighth century the Hour was called "Matutinum, " or morning Office, and sometimes it was called *Gallicinum* or *Galli cantus* from being recited at cock-crow. This is the Office of daybreak and hence its symbolism is of Christ's resurrection. "Christ, the light of the world, rose from the tomb on Easter morning, like a radiant sun, trampling over darkness and shedding His brightness upon the earth. The hymns, psalms, antiphons and versicles of Lauds, all proclaim the mystery of Christ's Resurrection, and the light which enlightens our souls. The reform of the Psalter in 1911 has not always preserved this liturgical idea; nevertheless, the character of the Office has not been altered. Lauds remains the true morning prayer, which hails in the rising sun, the image of Christ triumphant—consecrates to Him the opening day. No other morning prayer is comparable to this" (Dom. F. Cabrol, *The Day Hours of the Church*, London, 1910).

Antiquity. The Christians, in their night vigils, followed the pious practices of the Jews, as to prayers at dead of night and at dawn, Hence, the Hour, Lauds is of great antiquity, coming, perhaps, from Apostolic times. It is found well established in the very earliest accounts of Christian liturgy.

The old writers on liturgy loved to dwell on pious congruities and parallelisms. They ask the questions, why did the early Christians pray at dawn and why is the practice continued? They answer at great length, I will try to summarise their holy themes. The early Christians prayed at dawn, 1. that in the New Law the figures of the Old may be fulfilled; 2. to honour the risen Saviour and to remind us of our resurrection; 3. to glorify Jesus typified by the physical light. "I am the Light of the world" (St. John, viii. 12); 4. because at dawn, after rest, body and soul are refreshed and ready to devote all their powers to God, free from distractions and noise. Each dawn, revealing God's wondrous work, should hear God's praises in the most sublime words ever uttered, the Psalms (e. g., *Dominus regnavit, Jubilate Deo*, etc., etc.); 5. because God seems more disposed to hear prayers made at that hour. For, He has said, "Yet if thou wilt arise early to God and wilt beseech the Almighty... He will presently awake unto thee and make the dwelling of thy justice peaceable" (Job, viii. 5-6). "I love them that love me; and they that in the morning early watch for me shall find me" (Proverbs viii. 17).

Structure. If Lauds succeeds Matins immediately, *Pater Noster* and *Ave Maria* are omitted, and the Hour begins with *Deus in adjutorium.* At these words it is a practice but not an obligation to make the sign of the cross from head to breast (see Vespers, *infra*). Then the Gloria Patri, Sicut erat, Amen, Alleluia are said before the antiphons and psalms. But if a notable delay—say, of ten minutes' duration—be made between the end of Matins and the start of Lauds, the *Pater Noster* and *Ave Maria* begin Lauds. After the psalms, comes the Capitulum, the Hymn, Versicle and Response, antiphon to Benedictus, Canticle *Benedictus Dominus Deus Israel, Gloria Patri, Sicut erat*, Antiphon to Benedictus repeated, *Dominus vobiscum, Et cum spiritu tuo, Oremus*, collect, commemorations preceded by versicle, response and *Oremus* before each. Then *Dominus vobiscum, Et cum spiritu tuo, Benedicamus Domino, Deo Gratias, Fidelium animae, Amen*. If another Hour do not succeed immediately, *Pater Noster* (said silently), *Dominus det nobis* (with a sign of the cross) *suam pacem, Et vitam aeternam. Amen*. Then is said the antiphon of the Blessed Virgin, Alma Redemptoris or Ave Regina, or Regina Coeli, or Salve Regina, according to the part of the ecclesiastical year for which each is assigned, with *versicle, response, oremus, collect, Divinum auxilium*.... Amen.

Rubrics. In the paragraphs dealing with the structure of this hour is given the rule for saying *Pater Noster* and *Ave*, The Psalms for Lauds in the new Breviary follow these rules: —

General Rule: Psalms of the current day.

Exception: Sunday Psalms on the excepted Feasts.

In applying the general rule to Sundays and week days, it will be seen that the Psalter contains two sets of Psalms for Lauds. The use of the two sets is as follows: —

Sundays:
   (i) Throughout the year: first set of Psalms.

   (ii) Sundays from Septuagesima to Easter: second set of Psalms.

Ferias: The first set of Psalms is to be used on: —

   (i) Ferias throughout the year, not including those in Advent, Septuagesima, Sexagesima and Quinquagesima weeks.

   (ii) Ferias in Paschal time.

   (iii) Feasts at any season of the year.

   (iv) Vigils of Christmas and Epiphany.

The second set of Psalms is to be used on: —

   (i) Ferias of Advent.

   (ii) Ferias from Septuagesima to Wednesday in Holy Week, inclusive.

(iii) Vigils (common) outside Paschal time, when the Office of Vigil is said (*New Psalter and Its Uses*, p. 188).

On Maundy Thursday, Good Friday and Holy Saturday, the Psalms of the Feria are to be said. But the Canticle of Moses (Deut, 33) is not said on Holy Saturday.

Antiphons. As a general rule antiphons of the current day of the week are to be said.

Exceptions.
            (1) On excepted Feasts,
            (2) non-excepted Feasts which have proper antiphons,
            (3) Holy Week has special antiphons,
            (4) Six ferias before Christmas have special antiphons.

In Paschal time, all psalms and the canticles are recited under one antiphon.

Antiphon of Benedictus (1) Sunday antiphons are proper. (2) Ferias throughout the year have antiphons of current feria. But Ferias in Advent, and in Lent, in Passiontide, Paschal time and September Ember days have proper antiphons. (3) Feasts have antiphons from proper or from common.

Capitulum (Title XXIX.). *Etymology, meaning and synonyms.*

The word *capitulum* comes from the Latin, and means a little chapter, a heading, a beginning, an abridgment, because this little chapter is a little lesson, a brief extract from Sacred Scripture, the head or the beginning of the Epistle of the Mass of the Feast (Gavantus, Bona). It is found in every Hour, except Matins. It is known by other names, the summarium, collectio, collatio, lectio brevis, epistoletto, lectiuncula, Versiculus brevis.

Antiquity. Some authors hold that this usage of reading a brief extract from Sacred Scripture is of Jewish origin. For, the Jews were accustomed to interpose brief readings from Scripture prose in their psalm chanting service. The *capitulum* is found in Christian services of the fourth century; and St. Ambrose (340-397) is said to have instituted the *capitula* of Terce, Sext and None. This new practice spread quickly and several councils recommended or ordered the usage—e. g., the Council of Agde In 506 A. D.

Remarks. The *Capitulum* is said always except from Holy Thursday to the Vespers of Saturday preceding Low Sunday, and in Requiem Offices. In Compline it is said after the Hymn.

The *Capitulum* of Lauds is ordinarily taken from the beginning of the Epistle of the Mass of the day of the feast. Sext and None generally have their *capitula* drawn from the middle and end of the same Epistle extract. Terce has generally the same words for the *Capitulum*, as Vespers and Lauds, because it is the grandest and most sublime of the little Hours. The *Capitulum* is said without a blessing being sought, because it is (in choir) read by the Hebdomadarius, who there represents the person of Christ, just as the *Capitulum* does too, and for Whom it would not be consonant to ask a blessing. It concludes without *Tu autem*, because these words are correlative of *Jube*. And since it is such a short lesson it is easy to recite it without fault or sin, the more so as it is read by the Hebdomadarius, who should be advanced in perfection. It is short, whilst the lessons of Matins, the night Office, are long, because the day is specially given to toil and the night to contemplation. During the recital of this little lesson all turn to the altar through respect for Christ, figured by the *Capitulum*. Sometimes the words of the *Capitulum* are from the Itala version and not from the Vulgate.

Psalms and Canticles of Lauds. The Office of Lauds now consists of four Psalms and a canticle, followed by a little chapter, a hymn, versicle, antiphon, of Benedictus, the canticle, Benedictus and prayer. One of the characteristics of Lauds is the canticle taken from the Old Testament. Fourteen canticles taken from the Old Testament now find a place in our Breviaries. Formerly, only seven canticles from the Old Testament were given in the Psaltery (cf. *supra*, p. 149).

"If, according to the new distribution of the Psalter, the Psalms for Lauds do not refer so directly to the symbolism of sunrise, they are nevertheless more varied and are generally well chosen. The canticles inserted among the Psalms have also been changed. The whole selection is worthy of note. It contains, besides those given in the former arrangement of the Psalter, others which are very beautiful and admirably prayerful.

"The hymns for Lauds, all ancient and varying with the seasons, form a fine collection. Their theme is one: the rising of the sun as a symbol of Christ's resurrection, and the crowing of the cock, which arouses the sluggish and calls all to work. Some of these hymns are of considerable poetical merit: that for Sunday, *Aeterne Rerum conditor*, is a little masterpiece.

"The 'Benedictus' corresponds with the *Magnificat* of Vespers. Both are sung with the same solemnity and are of the same importance; they form as it were the culminating point of their respective Hours, and for feast days the altar is incensed while they are chanted.

"The 'Benedictus' or Canticle of Zachary recalls the Precursor's mission of proclaiming the Messiah and the new alliance. It is altogether appropriate to the Office of daybreak, as ushering in the dawn of a new era. The closing verse speaks of the light which the announcement of the Messiah shed upon the nations 'sitting in darkness and in the shadow of death'" (Dom Cabrol, Introduction to *Day Hours of the Church*).

"This Canticle of Zachary (St. Luke i. 68-79) naturally falls into two parts. The first (verses 68 to 75, 'Benedictus Dominus... diebus nostris') is a song of thanksgiving for the fulfilment of the Messianic hopes of the Jews, to which is given a Christian sentiment. The power, which was of old in the family of David for the defence of the nation, is being restored, and in a higher and more spiritual sense. The Jews mourning under the Roman yoke prayed for deliverance through the house of David. The 'deliverance, ' a powerful salvation ('cornu salutis nobis') was at hand so that the Jews were seeing the fulfilment of God's promise made to Abraham, and this deliverance, this salvation was such that 'we may serve Him without fear in holiness and justice, all our days' (St. Luke i. 75).

"The second part of the canticle (verses 76-80, 'Et tu puer... ad dirigendos pedes nostros') is an address by Zachary to his own son, who was to take an important part in the scheme of the powerful salvation and deliverance by the Messiah. This canticle is known as the canticle of joyous hope, hence its use at funerals at the moment of interment, when words of thanksgiving for the Redemption are specially in place as an expression of Christian hope" (*Catholic Encyclopedia*, art. "Benedictus").

Oratio (Title XXX.). The word *oratio* has various meanings. In the liturgy it is translated by the word "collect. " The word "collect" means either that the priest who celebrates Mass collects in a short form the needs, the thanksgivings and the praises of the people, to offer them up to God; or most probably "the original meaning seems to have been this: it was used for the service held at a certain church on the days when there was a station held somewhere else. The people gathered together and became a collection at the first church; after certain prayers had been said they went in procession to the station church. Just before they started, the celebrant said a prayer, the *oratio ad collectam* (*ad collectionem populi*), the name would then be the same as *oratio super populum*, a title that still remains in our Missal, in Lent, for instance, after the Post-Communion. This prayer, the collect, would be repeated at the beginning of Mass at the station itself. Later writers find other meanings for the name. Innocent III. says that in this prayer the priest collects all the prayers of the faithful" (*De Sacr. Altar. Mystic.* ii., 2). See also Benedict XIV. (*De SS. Missae Sacr.* ii., 5, —Dr. A. Fortescue, *Cath. Encyl.*, art. "collect").

Antiquity of collects. No one can say with certainty who the composers of the collects were. All admit the antiquity of these compositions. In the fourth century certain collects were believed to come from apostolic times; indeed, the collects read in the Mass on

Good Friday, for Gentiles, Jews, heretics, schismatics, catechumens and infidels bear intrinsic notes of their antiquity. Other liturgical collects show that they were composed in the days of persecution. Others show their ages by their accurate expression of Catholic doctrine against, and their supplications for, heretics, Manicheans, Sabbelians, Arians, Pelagians and Nestorians. St, Jerome in his Life of St. Hilarion (291-371) writes, "Sacras Scriptures memoriter tenens, post orationes et psalmos quasi Deo praesente recitabat. " It is said that St. Gelasius (d. 496), St. Ambrose (d. 397), St, Gregory the Great (d. 604) composed collects and corrected existing ones. The authorship and the period of composition of many of the Breviary collects are matters of doubt and difficulty. Even the date of the introduction of collects into the Divine Office is doubtful. In the early Christian Church there seems to have been one and only one prayer, the *Pater Noster*, in liturgical use. St. Benedict laid it down in his rule that there should be none other. It is generally held by students of liturgy that the collects were originally used in Mass only and were introduced into the Office at a time much later than their introduction into the Mass books.

In the Masses for Holy Week we see the collects in their oldest existing form. The rite of the Mass has been shortened at all other seasons, and there remains now only the greeting, *Oremus*, and the collect itself. The *Oremus* did not refer immediately to the collect, but rather to the silent prayer that went before it. This also explains the shortness of the older collects. They are not the prayer itself, but its conclusion. One short sentence summed up the petitions of the people. It is only since the original meaning of the collect has been forgotten that it has become itself a long petition with various references and clauses (compare the collects for the Sundays after Pentecost with those of modern feasts)—(*Cath. Encyl.* , art. "Collects").

The following examples which are not extreme, may help to make clear and emphatic the matter of the shortness of the old and the length of the new collects.

"Protector in te sperantium, Deus, sine quo nihil est validum, nihil est sanctum: multiplica super nos misericordiam tuam; ut te rectore, te duce, sic transeamus per bona temporalia, ut non amittamus aeterna. Per Dominum. "

Translation—"O God, the Protector of all that hope in Thee, without Whom nothing is sure, nothing is holy, bountifully bestow on us, Thy mercy, that Thou being our ruler and our guide, we may so pass through temporal blessings that we lose not the eternal. Through our Lord... " (Collect for third Sunday after Pentecost.)

"Omnipotens et misericors Deus qui beatam Joannam Franciscam tuo amore succensam admirabili spiritus fortitudine per omnes vitae semitas in via perfectionis donasti, quique per illam illustrare Ecclesiam tuam nova prole voluisti: ejus meritis et precibus concede ut qui infirmitatis nostrae conscii de tua virtute confidimus coelestis gratiae auxilio, cuncta nobis adversantia vicamus. Per Dominum... "

Translation-"Almighty and merciful God Who inflaming blessed Jane Frances with love, didst endow her with a marvellous fortitude of spirit to pursue the way of perfection In all the paths of life, and wast pleased through her to enrich Thy Church with a new offspring, grant by her merits and intercession that we, who, knowing our own weakness, trust in Thy strength, may by the help of Thy heavenly grace overcome all things that oppose us. Through our Lord" (Collect of St. Jane Frances Fremiot De Chantal, August 21).

Rubrics. In Vespers and Lauds the collect is said after the antiphons of the *Magnificat* and *Benedictus,* unless the *Preces* (q. v.) are to be said in these hours. Then the *Preces* are said after the antiphons, and the collects follow after them immediately. The collect of a ferial Office is found in Office of the previous Sunday, except in ferias of Lent and Rogation days which have special and proper collects.

At Prime and the other Hours the collect is said after the little respond, unless the *Preces* be recited. They precede the collect. At Compline the collect is said after the antiphon *Salva nos* if the *Preces* be not recited.

At Prime and Compline the collects of the Psalter are never changed except during the last three days of Holy Week. In this triduum, in all hours up to and including None on Holy Saturday the collect is said after the Psalm *Miserere.*

Before reciting the collect in the Office, everyone in deacon's orders or in priesthood says *Dominus vobiscum, Et cum spiritu tuo,* and this is said even if the Office be said privately. All others reciting the Office say *Domine exaudi orationem meam. Et clamor meus ad te veniat.* Then the word *Oremus* is prefixed to the recitation of the collect, and at the end, *Amen* is said. If there be only one collect, the *Dominus vobiscum* or the *Domine exaudi* with the responses *Et cum spiritu tuo; Et clamor meus ad te veniat* is repeated after the *Amen*. But if there be more than one collect, before each is said its corresponding antiphon and versicle and also the word, *Oremus*. After the last collect is said, the *Dominus vobiscum* and *Et cum spiritu tuo* are repeated. Then we add *Benedicamus Domino; Deo Gratias, Fidelium animae....* This latter verse is not a constant sequel to the *Benedicamus*, as we see in Prime, where the verse *Pretiosa* succeeds it; and again in Compline it is succeeded by *Benedicat et custodiet*. The concluding words of the prayers or collects vary. If the prayer is addressed to God the Father, the concluding words are *Per Dominum* (see the collects given above). If the prayer be addressed to God the Son, the concluding words are *Qui vivis et regnas*—e. g., Deus qui in tuae caritatis exemplum ad fidelium redemptionem .... Qui vivis et regnas (Collect for St. Peter Nolasco's feast, 3ist January). If in the beginning of the prayer mention is made of God the Son, the ending should be *Per eundem, e.g.,* Domine Deus noster? qui, beatae Brigittae per Filium tuurn unigenitum secreta coelestia revelasti;... Per eundem Dominum (collect for feast, 8th October). But if the mention of God the Son is made near the end of the collect, the ending is *Qui tecum vivit et regnal, e.g.* , "Famulorum tuorum, quaesumus, Domine.... Genitricis Filii tui Domini nostri intercessione salvemur: Qui tecum vivit et regnat" (collect of Assumption, 15th August). If the name of the Holy Ghost occur in the prayer, the conclusion is, *In unitate ejusdem Spiritus sancti, e.g.* , "Deus, qui hodierna die corda... in eodem spiritu recta... *in imitate ejusdem Spiritus*" (collect: for Pentecost Sunday).

The following lines, giving the rules for terminations, are well known and are useful, as a help to the memory: —

> *Per Dominum* dicas, si Patrem quilibet oras
> Si Christum memores, *Per eundem*, dicere debes
> Si loqueris Christo, *Qui vivis* scire memento;
> *Qui tecum*, si sit collectae finisin ipso
> Si Flamen memores *ejusdem* die prope finem

When there are several collects an ending or conclusion is added to the first and last only. *Dominus vobiscum* is said before the first collect only, but each collect is preceded by the word *Oremus*, unless in the Office for the Dead.

Explanation of the Rubric. Where a feast is transferred either occasionally or always and its collect contains words such as *Hanc diem, hodiernom diem*, it is not allowed to change the wording, without permission of the Congregation of Rites (S. R.C., 7th September, 1916).

If the collect of a commemoration be of the same form as the prayer of the feast, the former is taken from the common of saints, in proper place.

Dominus vobiscum. This salutation is of great antiquity. It was the greeting of Booz to his harvestmen (Ruth, ii. 4). The prophet used the selfsame salutation to Azas. And the Angel Gabriel expressed the same idea, *Dominns tecum*, to the Blessed Virgin. It was blessed and honoured by our Lord Himself, when to His apostles he said "Ecce ego vobiscum sum omnibus diebus" (St. Matt. 28. 20). This beautiful salutation passed into Church liturgy at an early date, probably in apostolic times. Its use in liturgy was mentioned at the Council of Braga (563), and it is found in the Sacramentarium Gelasianum (sixth century). These words are called the divine salutation. They mean that the priest who utters them is at peace with all clergy and people and thus wishes God to remain with them—the highest and holiest of wishes. For the presence of God, Who is the source of every good and the author of every best gift, is a certain pledge of divine protection and of that peace and consolation which the world cannot give. This formula is used even in private recitation of the Office, as the priest prays in union with and in the name of the Church.

The words *Et cum spiritu tuo* add a new and further significance to the salutation; for it is the spirit, the human soul, that prays, and when the spirit prays in the name of the Church for her children, its work is a work of high spiritual order, demanding the use of all the soul's powers,

Oremus. This exhortation is of very great antiquity, and in this form is found in the liturgies of St. James and of St. Mark. In those days it was said by the priest in a loud voice. The priest, the mediator, following the example of the great Mediator, Christ, calls others to join with him in prayer. St. Augustine tells us, that sometimes after pronouncing the word *Oremus*, the priest paused for a while and the people prayed in silence, and then the priest "collected" the united prayers of the congregation and offered them to God, hence the name *collect* (St. Augustine, Epistle 107), (*cf.* Probst., *Abendl Messe*, p. 126).

Invocation and Conclusion. Prayer is addressed generally to God the Father. This practice is in accordance with the example and doctrine of Christ, "Father, I give Thee thanks" (St. John, xi, 41); "Amen, amen, I say to you; if you ask the Father anything in My name, he will give it to you" (St. John, xvi. 23). "And He taught us to say 'Our Father. '" In the early ages of the Church, seldom was prayer addressed to God, the Son. Innocent III. tells us that the reason for the practice was a fear that such prayer might lead the catechumens, the Jews or the Pagans converted to Christianity, to allege or to believe that Christians worshipped several Gods. However, with the advent of the early heresies, it became necessary to formulate prayers witnessing the divinity of Christ and His equality in all things to the Father and the Holy Ghost. In some of the great prayers of the liturgy, the three Persons of the Holy Trinity are named to show their equality and unity of nature and substance. Nearly all the prayers of this kind are the products of the Church during the storms of early heresy against the divinity, nature or personality of Christ.

The conclusions of the prayers generally contain the words *Per Dominum nostrum Jesum Christum*, because all graces come through Jesus Christ, our Lord and Saviour, Who pleads, as Mediator between God and Man, as He Himself has said, "No man cometh to the Father but by Me" (St. John, xiv. 6).

Hence, in every collect, we may distinguish five parts: the invocation, the motive, the petition, the purpose, the conclusion.

(1) The Invocation takes some form such as *Deus, Domine*.

(2) The motive is commonly introduced by the relative *qui*; e. g., Deus, *qui corda fidelium sancti spiritus illustratione docuisti*.

(3) The petition, the body or centre or substance of the prayer, is always noted for the solemn simplicity of language, which marks liturgical prayer, e.g., *Multiplica* super nos misericordiam tuam.

(4) The purpose is an enforcement of the petition. It has reference, generally, to the need of the petitions and is marked usually with the word *ut*. "Multiplica super nos misericordiam tuam, *ut* quae, nobis

agendis praecipis, te miserante adimplere possimus" (prayer for feast of St. Patrick).

(5) The *conclusion* varies, e.g., "Per Dominum nostrum, " "Per eundem Dominum, " etc.

"Those who pay intelligent attention to the liturgical chant at High Mass, and in particular to the chant of the celebrant, will be able to discover for themselves that the intonations used in the singing of the collect and the Post-Communion serve, as a rule, to mark off two at least of the main divisions indicated. Two inflections, a greater and a lesser, occur in the body of the prayer, the greater for the most part coming at the close of the 'motive, ' while the lessor concludes the 'petition' and produces the purpose of the prayer. When the prayers are correctly printed, as in the authentic 'Missale Romanum, ' the place of the inflexions is indicated by a colon, 'punctum principals, ' and a semicolon, 'semi-punctum, ' respectively. These steps, it will he observed, indicate, not precisely 'breaks in the sense' (as Haberl incorrectly says) but rather the logical divisions of the sentence, which is not quite the same thing" (Father Lucas, S.J., *Holy Mass*, chap, vi.).

The question is often asked, why *Dominus vobiscum* is said after the collect, or prayer. Writers on liturgy reply that it is so placed because Christ frequently used the salutation *Pax vobis*, and the priest in public prayer holds the place of Christ, and as he, the priest, used this formula of salvation before the collect to obtain the spirit of prayer and the grace of God, he repeats it so that these gifts may be retained.

In the collects, the fatherland of the saints is rarely found, because the saints' true home and fatherland is heaven, where they were born again to life eternal, and their fatherland is not this valley of exile where they spent their temporal life. Nor are their surnames given in the collects (see the collect of St. Jane Frances Fremiot de Chantel given on p. 180). But it is not infrequent in the collects to find certain appellations characterising a saint or noting some special prerogative or wonderful gift of grace. The Church's collects record the wonderful gifts of St. John Chrysostom ("the golden-mouthed"), St. Peter Chrysologus ("qui ob auream ejus eloquentiam Chrysologi cognomen adeptus est") (*Rom. Brev.*). Sometimes the nation or earthly home of a saint is given in a collect to distinguish one saint from another. This is seen in the case of saints bearing the name of

Mary, which if used absolutely or unqualifiedly refers to the Mother of God. See the collects for St. Mary Magdalen, St. Mary of Egypt, etc.

The collect or prayer is placed at the end of the Hours to collect or gather up the fruits of all the prayers that precede; to beg from God that His grace may follow our actions as it precedes them; that the prayer may be a shield and buckler against all temptations which may be encountered. The prayers at Prime and at Compline never vary, to remind us, the old writers tell us, that all our acts should be invariably referred to God. In the early ages of the Church, all public prayers, both in Mass and in Office were offered up by both priests and people with outstretched arms. This practice is observed still, in a certain way, in Mass.

Benedicamus is the prayer to thank God for all His graces.

Fidelium animae. This prayer is said after every Hour, unless where the hour is said in choir and followed immediately by Mass. It Is omitted, too, before the Litany.

De Precibus (Title XXXIV.). These are prayers which are said at some of canonical Hours, before the collect or oratio. They commence with Kyrie eleison or Pater Noster. They consist of versicles and responses and these differ from other versicles and responses, which are generally historic, e.g., In omnem terram exivit sonus eorum, Amavit eum Dominus et laudavit eum. But the versicles and responses of the *preces* are always a call to God or an exhortation to praise God (e. g., Fiat misericordia tua, Domine), super nos, Quemadmodum speravimus in te (see Prime, infra, page 193). These prayers are of great antiquity, mention of them being found in the works of Amalare (ninth century).

They are said in some Offices in Vespers, Compline, Lauds, Prime and Little Hours. Before the reform of the Breviary by Pope Pius X,, the Preces at Vespers contained six short prayers and the Psalm, Miserere. In the new Breviary nine short prayers are given in the Preces—the six former prayers being retained and three new ones, Pro Papa; Pro antistite; Pro benefactoribus, being added. The Miserere is omitted. The same additions were made in Lauds and the Psalm, De Profundis omitted.

In Prime and the Little Hours, the preces are unchanged standing in the new Breviary as in the old.

Rubrics. The Preces are recited in the Office of—

(1) Prime and Compline on certain days;

(2) Lauds, Prime, Terce, Sext, None, Vespers and Compline of certain feasts.

The preces feriales at Lauds and Vespers are the same in structure. They have the same structure in Terce, Sext, None, but differ in character. The preces dominicales at Prime and Compline have a form of their own, additions being made in the preces of Prime when said on a feria.

1. The Preces Feriales are said at Lauds on Ferias of Lent, Advent and Passiontide, Ember days, except Ember day at Pentecost and on Vigils (except on Vigil of Christmas, Epiphany, Ascension, Friday after Ascension and Vigil of Pentecost)—when the Office on those days is of the current feria.

2. At Prime (i) Preces Dominicales are said in all semi-doubles, simples, Ferial Offices.

(i) They are said at Little Hours if said at Lauds.

(ii) At Prime, Preces Feriales are said if they have been said at Lauds.

3. At Vespers Preces Feriales are said (1) on ferias of Advent and Lent when office is of feria.

4. At Compline, Preces Dominicales are said on all (i) semi-doubles, (ii) simples, (iii) all Ferias, *unless* at Vespers a double or an octave was celebrated.

SOME TEXTS AND INTENTIONS WHICH MAY HELP TOWARDS THE DEVOUT RECITATION OF LAUDS.

1. "And very early in the morning, the first day of the week, they come to the sepulchre, the sun being now risen. "

They said to one another, "Who shall roll us back the stone from the door of the sepulchre? " (St. Mark, xv.).

2. "And looking, they saw the stone rolled back.... And entering the sepulchre they saw a young man sitting on the right side, clothed with a white robe; and they were astonished. Who sayeth to them, Be not affrighted; you seek Jesus of Nazareth Who was crucified. He is risen, He is not here" (St. Mark, xv.).

3. "Behold Jesus sayeth to her (Magdalen) 'Woman, why weepest thou? '"

4. "Behold Jesus met them (the women) saying to them 'All hail. '"

(5) "See my hands and feet, that it is I myself, handle and see" (St. Luke, xxiv.).

6. "Bring hither thy hand and put it into My side and be not faithless. "

7. "My Lord and my God" (St, John, xx.).

General Intentions. The wants of the Church, peace among nations — vocations to the priesthood — Church students — souls in Purgatory.

Personal Intentions. A glorious resurrection; fervour in saying the Office; fervour in saying Mass; fervour in priestly work; forgiveness of all sin.

Special Intentions. For Catholic Ireland; for the conversion of America; for peace throughout the world.

PRIME (TITLE XV.).

Etymology. The name *Prime* is derived from the Latin *prima* because this part of the Office was said at the first hour of the day, 6 a. m., with us, following the old Roman distribution of the day.

Origin. It was stated by some writers that this Hour was established by St. Clement and should therefore date from almost apostolic times. But modern writers, following the statement of Cassian, date the origin of this Hour from about the year 382. It was believed, too, that the monastery indicated by Cassian as the cradle of Prime was the monastery of Bethlehem, St. Jerome's monastery. But it was probably established not there, but in a monastery in the neighbourhood, Dair-er-Raociat (convent of the shepherds) or in Seiar-en-Ganheim (enclosure of the sheep). Cassian tells us the reason that led to the introduction of this Hour. Lauds ended at dawn, and the monks retired to rest. As no other choir work called them until Terce, at 9 a. m., some of them were inclined to rest until that hour and to neglect the spiritual reading and manual work laid down by their rule. To prevent this prolonged rest, it was decided to introduce a short choir service, the recital of a few psalms, and then the monks went to work until Terce (*Cath. Encyclopedia*, "Prime").

Contents. Originally the matter for Prime was drawn from Lauds and was a repetition of part of Lauds. Prime consists of two parts. The first part consists of hymn, psalms, little chapter and collect. The prayers and confiteor inserted before the collect and said on certain days are adjuncts. The second part contains the Martyrology (when Prime is said in choir) and other prayers peculiar to the Hour. "The reason for this divergence may be traced to the fact that Prime is of monastic institution and the second portion, which is said in the chapter house, has reference to monastic customs. The Martyrology and Necrology having been read, prayers were said for the dead recommended to the Community, as benefactors, friends, patrons, protectors, etc. Then followed a special prayer in preparation for manual labour of the day, and a chapter of the rule was read, on which the Abbot briefly commented or else gave some admonition to the Community. This monastic character will be easily recognised by a glance at the formulas used. The prayer, 'Sancta Maria et omnes sancti' forms a natural conclusion, to the reading of the Martyrology, The 'Deus in adjutorium, ' the 'Pater Noster' with accompanying versicles, and the collect, are the prayers before manual labour: 'Respice, ' etc., Look, O Lord, upon Thy servants and upon Thy works... and direct Thou the work of our hands. 'Dirige et sanctificare, ' etc., 'Vouchsafe to direct and sanctify our senses, words and actions, ' etc. Whilst the 'Dominus nos benedicat' and the 'Fidelium animae' are the conclusion of the prayers for the dead" (Dom Cabrol, Introduction to the *Day Hours of the Church*).

Structure: -i. Pater, Ave, Credo, silently. 2. Deus in adjutorium.... Domine ad adjuvandum .. with sign of the cross, Gloria Patri.... Sicut erat.... 3. Hymn, *Jam lucis*. 4. Antiphon, first words only. 5. Psalms for the Sunday or feria as rubrics direct, with the Athanasian Creed if it be ordered, then the antiphon in full. 6. Regi saeculorum... or, Pacem et veritatem.... Deo Gratias, Christie, Fili Dei vivi.... 7. Preces, if they are ordered in the Office of the Day, Preces Dominicales or Preces feriales as rubrics direct. These include versicles, responses, confiteor, misereatur... indulgentiam... versicles responses. 8. Dominus vobiscum. Et cum spiritu tuo. Oremus, Domine Deus..... Amen. Dominus vobiscum, Et cum spiritu tuo. 9. Benedicamus Domino, Deo Gratias. 10. In choir, the martyrology is here read, 11. Pretiosa... mors.... 12. Sancta Maria et omnes Sancti.... 13. Thrice, Deus in adjutorium meum intende, Domine ad adjuvandum... without the sign of cross, Gloria Patri.... Sicut erat. 14. Kyrie Eleison, Christe Eleison, Kyrie Eleison, Pater Noster, qui es in coelis... (in silence). Et ne nos inducas in tentationem. Sed libera nos a malo. 15. Respice in servos tuos.... Et sit splendor.... 16. Gloria Patri.... Sicut erat.... Oremus, Dirigere et sanctificare.... 17. Jube, Domine.... Deus et actus nostros.... Amen. 18. Lectio brevis, which in feast offices is the Capitulum from None. 19. Adjutorium nostrum in nomine Domine (with sign of cross on forehead, breast and shoulders); Qui fecit.... 20. Benedicite, Deus; Domine nos benedicat... in pace, Amen. To the lectio brevis at Prime, Tu autem Domine, miserere nobis, is added.

The Athanasian Creed. In the Roman Breviary prior to the reform of 1911, the title given to the formula of faith was Symbolum S. Athanasi. In the new Breviaries the title stands Symbolum Athanasianum. Why was the change made?

During the past two hundred years the authorship of this formula has led to great discussion and its reading has led to much bitter and heated controversy in Anglican and Protestant churches. Many contended for its retention in Protestant services and many rejoiced at its partial exclusion, its truncated revision and clamoured for its rejection everywhere from service. Controversy led to the study of its origin. In 1872 a Protestant author, Ffoulkes, maintained that it was not composed by St. Athanasius (296-373) but by Paulinus of Aquileia (A. D. 800). But the literature of the age of Charlemagne proves that this creed had at the beginning of the ninth century an antiquity of at least more than a century (Ommaney, *History and Structure of the Athanasian Creed*, Oxford, 1897). Scholars, basing their opinions on words found in the *Expositio Fidei Fortunati*, date the origin of this symbol from the fifth century. It contains certain expressions which a writer subsequent to the Council of Chalcedon (451) would have been most unlikely to employ, and omits certain expressions which such a writer would have been most unlikely to omit. However, it is likely that the creed dates from the fifth century.

Who its author was, is quite doubtful. It was not St. Athanasius, it may have been St. Hilary of Aries, or St. Vincent of Lerins, or some local bishop in southern France, "But let us only suppose that the real author was some local bishop—or the theologian employed by some local bishop—and that it was composed in the first instance for purely local use in some district of southern France—then does not the difficulty disappear, and are not the facts of its silent and gradual adoption suitably explained? Not coming from an author of wide reputation, it would not at first have attracted much attention and would have been used only in the locality of its origin; from there its use would have spread to neighbouring districts; as it got more known it would have been more widely adopted, and the compactness and lucidity of its statements, and the enthusiasm-inspiring character of its style would have contributed to make it highly prized wherever it was known. Then would come speculation as to its authorship, and what wonder if in uncritical times an Athanasian authorship was first guessed, then confidently affirmed and believed? " (Father Sydney F. Smith, S.J., *The Month*, October, 1904).

This opinion is only one of several held by Catholic scholars. Dom Morin holds strongly, and gives very good reasons for his view, that it was written by Martin of Braga between the years 550 and 580. It was written, he says, for the people of Galicia in Spain, who had been recently converted from Arianism (*Journal of Theological Studies*, April, 1911). It was adopted into Gallican liturgy and office about 980, and in the Roman office only when the Curial Breviary was adopted.

"The liturgical use of the Athanasian Creed was Frankish in origin (ninth century) and spread through the influence of the Cluniac reform (tenth century), but only found its way to Rome in the Supplementary prayers in the twelfth and thirteenth century" (Burton and Myers, *op. cit.*, p. 51).

Rubrics. Athanasian Creed, to be said (1) Trinity Sunday, (2) Sundays after Epiphany, (3) Sundays after Pentecost unless there be in (2) and (3) the commemoration of a double, or of an octave.

Why is prayer offered at this first hour of the day?

Writers on liturgy answer, 1st to offer to God the first fruits of our day, of our work, of our devotion, following in this the example of

Christ, Who from His first entry into the world offered Himself to His Father for the salvation of mankind. 2d To beg of Him to keep us safe during the day, 3d To beg of Him to keep us free from sin, "ut in diurnis actibus nos servet a nocentibus. "

> "May God in all our words and deeds
> Keep us from harm this day.
> May He in love retain us still,
> From tones of strife and words of ill,
> And wrap around and close our eyes
> To earth's absorbing vanities.
> May wrath and thoughts that gender shame
> Ne'er in our breasts abide.
> And painful abstinences tame
> Of wanton flesh, the pride" (Hymn at Prime).

Rubrics. The Office of Prime begins in choir with the silent recitation of *Pater Noster, Ave, Credo.* Then, if in choir (aloud) Deus in adjutorium.... Domine ad adjirvandum.... Gloria Patri.... Alleluia, or Laus tibi.... Then the hymn *fam lucis* is said. The antiphon for the day is said as far as the asterisk (*), then the Psalms of the day's Office as arranged in the new Pian Psaltery, according to the day of the week, except on some special feasts, when the Psalms at Prime are the Sunday psalms. When the *ordo recitandi* marks an Office as *officium solemne* (an excepted feast), the psalms at Lauds and Hours are the Sunday psalms; and at Prime the psalm *Deus in nomine tuo* (Psalm 53) takes the place of Psalm *Confitemini* (Psalm 117). At Prime, and at the small Hours, Terce, Sext, None, only one antiphon is said. It is said in full at the end of the last Psalm in each Hour.

The Capitulum, the little Responsory, *Christe, Fili Dei vivi...* is then said. In this responsory the versicle *Qui sedes ad dexteram Patris* is sometimes changed, e.g., in paschal time it is, *Qui surrexisti a mortuis.*

The manner of reciting this responsory is sometimes not correctly understood, owing, perhaps, to its printed form in some Breviaries. The normal method is to repeat the *whole* response, then say the versicle, and then the second portion of the response; then the *Gloria Patri el Filio et Spiritui Sancto, without the Sicut erat,* is said, and the response repeated. The versicle *Exsurge* and the response *Et libera* are then said. This is the method of recitation in all the small Hours and at Compline.

After this responsory, if the Office be of double rite or be an Office within an octave, or on the vigil of Epiphany or on Friday or Saturday after Ascension, or on a Sunday on which a double is commemorated, or an octave is celebrated, or on a semi-double feast within an octave, *Dominus vobiscum, Et cum spiritu tuo,* and the prayer *Dominus Deus omnipotens* is said. But if the Office be not any of these mentioned just now, the responsory is followed by the *Preces.*

Preces (Title XXXIV.) In the Breviary there are two sets of preces, the Preces Dominicales for Sunday and the Preces Feriales for ferial Offices. These ferial preces of Prime differ from the ferial preces of Lauds, and are said in Prime when the ferial preces are said in Lauds, That is, on the ferias of Advent, Lent, Passiontide, Ember days and Vigils. The ferial preces of Lauds are found in the Breviary, immediately after the second set of Psalms for ferial Lauds and after the short responsory in the psalm arrangements for the days of the week. (See Lauds, *supra*, p. 188.)

These prayers were introduced at a very early stage of Christian liturgy. St. Isidore writes that they come from Greek liturgy and the opening words *Kyrie eleison* seem to indicate remnants of an old litany. Formerly they were read oftener during the liturgical year than we now are called on to repeat them. They are sometimes referred to as the *preces flebiles*, tearful prayers, because they are said in times of penance, and are formed to excite tears. In choir recitation they are said kneeling. When the preces or the preces feriales are said the sign of the cross is made from the forehead to the breast, at the words *Adjutorium nostrum in nomine Domini.* Then the Confiteor is said.

The Confiteor was from an early date a prayer said privately as a preparation for Mass. It is found in several forms; *Confiteor Deo, beatae Mariae, omnibus sanctis et vobis* (Sarum Missal), but since the time of St. Pius V. (1566-1572) our present form alone was followed and allowed (S. R. C., 13th February, 1666). If the Office be recited privately or with one or two companions, the *confiteor* is said once only and simultaneously in the preces, and the words *vobis fratribus* and *vos fratres*, which priests say in the opening prayer of Mass are omitted. It should be remarked, too, that the *Misereatur* and *Indulgentiam* have not in this location *vestri, vestris, vos,* but *nostri, nostris, nos.* Sometimes errors in this part of the recitation of the

Office are unnoticed, and this pronoun error makes the formula meaningless.

After the *Indulgentiam* come the concluding versicles of the preces, Dignare... sine peccato... miserere... miserere... Fiat... Quemadmodum... Domine... Et... Dominus vobiscum, Et cum spiritu tuo, and the prayer *Domine Deus Omnipotens...* Amen.... Dominus vobiscum, Et cum spiritu tuo.... Benedicamus Domino, Deo gratias. If the Office be said in choir, the martyrology is read at this part of Prime. The reading of the martyrology is not of obligation in private recitation of the Office; but the reading of it was highly recommended, even in private recitation, by Pope Gregory XIII. (14th January, 1584; see his words in the beginning of the Martyrology).

Then are said, Pretiosa... mors... sancta Maria... Deus in adjutorium... Domine ad adjuvandum (both the latter being repeated thrice)... Gloria Patri... Sicut erat... Kyrie eleison... Christe eleison... Kyrie eleison... Pater Noster (silently) until words "Et ne nos"... Sed libera... Respice... Et sit... Gloria Patri... Sicut erat... Oremus, Dirigere et... Amen, Jube Domine... Dies et actus... Amen.

The short lesson which, on all feasts, is the same as the chapter which is said at None will be found in the proper or common, under that Hour, The new Psalter and new rubrics made no change in this matter. Hence, for example, on the feast of SS. Peter and Paul the short lesson at end of Prime is taken from None of the feast, "Et Petrus ad se reversus"; the short lesson for Prime on the feast of St. Aloysius is "Lex Dei ejus" and not the short lesson printed in the Psalter under the day's Office.

On all Sundays and week days it varies according to the season. Thus—

1. From the 14th January until the first Saturday in Lent, from Monday to Wednesday in Trinity week, from the Friday after the octave of Corpus Christi until the Saturday before Advent, the short lesson is "Dominus autem" (II. Thess. iii.),

2. From the first Sunday of Advent until the 23rd December inclusive it is "Domine miserere" (Isaias xxxiii,).

3. From the first Sunday of Lent until the Saturday before Passion Sunday inclusive it is "Quaerite Dominum" (Isaias iv.).

4. From Passion Sunday until Wednesday in Holy Week it is "Faciem meam" (Isaias, 1.),

5. From Easter Sunday to the Vigil of Ascension inclusive, the short lesson is "Si consurrexists" (Coloss. iii.).

At the end of the short lesson the words "Tu autem Domine, miserere nobis; Deo gratias" are added, and after these words are said "Adjutorium nostrum... Qui fecit... Benedicite Deus" and the Blessing, "Dominus nos benedicat... requiescant in pace, Amen. " Then *Pater Noster* is said silently, unless another Hour is to follow immediately.

TEXTS AND INTENTIONS FOR PIOUS RECITATION OF PRIME.

1. "Herod and his army set him at nought" (St. Luke, c. 25).

2. "Not this man, but Barrabas. Crucify Him. "

3. "I find no cause in Him. I will chastise Him and let Him go" (St. Luke).

4. "But Jesus he delivered up to their will" (St. Luke, c. 23).

5. "Shall I crucify your King?, " (St. John, 19).

General Intentions. The Pope and his intentions; the propagation of the Faith; the priesthood; the Catholic laity; Catholic Missions in the East; Catholic Europe.

Personal Intentions. The spirit of meekness and humility; greater devotion to the Eucharist; greater love of the Blessed Virgin; the priestly vows.

Special Intentions. For our friends; for the sick and sorrowful; for the Church in Scotland; for our enemies; for the priesthood of America.

CHAPTER III.

TERCE, SEXT, NONE (TITLE XVI.).

TERCE.

Etymology. The word Terce comes from the Latin word *tertia (hora)*, third. Because this little Hour was said at the third hour of the Roman day, that is, about 9 o'clock in the forenoon,

Structure. It consists of Pater Noster, Ave, Deus in adjutorium, Gloria Patri... Sicut erat... Amen, Alleluia, Hymn, opening words of the antiphon, the three psalms, antiphon in full, capitulum, response, Dominus vobiscum, Et cum spiritu tuo, Oremus, collect, Dominus vobiscum, Et cum spiritu tuo, Benedicamus... Deo gratias, Fidelium animae.... Amen. And Pater Noster is said silently if another Hour is not begun immediately.

Terce is called the golden Hour, *hora aurea*, because at this time of the day, the third Hour, the Holy Ghost, who is typified by gold, descended on the apostles. It is called sometimes the sacred Hour (*hora sacra*) because in conventional churches it is recited immediately before Holy Mass. It is the most solemn of all the small Hours.

Antiquity. The custom of praying at these three hours, terce, sext and none, is very ancient. It was in use amongst the devout Jews, and the early converts to Christianity retained the practice. The Apostolic Constitutions contain the words "Preces etiam vestras facite hora tertia. "

Why does the Church wish us to pray at the third hour?

The question is asked by liturgists of olden times. Their replies are: —

1. to remind us of the hour when our Saviour was condemned (St. Mark, c. 15).

2. to remind us of the hour at which the Holy Ghost descended on the Church.

3. as the Church's hymn tells us that at this hour of the day when men are engrossed in worldly affairs, they especially need God's help,

"Come, Holy Ghost, Who ever One,
Reignest with Father and with Son.
It is the hour, our souls possess
With Thy full flood of holiness.
Let flesh and heart and lips and mind
Sound forth our witness to mankind.
And love light up our mortal frame
Till others catch the living flame,
Now to the Father, to the Son,
And to the Spirit, Three in One,
Be praise and thanks and glory given,
By men on earth, by saints in heaven. Amen."

(Translation by Cardinal Newman of St. Ambrose's hymn, *Nunc sancte*).

TEXTS AND INTENTIONS FOR PIOUS RECITATION OF TERCE.

1. "Therefore, Pilate took Jesus and scourged Him. "

2. "And the soldiers plaiting a crown of thorns put it on His head; and they put on Him a purple garment. "

3. "And they came to Him and said, 'Hail, King of the Jews, ' and they gave Him blows" (St. John).

4. "Jesus, therefore, came forth bearing the crown of thorns and the purple garment, and he (Pilate) sayeth to them 'Behold the Man! '"

General Intentions. The Pope's Intentions; the conversion of heretics; the conversion of the Jews.

Personal Intentions. Devotion to the Holy Ghost; devotion to the Passion.

Special Intentions. Vocations in America and Australia; for the Irish people throughout the world; for the souls of our deceased penitents.

SEXT.

Etymology. The word Sext comes from the Latin word *sexta, (hora)*, the sixth hour, because the little Hour should be said at what was the sixth hour of the Roman day, about mid-day with us.

Structure. The structure of this hour is similar to that given in Terce above, the hymn, antiphon, psalms, little chapter and responses differing, but the order and form being similar in both.

Antiquity. The Psalmist wrote, "Vespere et mane et meridie narrabo et annuntiabo, et exaudiet vocem meam" (Ps. 54). This practice of devout Jews was maintained by the early Christians and in the Acts of the Apostles we read, "Ascendit Petrus in superiora ut oraret circam horam sextam" (Acts x, 9). At this hour, the Christians met for public, joint prayer.

Why does the Church wish us to pray at the sixth hour of the day?

1. Because at this hour Christ instructed the Samaritan woman, the type of the Gentiles; and He promised to give the living water, springing up unto life everlasting, which was His blood, poured out on Calvary at the sixth hour.

2. Because at this sixth hour Christ was raised on the cross for our salvation and it is right and just, daily, to remember Him and His great love for us. Besides, it is to realise His words "And if I be lifted up from the earth, I will draw all things to myself" (St. John xii. 32). And the Church, in the opening words of Sext for Sunday, impresses this idea on us "Deficit in salutare meum anima mea, " "My soul hath fainted after thy salvation" (Ps. 118).

3. To ask God to grant us health and peace of heart, as the hymn for Sext sings: —

> "O God, Who canst not change nor fail,
>   Guiding the hours as they go by,
>   Brightening with beam the morning pale,
>   And burning in the midnight sky,
>   Quench Thou the fires of hate and strife,
>   The wasting fever of the heart;
>   From perils guard our feeble life,
>   And to our souls Thy grace impart.

Grant this, O Father, only Son,
And Holy Ghost, God of Grace,
To whom all glory, Three in One,
Be given in every time and place—Amen."

(Translation by Cardinal Newman of St. Ambrose's
hymn, *Rector potens*).

TEXTS AND INTENTIONS FOR THE PIOUS RECITATION OF SEXT.

1. "And they took Jesus, and after they had mocked Him, they took off the purple from Him and put His own garments on Him and led Him out to crucify Him" (St. Mark, c. 15).

2. "Bearing His own cross, Jesus went forth to that place called Calvary. "

3. "Daughters of Jerusalem, weep not for Me, but for yourselves. "

General Intentions. The wants of the Church; for peace and goodwill amongst all States and peoples; for the Pope; for Church students.

Personal Intentions. For patience; for fraternal charity; for the love of the practice of mortification.

Special Intentions. For Catholic schools; for increase in number of daily communicants; for the success of catechists and their work.

NONE.

Etymology. The word *None* comes from the Latin word *nona*, ninth (*hora nona*), because this part of the Office was said at the ninth hour of the Roman day, that is, about three o'clock in our modern day.

Antiquity. This hour was set apart in Apostolic times for joint prayer, "Now Peter and John went up into the Temple at the ninth hour of prayer" (Acts iii. 1).

Structure. See note under this head at Terce.

Why does the Church desire prayer at the ninth hour?

1. In this she follows the example of her Founder, Christ, Who prayed at the ninth hour. "At the ninth hour, Jesus cried out with a loud voice, saying 'Eloi, Eloi, lamma sabacthani? ' which is, being interpreted, 'My God, my God, why hast Thou forsaken me? '" (St. Mark xv. 34).

2. That ninth hour was the long-wished-for and long-watched-for hour when reconciliation between earth and heaven was complete.

3. To beg from God light and grace, especially towards the end of life, for the day's decline in the afternoon is a figure of the waning of spiritual and corporal life. The hymn for None expresses this: —

> "O God, unchangeable and true,
> Of all the light and power,
> Dispensing light in silence through
> Each successive hour;
> Lord, brighten our declining day,
> That it may never wane
> Till death, when all things round decay,
> Brings back the morn again.
> This grace on Thy redeemed confer,
> Father, Co-equal Son,
> And Holy Ghost, the Comforter,
> Eternal Three in One—Amen."

> (St. Ambrose's hymn, translated by Cardinal Newman).

TEXTS AND INTENTIONS TO AID THE PIOUS RECITATION OF NONE.

1. "Come down from the cross" (St. Matthew, c. 27).

2. "Lord, remember me when Thou shalt come into Thy Kingdom" (St. Matthew, c. 23).

3. "My God, my God, why has Thou forsaken me? " (St. Matthew, c. 27).

General Intentions. All the intentions of the Sacred Heart; the conversion of Britain; the Church in America.

Personal Intentions. Fervour in preparation for Mass; fervour in thanksgiving after Mass; fidelity to professional duties and studies.

Special Intentions. The temporal welfare of Ireland; to beg a blessing on her priests; to beg a blessing on her Church students; to beg a blessing on her Catholic laity; to beg a blessing on her elementary schools.

CHAPTER IV.

VESPERS AND COMPLINE.

Etymology. The word *vespers* comes directly from the Latin *Vesper*; *Vespera* or *Espera* was a name given to the star Venus, which rising in the evening was a call to prayer. This Hour is recited after None and before Compline. In structure, it resembles Lauds, Pater Noster, Ave, Gloria, Five Psalms with antiphons, Capitulum, Hymn, Versicle, antiphon, Magnificat, antiphon and collect.

It had several synonymous names. It was called *Duodecima Hora* (Antiphonary of Bangor), because it was said at the twelfth hour of the day, six o'clock, or, perhaps, the name came from the twelve psalms which made up the Hour in some churches. It was known, too, by the names *Lucernarium, hora lucernalis,* the hour of the candles; because at this hour a number of candles were lighted, not only to shed light but for symbolic purposes. It was sometimes referred to as *hora incensi*, from the custom of burning incense at this evening service, and sometimes it is called *gratiarum actio* (St. Isidore), because it gives thanks to God for the graces given during the day. It came to mean not the evening Hour, but the sunset Hour. And in the sixth century it was celebrated before daylight had gone and before there was any need for artificial light. In the fourth century it was recited by torchlight.

Antiquity. The Jews honoured God by special and solemn evening service. Their feasts by God's command began in the evening. "From evening unto evening you shall celebrate your sabbaths" (Lev. xxiii, 32). And David sang "Evening and morning and at noon I will speak and declare" (Psalm 54:32). The eariy Christians faithfully followed the practice.

"In the sixth century, the order of Psalms, etc., in Vespers differed little from the Vespers in our modern Breviaries. Long before the sixth century there were evening Offices in various forms. Its existence in the fourth century is also confirmed by St. Augustine, St. Ambrose, St. Basil, St. Ephraem... Before the fourth century we find allusions to the evening prayer in the early Fathers, Clement I. of Rome, St. Ignatius, St. Clement of Alexandria, Tertullian, Origen, the Canons of St. Hippolytus, St. Cyprian (for texts see Baumer-Biron; 1. c. t. 20 seq. 73-74, 76, 78)" — (Dorn Cabrol, *Cath. Ency.*, art "Vespers").

Why do we offer up public prayer in the evening? The old liturgists reply: —

1. To imitate the devout Christians of apostolic times.

2. To honour Jesus, the true Sun of the world, Who hid Himself at His Incarnation, and in His life, and Whose glory was hidden in His Passion.

3. To thank Christ for the Eucharist, which He instituted in the evening of His earthly life,... "and they prepared the Pasch. But when it was evening (vespere autem) He sat down with His twelve disciples" (St. Matthew, xxvi. 20). At this vesper meeting He gave to priests the power to offer the sacrifice of the Mass, to change bread and wine into His body and blood. At this vesper service, too, Christ and His apostles celebrated the divine praises, "Hymno dicto" (St. Matthew xxvi. 30).

4. In the evening our Lord's body was taken down from the cross.

5. At the approach of evening Christ appeared to His disciples at Emmaus and revealed to them His divinity. "Stay with us because it is towards evening (advesperascit) and He went in with them. He took bread and blessed and brake and gave it to them and their eyes were opened and they knew Him" (St. Luke xxiv. 29-30). At Vespers we thank God for the Eucharist.

The hymns at Vespers date for the most part from the sixth century. They are of great beauty and have the peculiar characteristic of telling of the days of creation. Thus St. Gregory's (?) fine hymn, *Lucis Creator optime*, in Sunday's Vespers, refers to the creation of light; Monday's hymn, *Immense coeli Creator*, refers to the separation of land and water; Wednesday's hymn (written probably by St. Ambrose), *Coeli Deus sanctissime*, refers to the creation of the sun and moon; the hymns for Thursday's vespers, *Magnae Deus potentiae*, refers to the creation of fish and birds; Friday's hymn, *Hominis superne conditor* (St. Gregory), refers to the creation of the beasts of the earth; Saturday's hymn (St. Ambrose) is an exception, as it refers to the Trinity. All these hymns have been beautifully translated into English and the text and translations repay study.

Sunday's hymn, *Lucis Creator optime*, stands thus in translation: —

"O blest Creator of the light,
Who makest the day with radiance bright,
And o'er the forming world didst call
The light from chaos first of all.

Whose wisdom joined in sweet array
The morn and eve and named them day,
Night comes with all its darkening fears;
Regard Thy people's prayers and tears,

Lest sunk in sin, and whelmed with strife,
They lose the gift of endless life;
While thinking—but the thoughts of time,
They weave new chains of woe and crime.

But grant them grace that they may strain
The heavenly gate and prize to gain;
Each harmful lure aside to cast,
And purge away each error past.

O Father, that we ask be done,
Through Jesus Christ, Thine only Son;
Who, with the Holy Ghost and Thee,
Doth live and reign eternally. Amen."

(Translation by Dr. J.M. Neale).

Structure. Vespers, in structure, resembles Lauds and consists of five Psalms. It begins with Pater Noster, Ave (said silently), Deus in adjutorium,... Domine ad adjuvandum.... Gloria Patri.... Sicut erat. Alleluia or Laus tibi.... Antiphon begun only if the feast be not double; if feast be a double the antiphon is said in full before and after each psalm. If feast be a semi-double or simple the antiphon is intoned at the beginning and is said in full at end of each psalm and then only. Then are said Capitulum, Deo gratias, Hymn, versicle and response, antiphon to Magnificat, the canticle Magnificat, Gloria Patri.... Sicut erat.... Dominus vobiscum.... Et cum spiritu tuo, Oremus, collect, commemoration if any made by versicle and response and antiphon of Magnificat proper to commemoration with collect, Dominus vobiscum, Et cum.... Benedicamus Domino; Deo gratias, Fidelium animae.... Amen. If Compline be not said immediately after Vespers, Pater Noster is added.

At the opening words of the *Magnificat, Nunc Dimittis* and *Benedictus*, it is a practice with many priests to make the sign of the cross from forehead to breast, as at *Deus in adjutorium* (*cf.* Ceremoniale Epis. lib. II. i. 14). This custom, where it exists, should be preserved (S. R.C., April, 1867).

Writers on liturgy tell us that the number of Psalms in Vespers have a symbolic meaning, typifying the five wounds of the Saviour, the last of which, the wound in the side, was inflicted on the evening of Good Friday, and the others, as the Church says in the hymn *Vergente mundi vespere*, at the waning of the day of the Old Law, before the dawn of salvation (Honorius of Autun, circa 1130). Other writers say that these five psalms should produce acts of contrition for the sins committed during the day, by the five senses; and that they should be for us, morally, what the five lighted lamps were for the wise virgins in the Gospel parable (Amalare of Metz, circa 850).

Magnificat. Author. The Blessed Virgin Mary is the author of this canticle. "The witness of the codices and of the Fathers is practically unanimous for the Vulgate reading: 'Et ait Maria, ' but apart from this, the attribution of the *Magnificat* to Elizabeth would in St. Luke's context be highly abnormal" (Dr. H. T. Henry, *Cath. Encyc.*, word, *Magnificat*)—The Roman Breviary entitles it *Canticum Beatae Marine Virginis.*

It is divided by commentators into three parts (St. Luke 1, vv. 46-49; 50-53; 54-55). It "is in many places very similar in thought and phrase to the Canticle of Anna (I. Kings ii. 1-10) and to various psalms (Ps. 33, vv. 3-4; Ps. 39, v. 9; Ps. 70, v. 9; Ps. 125, vv. 2-3; Ps. 110, v. 9; Ps. 97, v. 1; Ps. 117, v. 16; Ps. 32, v. 10; Ps. 92, v. 7; Ps. 33, v. 11; Ps. 97, v-3; Ps. 131, v. 11). Similarities are found in Hab. c. III. v. 18; Mal. c. III. v. 12; Job. c. 5, v. 11; Is, c. 41, v. 8; Is. c. 149, v. 3, and Gen. c. 17, v. 19. Steeped thus in scriptural thought and Phraseology, summing up in its inspired ecstasy the economy of God with His chosen people, indicating the fulfilment of olden prophecy, and prophesying anew until end of time, the Magnificat is the crown of the Old Testament singing, the last canticle of the Old and the first of the New Testament. It is an ecstasy of praise for the inestimable favour bestowed by God on the Virgin, for the mercies shown to Israel, and for the fulfilment of the promises made to Abraham and the patriarchs" (Dr. Henry, *loc. cit.*).

It is found universally in the ancient liturgies and affords a proof of the apostolic and universal praise of the Blessed Virgin. Durandus (thirteenth century) gives some reasons for the assignment of the Magnificat to Vespers. Because Vespers is the grandest liturgical Hour; because Mary probably arrived at the house of Elizabeth in the evening; because it was in the moral evening of the world that Mary consented to be the Mother of God; because she is the star of the sea, etc. The following interesting reason for the use of the Magnificat at Vespers is given by St. Bede (works 5, 306). "It comes to pass, by the bounty of the Lord, that if we were at all times to meditate upon the acts and sayings of the Blessed Virgin, the observance of chastity and the works of virtue will always continue with us. For, the excellent and salutary custom has grown up in Holy Church that all shall sing her hymn (the Magnificat) every day with the Vesper Psalms, in order that the recalling of the Lord's incarnation, by this means, may the oftener incite the souls of the faithful to devotion and that the consideration of the example set by His Mother may confirm them in the stability of virtue. And it is meet that this should be done at Vespers, so that the mind wearied in the course of the day, and distracted by various opinions, may, at the approach of the season of quiet, collect itself in oneness of meditation and through the wholesome reminder may hasten to cleanse itself, by the prayers and tears of the night, from everything useless or harmful which it had contracted by the business of the day. "

Suffrages of the Saints. (Title XXXV.) In Sec. 2 of rubrics of the new Breviary we read, "Deinceps, quando facienda erunt suffragia sanctorum, unum fiet suffragium, juxta formulam propositam in Ordinario novi Psalterii. " Thus were abolished the old formulae of suffrages and a new one inserted.

Antiphon Beata Dei Genitrix.... V. Mitificavit .... R. Et exaudivit.... Oremus, A cunctis....

This will be said at Lauds and Vespers outside Paschal time (1) on all Sundays and ferias, (2) on semi-doubles and simples, except (*a*) in Advent and Passiontide, (*b*) when there is a commemoration of a double, a day within an octave. In Paschal time the Commemoration is of the Cross.

In this prayer the names of the Holy Angels and of St. John the Baptist, if they be titulars, are inserted before the name of St. Joseph. At the letter N. in the prayer, the name of the titular saint of the particular church should be inserted; but churches dedicated by the title of a mystery (e. g., the Ascension) are not to be named in this prayer (S. R.C., March, 1912).

TEXTS AND INTENTIONS TO AID THE PIOUS RECITATION OF VESPERS.

1. "Woman, behold thy Son; Behold Thy mother" (St. John, c. 19),

2. "I thirst" (St. John, c. 19).

3. "And they, putting a sponge full of vinegar about hyssop, put it to His mouth" (St. John, c. 19).

General Intentions. The conversion of sinners; the wants of the Church; those in death agony; spread of Eucharistic devotion; daily Communion; priest adorers; reparation for bad Communions; reparation for impieties and irreverences towards the Eucharist.

Personal Intentions. Regularity in visits to Blessed Sacrament; Fervour in Mass and in administering Holy Communion; a happy death; true and deep devotion to Mary.

Special Intentions. The Irish Daily Mass Crusade; Total Abstinence; devotion to the Passion; devotion to the agonising Heart of Jesus.

COMPLINE.

Etymology and synonym. The word compline comes from the Latin word *complere*, to complete, to finish, because this Hour completes or finishes the day Hours of the Office. It bore several names, *Completa* (St. Isidore), *Initium noctis* (St. Columbanus), *Prima noctis hora* (St. Fructeux).

Antiquity. The origin of this Hour has given rise to a great deal of controversy. Both Baumer and Battifol in their histories of the Breviary attribute the origin of this Hour to St. Benedict (480-543). Other scholars attribute its origin to St. Basil, and hence date it from the fourth century. It is admitted that before the time of St. Basil, Bishop of Caesarea (370-379) this Hour was in existence. Some hold that St. Basil established the Hour in the East and St. Benedict in the West. The latter certainly invested the Hour with the liturgical character and arrangement which were preserved by the

Benedictines and adapted by the Roman Church. The Compline of the Roman Church is more ornate and solemn than the liturgy assigned to this Hour by St. Benedict, which was very simple. The addition of the response *In manus tuas Domine*, the *Nunc dimittis* and its anthem of the Blessed Virgin make this Hour one of great beauty.

Structure, The structure of the Hour seems to point to its monastic origin, "The reader begins, 'Pray, Father, a blessing' (jube, domne benedicere); the blessing, 'The Lord Almighty grant us a quiet night and a perfect end. Amen. ' 'Noctem quietam.... ' Then follows a short lesson, which the Father Abbot gave to his monks. 'Brethren, be sober and watch; because your adversary, the devil, as a roaring lion, goeth about, seeking whom he may devour, whom resist ye, strong in faith. But Thou, O Lord, have mercy on us. ' And the monks answer 'Thanks be to God. ' 'Fratres sobrii estote et vigilate.... ' Then the *Pater Noster* (silently), and the presiding priest, who was the Abbot or his deputy, said the confiteor and the choir answered *Misereatur....* 'May Almighty God have mercy upon thee and forgive thee thy sins, and bring thee to life everlasting. ' The choir then repeats the Confiteor and the priest replies 'Misereatur vestri.... ' 'May Almighty God have mercy upon you, forgive you your sins and bring you to life everlasting. '" Of course, in private recitation, or where two or three recite the Office, these prayers are said only once, and in the Confiteor, *tibi pater* and *te pater* are omitted, and *nostri, nostris, nos, nostrorum, nobis,* are said in the Misereatur and Indulgentiam.

Then the *Converte nos Deus.... At averte iram tuam.... Deus in adjutorium.... Domine ad adjuvandum.... Gloria Patri....* Antiphon (begun only) and three psalms, which vary, are said, *Gloria Patri.... Sicut erat...* being said at the end of each. *In manus tuas...* is said twice. *Redemisti nos.... Commendo spiritum meum; Custodi nos... sub umbra.... Salva nos; Nunc dimittis.... Gloria Patri, Salva nos Domine vigilantes, custodi nos... pace.* (Preces are said here if rubric orders; i. e., *Kyrie eleison, Christie eleison... ad te veniat*); *Dominus vobiscum, Et cum.... Benedicamus Domino, Deo gratias; Benedicat et custodiat nos omnipotens.* Amen; then the anthem of the Blessed Virgin, *Alma Redemptoris Mater* (from Saturday before first Sunday of Advent to the feast of the Purification, inclusive) with its antiphon; in Advent, *Angelus Domini*, response, *Et concepit*, Oremus and prayer, *Gratiam tuam*, or with antiphon (after Advent) *Post partum...* and response, *Dei genetrix, Oremus, Deus qui salutis*. After the Purification, until Holy Thursday the anthem is *Ave regina coelorum*, with versicle *Dignare me*

..., *Da mihi*, Oremus, *Concedemisericors*. From Holy Saturday until Saturday after Pentecost, the anthem is *Regina coeli* with versicle, *Gaude...* and response, *Quia surrexit....* Oremus and prayer, *Deus qui per resurrectionem*. From Holy Trinity Sunday to the Saturday before Advent, the antiphon is *Salve Regina* with versicle, *Ora pro nobis...* response, *Ut digni*, Oremus and prayer, *Omnipotens semipeterne Deus*. Then the versicle *Divinum auxilium....* Amen. *Pater Noster, Ave, Credo*, in silence, are said. The *Sacro-sanctae* is added (see pp. 133-135).

The study of the component parts of this Hour are of great interest. After the Abbot had given his blessing and begged of God to grant the two-fold favour of a quiet night and a good death, a monk read from Holy Scripture, and when a suitable portion was read, or at the end of a Scripture chapter or theme, the Abbot said, "Tu autem, " and the reader "Tu autem, Domine, miserere nobis. " This was to ask God to pardon faults both of reader in his reading and of monks, who, perhaps, were drowsy and inattentive. The Abbot terminated the exercise by the *Adjutorium nostrum* (the *Pater Noster* is of more recent introduction). Monks who were absent substituted for the Scripture lesson which they had missed, the pithy extract from St. Peter, "Fratres; sobrii estote, " which we now read. The whole company of monks and their abbot then proceeded to the chapel where each made his examination of conscience, and at a sign from the abbot, the monks, two by two, in a subdued tone of voice, said the *Confiteor, Misereatur, Indulgentiam* and *Converte nos*. Gavantus and Merati hold that the *Converte nos* does not belong to this introductory matter, but formed part of Compline proper. This prayer is very beautiful: "Convert us, O God, our Saviour. And turn away Thine anger from us. Incline unto my aid, O God; O Lord, make haste to help us. Glory be to the Father,... Praise be to God. "

The new arrangement of the Psalter did not retain the old traditional psalms, 4, 90, 133, in Compline, except for Sundays and solemn feasts. But the selection of psalms accords well with the idea of the hour—night prayer—and with the other prayers, which go to make up the close of the Office of the day. The hymn, *Te lucis*, so chastely simple, has ever been admired. Its ideas suit so admirably for the prayer before sleep and for reminding us of sleep and her sister death and the solemn petition made to God to be our guardian and defence in the solemn hour of death, are simply and solemnly set out in this daily hymn. How beautiful it reads in Father Caswall's translation: —

"Now with the fast departing light,
Maker of all, we ask of Thee
Of Thy great mercy, through the night,
Our guardian and defence to be.

Far off let idle visions fly,
No phantom of the night molest:
Curb Thou our raging enemy,
That we in chaste repose may rest.

Father of mercies! hear our cry;
Hear us, O sole-begotten Son!
Who, with the Holy Ghost most high,
Reignest while endless ages run."

In Passiontide, the Breviary gives us the last verse, Deo Patri, and the translation renders it: —

"To Thee, Who dead again dost live,
All glory, Jesus, ever be,
Praise to the Father, infinite,
And Holy Ghost eternally. "

Little Chapter. This is a beautiful call to our Lord to remind Him, as it were, that we are His own, that we bear His name. In this invocation we express our confidence in Him and ask Him not to abandon us, but to dwell with us. "But Thou, O Lord, art among us, and Thy holy name is invoked upon us; forsake us not, O Lord our God"; and for past protection the Church adds to their invocation, taken from the prophet Jeremias, the words of gratitude, "Thanks be to God. "

The Response. "In manus tuas, Domine, commendo spiritum meum... nos. " "Into Thy hands, O Lord, I commend my spirit. Into Thy hands I commend my spirit. For Thou hast redeemed us, O Lord God of Truth. I commend my spirit. Glory be to the Father and to the Son and to the Holy Ghost. Into Thy hands, O Lord, I commend my spirit. Keep us, O Lord, as the apple of Thine eye. Protect us under the shadow of Thy wings. " No more sublime prayer exists in the liturgy than this response, which the Church orders us to say nightly. She wishes, in its daily recital, to prepare us for death, by reminding us of the sentiments and words of our dying Lord on the cross, "Into Thy hands I commend my spirit" (Ps. 30, v. 6), and by asking Him Who redeemed us on the bitter tree, to keep us safe as the apple of His eye and to protect us "under the shadow of His wings" (Ps. 40, v, 6). These solemn words of our dying Saviour have been, in all ages, and in all lands, the death prayer of many of those whom He redeemed, with the great price. St. Stephen, the proto-martyr, prayed "Lord Jesus receive my spirit. " "Into Thy hands I commend my spirit, " prayed St. Basil in his death agony. "Into Thy hands I commend my spirit, " prayed thousands of God's servants, heroes and heroines, e.g., Savanarola, Columbus, Father Southwell, the martyr Mary, Queen of Scots, and countless other servants of God.

Nunc Dimittis. The canticle *Nunc dimittis* is the last in historical sequence of the three great canticles of the New Testament. It was spoken at the presentation of Christ, by Simeon, "This man was just and devout, waiting for the consolation of Israel; and the Holy Ghost was in him. And he had received an answer from the Holy Ghost, that he should not see death before he had seen the Christ of the Lord. And he came by the spirit into the temple. And when His parents brought the child Jesus to do for him according to the custom of the law. He also took Him in his arms and blessed God and said 'Now thou dost dismiss thy servant, O Lord, according to thy word in peace.... '" (St. Luke ii. 29-33). This sublime canticle uttered by the holy old man at the close of his days is placed fittingly in the priest's Office at the close of the day. It breathes his thanks, expresses his love and his wish to die, having seen the Saviour.

Before the canticle are said the opening words of the antiphon, "Salva nos"; and it is repeated in full at the end. "Save us, O Lord, while we are awake, and guard us when we sleep, that we may watch with Christ and rest in peace. "

The prayers, Kyrie eleison, Christie eleison, etc., are said always except when a double office or a day within an octave has been commemorated at Vespers. The prayer, *Visita quaesumus* is found in Breviaries of the thirteenth century and was introduced probably by the Friars Minor. The words *habitationem istam* are said to indicate that it is a prayer not only for the chapel of the friars, but for their dwellings on journeys. It was said in choir by the abbot or presiding priest. Like all prayers for Compline it begs God to drive far away the snares of the enemy; it begs Him to let His angels dwell in that house to keep the dwellers therein, in peace; and finally, it begs Him to "let Thy blessing be always upon us. Through Jesus Christ, Thy

Son, our Lord, Who liveth and reigneth with Thee in the unity of the Holy Ghost, God, world without end. Amen. "

After the Dominus vobiscum and its response, the abbot or presiding priest gave the solemn blessing "Benedicat et custodiet..., May the Almighty and merciful Lord, the Father, the Son and the Holy Ghost, bless and preserve us. Amen. "

Then one of the anthems of the Blessed Virgin Mary is said. From the Saturday before Advent until the feast of the Purification, inclusive, is said the anthem "Alma Redemptoris Mater"; translated by Father Caswall, it reads: —

> "Mother of Christ, hear Thou thy people's cry,
> Star of the deep and portal of the sky,
> Mother of Him who Thee from nothing made,
> Sinking we strive and call to Thee for aid.
> Oh, by that joy which Gabriel brought to Thee,
> Thou Virgin first and last, let us Thy mercy see. "

The Latin hexameters are attributed to Hermanus (circa 1054). It has been translated by several poets great and small, and is well known in Newman's translation, "Kindly Mother of the Redeemer. " It was a popular hymn in Norman Ireland and in Catholic England, as we see in Chaucer's "Prioress's Tale. " After this anthem are said its versicle, response, and prayer *Oremus, Gratiam tuam quaesumus.*

From the first Vespers of the Nativity, the versicle, response and prayer said are "Post partum... ; Dei Genetrix.... Oremus, Deus qui salutis. "... From the end of Compline on February 2nd until Holy Thursday exclusive the antiphon is "Ave Regina coelorum. " It appears to be of monastic origin, and St. Jerome attributes it to St. Ephraem. Its expressions are borrowed from the works of St. Ephraem, of St. Athanasius and of other doctors, and its theme is Mary, as Queen of Heaven, the dawn of our salvation, and an extolling of her beauty.

From Compline of Holy Saturday, inclusive, until None of the Saturday after the feast of Pentecost, inclusive, the "Regina coeli" is said. It is a very old composition, but its author is unknown. Some authors attribute it to St. Gregory the Great (590-604). Others, following a venerable tradition, say that the three first lines were the composition of angels, and the fourth, Ora pro nobis Deum, alleluia, was added by Pope Gregory. The legend tells us that when in the year 596 Rome was desolated by the plague, Pope Gregory the Great exhorted his people to penance and prayer, and carrying in his hands the picture of the Blessed Virgin, said to be painted by St. Luke, he led them in procession to the church, Afa Coeli, on Easter morn. When the procession was passing Adrian's Mole, angel voices were heard chanting the Regina Coeli, and the Pope astonished and rejoiced added the words "Ora pro nobis Deum, Alleluia, " and immediately a shining angel appeared and sheathed his sword, the plague ceased on that very day (Gueranger, *Liturgical Year*, "Paschal Time, " Part I., p. iii; Duffy, Dublin). Attempts at translation have been indifferent.

From the first Vespers of the feast of the Most Hoiy Trinity to the None of the Saturday before Advent, the Salve Regina is said. The authorship was assigned to St. Bernard (1091-1153). But scholars reject this theory. It is assigned to Petrus de Monsoro (circa 1000) and to Adehemar, but the claims of both are doubtful. In 1220 the general chapter of Cluny ordered its daily chanting before the high altar, after the Capitulum. The use of the anthem at Compline was begun by the Dominicans about 1221 and the practice spread rapidly. It was introduced into the "modernised. " Franciscan Breviary in the thirteenth century. The Carthusians sing it daily at Vespers; the Cistercians sing it after Compline, and the Carmelites say it after every Hour of the Office. It is said after every low Mass throughout the world. It was especially obnoxious to Luther, who several times denounced it, as did the Jansenists also. It is recorded in the lives of several saints that the Blessed Virgin, to show her love for this beautiful prayer, showed to them her Son, at the moment they said "Et Jesum... nobis post hoc exilium ostende. "

Speaking of these antiphons of the Blessed Virgin, Battifol, in his *History of the Roman Breviary* (English ed.), writes: "We owe a just debt of gratitude to those who gave us the antiphons of the Blessed Virgin... four exquisite compositions, though in style enfeebled by sentimentality. "

After the antiphon of the Blessed Virgin the versicle and response are said. Then Oremus and prayer "Omnipotens sempiterne Deus... Divinum auxilium... Amen, " are said. Then the Pater Noster, Ave and Credo are said silently, and this finishes the Hour. The prayer Sacro-sanctae et individuae.... V. Beata viscera... R. Et beata ubera... Pater Noster and Ave are generally added though not of obligation.

They are to be said kneeling. The reading of this well-known and oft-repeated prayer, in its English translation, may bring fresh and fervent thoughts to priests, for it is a sublime prayer: —

"To the most holy and undivided Trinity, to the humanity of our Lord Jesus Christ crucified, to the fruitful virginity of the most glorious Mary ever a Virgin, and to the company of all the saints, be given by every creature, eternal praise, honour, power and glory, and to us the remission of all our sins. Amen. Blessed be the womb of the Virgin Mary, which bore the Son of the Eternal Father. And blessed be the breasts which gave suck to Christ our Lord. "

TEXT AND INTENTIONS TO AID THE PIOUS RECITATION OF COMPLINE.

1. "Into Thy hands, O Lord, I commend my spirit. "

2. "It is finished. "

3. "For this Thou hast redeemed us, O God of truth. "

General Intentions. The spread of the faith; the Pope; the Church in France and in Spain; for the Church in Australia.

Personal Intentions. A happy death; fervour in administering the last sacraments; devotion to St. Joseph, patron of a happy death.

Special Intentions, For the sick poor of Ireland; for persons dying without the last sacraments; for those dying all alone; for dying sinners.

THE LITTLE OFFICE OF THE BLESSED VIRGIN, (TITLE XXXVII.).

Origin. This Office dates from the eighth century at least. Pope Gregory II. (715-731) and Pope Gregory III. (731-741) ordered the monks to say this little Office in addition to their great Office. The practice was observed by St. John Damascene (676-787) and by St. Peter Damien (1007-1072). This usage was confined to monasteries only. At the end of the eleventh century the practice became almost universal. Pope Urban II. (1088-1099) besought the special aid of the Blessed Virgin in his crusade against the Turks and recommended all clerics to recite the little Office. Provincial councils prescribed its use and some canonists held it to be obligatory. However, the Bull *Quod a nobis* of Pope Pius V. (9 July, 1568) removed all obligation of the private recital of this Office, but he exhorted all to continue the practice and granted indulgences for its recitation.

PART IV.

NOTES ON SOME FEASTS.

CHAPTER I.

PROPER OF THE TIME.

ADVENT.

Advent (Latin, *advenire*, to come to) is a period beginning with the Sunday nearest to the Feast of St. Andrew (November 30) and embracing four Sundays. In the early Church there was a divergence of date and practice in Advent celebration. Thus, in France it began on St. Martin's Day (11 November) and ended with Christmas, France kept Advent with tri-weekly fasts. Rome did not, in very early days, observe the Advent fasts, but maintained the shorter period, containing only four Sundays. (Father Thurston, *The Month*, No. 498).

Several authors stated that this period of preparation for the celebration of Christ's birthday was instituted by Gregory the Great. It is now traceable to the fourth century in France; in Rome it was of later date. The Church, as is seen in the Advent Offices in the Breviary, instituted this part of the liturgical year to honour and to recall the two comings of Christ—His first coming in human form at Bethlehem, as Saviour; and His second coming, as Judge of all mankind. In her liturgy she expresses repeatedly both sentiments, a sentiment of joy and a sentiment of sorrow. The former she expresses by her *alleluias* and the latter by her omission of the *Te Deum* and by her recital of the ferial prayers, the prayers of tears and grief.

In the Advent Offices are many phrases which were fulfilled at the Incarnation: "Rorate coeli desuper et nubes pluant Justum; O Adonai, veni ad redimendum nos; Emitte Agnum, Domine, Dominatorum terrae; Orietur sicut sol Salvator mundi et descendet in uterum Virginis. " Centuries have passed since the Saviour came, and yet the Church wishes us to repeat the sublime prayers and prophecies which associate themselves with the coming of the Word made Flesh, and by our repetition to be animated with the ardent longings of olden days; and that by them we may awaken our faith, our hope, our charity, and obtain and augment God's grace in our souls.

Rubrics. The first Sunday of Advent has the invitatory hymn and the rest of the Office proper. The lessons are from Isaias, the prophet of the Incarnation. The first response to the lesson is unique in the Breviary for it has three verses (see p. 164). These three verses are spoken in the names of the holy people who lived before the law, during the law, and after the law. The Gloria Patri is added to honour the Holy Trinity, who has at length sent the long-watched-for Messias (Durandus). And the response is repeated from the beginning because the second coming of Christ is watched for, by His faithful (Honorius d'Autun). The *Te Deum* is not said, in order thereby to mark the sad thought of the second coming of Christ, then our judge.

Lessons. From the first Sunday of Advent until the first Sunday of August the lessons of the first and second nocturns are given in the Breviary in the Proprium de Tempore, after the Psaltery. The lessons of third nocturn for same period are given after those of second nocturn. The suffrages are not said in Advent. In Advent the lectio brevis is "Domine miserere. " In Sunday Matins special versicles are given. The preces are said at Lauds and Vespers in ferias of Advent and at the small Hours; preces are said, too, if they be said at Lauds.

The great antiphons are the antiphons of the Magnificat which begin on the 17th December. They are sometimes called the great O's, or the O antiphons, as each begins with this letter. They begin "O Sapientia, quae ex ore Altissimi prodiisti... " and continue "O Adonai, O radix Jesse, " etc.... They are the most beautiful antiphons in the liturgy, expressing the prayers and ardent hopes for the coming Saviour. They have formed the subjects of study for poets, scholars and liturgists, ancient and modern. It is asked why these antiphons introduce the Magnificat and not the Benedictus. And liturgists reply: Because the Incarnation was of Mary, and hence these heralds of the Infant King more appropriately introduce Mary's canticle rather than that of Zachary. And the old liturgists add that these antiphons are said at Vespers, the evening Hour, because the Messias was expected and watched for in the world's evening. They tell us, too, why there are seven great antiphons. They are to excite our piety during this octave preparatory to the birthday of Christ. This number seven typifies the seven gifts of the Holy Ghost; it represents the seven miseries of mankind, ignorance, eternal punishment, the slavery of the devil, sin, gloom and exile from our fatherland, which is Heaven. And those wonderful men of mediaeval days tell us why we have need of a Teacher, O Sapientia; of a Redeemer, O Adonai; of a Liberator, O Radix Jesse; of a Guardian, O Clavis David; of a brilliant Instructor, O Oriens; of a Saviour to bring us, Gentiles, back to our Great Father, God; O Rex gentium; a Herald to the Jews. Honorius of Autun tells that these antiphons refer to the seven gifts of the Holy Ghost and are arranged in the well-known order in which these gifts are always arranged in works of piety. He says that Christ came in the Spirit of Wisdom, O Sapientia, that in the word "Adonai" is indicated that Christ redeemed us in the Spirit of Understanding. He says, too, that the antiphon "O Radix" signifies the sign of the cross, and that Christ redeemed us in the Spirit of Counsel. "O Clavis" indicates that Christ opened Heaven and closed Hell in the Spirit of Strength or Fortitude. "O Orient" shows forth Christ enlightening us in the Spirit of Knowledge. "Rex gentiam" points out the holy King who saved men by the Spirit of Piety. "O Emanuel" refers to Christ coming in the Spirit of Fear, but giving us also the Law of Love.

These antiphons have formed the theme of the oldest Christian poem in Europe—Cynewulf's "Christ, " a work which is the admiration of modern scholars. They were celebrated with great pomp and joy in monastic life, the monks carrying their congruous symbolism into their recitation. For, to the gardener-monk was assigned, the chanting of "O Radix Jesse, " to the cellarer-monk, the "O clavis David"—typifying their work of root-growing and key keeping. (See *The Month*, No. 489; *The Irish Ecclesiastical Record*, December, 1918).

Christmas. Antiquity. "It was formerly taken for granted that Christ had actually been born on this day, and, accordingly, the learned were of opinion that the Church had observed it from the beginning, as the day of His birth. Even at the present day it will be dfficult for many to give up this idea. But there is no Christmas among the Christan feasts enumerated by Tertullian ([died] 220), Origen (185-254), and the recently published Testament of Jesus Christ. On the contrary, there is clear proof that even in the fourth and fifth centuries it was unknown in some parts of the Church, where its introduction, at a later period, can be proved historically" (*vide* Kellner, *op. cit.* , pp. 127-158).

Christmas is one of the great festivals. In Rome there were two night Offices. The first, celebrated at nightfall in the Papal chapel, begins with the antiphon of the first psalm in the nocturn. It has nine lessons and the *Te Deum*. About midnight a more solemn Office began, this time with the invitatory and psalm *Venite*. The first of these Offices became the Office of the vigil.

In the Office of Christmas Day the lessons are read without the title of the book (Isaias) from which they are taken, because their author's name was so often repeated during the Advent that each one knew their source, or because at Christmas God speaks to us by His Son, rather than by His prophet. In the first response the Gloria Patri is said, to thank God for the great favour He has bestowed on us—His Son, the Christ. In the third nocturn, *Alleluia* is added to the antiphons, because the third nocturn typifies the time of grace, in which we should express the joy that is ours in the birth of the Saviour. In this nocturn, too, are given three Gospel extracts, corresponding with the Gospels in the Mass of Christmas. Matins are separated from Lauds by the first Mass because, it is said at midnight, and Lauds is a day Office. At Prime the versicle of the little response is *Qui natus est*.

Rubrics. Christmas is a primary double of the First Class. The third of the new *Tres Tabellae* (S. C. R., January, 1912) in the new Breviaries gives the rules for concurrence of Vespers in the Octave of Christmas.

Feast of St. Stephen. The worship of St. Stephen may be said to be as old as the Church herself, since St. Paul gave him the title of Martyr of Christ (Acts XXII. 20). His name is to be found in the earliest liturgical sources, e.g., the Arian martyrology belonging to about 360 and in all calendars, ancient and modern, excepting the Coptic. His cultus received great impulse from the discovery of his relics at Kaphar Gamala, on the shore of Lake Genesareth, and the wonderful miracles wrought by them, A basilica in his honour was erected, in Rome in the fourth century.

St. John the Apostle. The commemoration of St. John on the 27th December was formerly united with that of St. James the Less. In time, St. John's feast only was celebrated on this date, and such was the case as early as the time of Bede.

The Circumcision. This festival was originally called *Octava Domini*, and hence it may be inferred that it was not an independent festival and passed unnoticed if it fell on a week day. Thus, in the

Homilarium of Charlemagne (786) it is referred to by this name. But very shortly after this, the name which we now use for the festival of the 1st January was used in Rome, and spread through the Church. In the early days of Christianity the first day of the civil year was given over to rejoicings, dancing, feasting and rioting. And these abuses lingered in France, though stripped of their pagan character, until the later middle ages. A remnant of them is found in the so-called Feast of Fools, which was held in churches, and which mocked several religious customs and ceremonies. These feasts lasted till the middle of the fifteenth century.

Epiphany. The name is derived from a Greek verb employed to describe the dawn, and the adjective derived from the Greek verb was applied in classic Greek, to the appearances of the gods bringing help to men. In Christian liturgy, the feast was instituted to celebrate the appearance, the manifestation of Christ, to the Gentiles, in the persons of the Magi. In later times, there were added to this commemoration of Christ's manifestation to the Gentiles, two further commemorations of his wonderful showings of His divine mission, viz., His manifestation in His baptism in the Jordan, a manifestation to the Jews, and His miracle at Cana, a showing forth to His friends and disciples. This feast is of early origin. Suarez thinks it should be attributed to the Apostles (*De Relig*. L. 2. ch. 5, n. 9); and Benedict XIV. held that it was established by the infant Church at Rome to draw off the Christians from the profane and sinful revelry which marked the pagan feast of this date. However, these statements are hardly accurate. "With regard to the antiquity and spread of the feast, it was unknown in North Africa during the third century, for Tertullian makes no reference to it; and even in the time of St. Augustine, it was rejected by the Donatists as an oriental novelty. In Origen's time, at least, it was not generally observed as a festival in Alexandria, since he does not reckon it as such. For Rome, evidence is wanting for the earliest times, but since the daughter Church of Africa knew nothing—of the festival at first, it may be inferred that originally it was not kept at Rome, but was introduced there in course of time. In Spain it was a feast-day in 380, in Gaul in 361... " (Kellner, *op. cit.* , p. 172).

In the antiphons for the Magnificat and the Benedictus it may be noticed that the three manifestations are given not in the same order. "This day is the Church united to the Heavenly Spouse, for Christ, in the Jordan, washes away her sins; the Magi run to the royal nuptials with their gifts, and the guests of the feast are gladdened by the water changed into wine" (Ant. of Benedictus). The Magi, seeing the star, said to each other: "This is the sign of the King: let us go and seek him, and offer him gifts, gold, frankincense and myrrh" (Ant. of Magnificat, 1st Vesp.), "We celebrate a festival adorned by three miracles: this day, a star led the Magi to the manger; this day water was changed into wine at the marriage feast; this day Christ vouchsafed to be baptised by John, in the Jordan of our salvation" (Ant. of Magnificat, 2nd Vesp.). Now, the baptism is the special event commemorated by the Easterns on this feast, and on account of its connection with the baptism, this feast has, amongst the Greeks, the secondary title of the feast of lights. And, in Ireland (Synodus II., St. Patricii, can. 20), contrary to the ancient custom of the Church, solemn baptism was administered on this feast day. This subject of the baptism forms the only theme of the ancient sermons bearing on this feast. On the other hand, the visit of the Magi is the sole event commemorated by St. Augustine in his six sermons delivered on this feast day. The third event, the marriage feast, is of later commemoration; and Maximus of Turin doubted if they all actually happened on the same day.

The Octave to the feast dates from the eighth century. It was customary on this date, in the Eastern Church, to read publicly the epistola festalis of the Patriarch of Alexandria arranging the date of Easter and the practice was ordered by the fourth Council of Orleans in 541.

In Epiphany the invitatory is not said in the beginning of Matins, in order, say the liturgists, not to repeat the inquiry made by Herod from the scribes about the birthplace of Christ, an inquiry and invitation inspired by hatred and anger. The invitatory is omitted, they tell us, that we, like the Magi, may come to Christ, without other than a silent invitation. Teachers of olden time used to urge those who were slow to believe to imitate the Magi. But, the invitatory is not quite omitted. It is read in the third nocturn, which typifies the law of grace, in which the Apostles and their successors invite all to praise and worship God. The psalms of the feast are taken from the psalms of each day of the week, but chiefly from Friday's psalms, perhaps because the Magi's visit was on that day.

SEPTUAGESIMA.

"During the age of the persecutions it was scarcely possible for Christians to observe any other festival than Sunday, and so it is not surprising that the two writers who have occasion to speak of the institution of the festivals of the Church, mention only Easter and Pentecost, both of which fall on a Sunday. To these Christmas was added in the fourth century and Epiphany somewhat earlier. These chief festivals, along with others soon added to their number, formed the elements for the organisation of a festal system in the Church, as centres round which the lesser festivals grouped themselves. The last step of importance, however, in the development of the Church's year was to connect these chief festivals with one another, so as to make them parts of a whole. The Sundays afforded a convenient means for effecting this. They were associated with the festal character of the nearest feast and were connected with it as links in a chain. The way for this development had been prepared by the season of preparation for Easter, and the Sundays in the fifty days between Easter and Pentecost— Quinquagesima—were marked with the festal character with which antiquity invested the whole period. All that was needed was, first of all, to connect Christmas, Easter and Pentecost; and, in the second place, the institution of a season of preparation before Christmas. This was accomplished between the sixth, and the eighth centuries.

"During the first six centuries the ordinary Sundays of the year had neither liturgical position or character, since they were not even enumerated. There was a sort of *commune dominicarum, i.e.* , a number of Masses existed from which one could be chosen at will for each Sunday. To these Sundays, which were called simply *dominicae quotidianae*, those after Epiphany and Pentecost belonged.

"They numbered altogether twenty-nine or thirty, according as the calendar gave fifty-two or fifty-three Sundays in the year.... The smaller number of these, six at most, come between Epiphany and Septuagesima, but the larger, twenty-three to twenty-eight, between Whit Sunday and Advent. The variation depends on the date of Easter. There is no historical circumstance forthcoming to give these a specially festal character.... " (Kellner, *op. cit.*, pp. 176, *et seq.*).

Septuagesima Sunday comes nine weeks before Easter. It cannot come before the 18th January, nor after the 22nd February. It is the first day of a period of mourning and penance, preparatory to the great penitential period of Lent. On the Saturday preceding Septuagesima two *alleluias* are added to the Benedicamus and Deo Gratias, to intimate that the period of rejoicing in the Saviour's birth has passed. Violet, the penitential colour, is used at Mass, and the chapters in Genesis recording the fall of Adam, warn man to think well, to humble himself and to do penance. Every part of the Office, the lessons, antiphons and hymns, bear the notes of mourning and penance.

LENT.

Lent. —The Teutonic word, *Lent,* originally meant the spring season. It has come to mean the forty days preceding Easter. Scholars used to maintain that this season of penance was of apostolic origin; but, modern scholars noting the diversity of practice and the diversity of duration in different churches and the Easter controversy, hold that it is not of apostolic origin, and that it dates from the third century or even from the fourth century. It is not mentioned in the Didascalia (circa 250 A. D.), but was enjoined by St. Athanasius upon his flock in 331.

EASTER AND PASCHAL TIME.

Easter is the chief festival of Christendom, the first and oldest of all festivals, the basis on which the Church's year is built, the connecting link with the festivals of the old covenant and the central point on which depends the date of the other movable feasts. Some of the very early Christian writers call it feast of feasts (festum festorum).

The English word Easter is from *Eastre,* the goddess of spring. In the liturgy we never find the word *Pascha,* always the words *dominica resurrectionis.* Pascha has no connection with the Greek [Greek: Pascho], but is the Aramaic form of *pesach.*

Some points regarding this festival are to be noted, its antiquity, its connection with Jewish feasts and Christian feasts, its preparation, character and duration.

Antiquity. No mention of this feast is in the *Didache,* in Justin's Dialogue with Trypho, or in his apologies. But in the year 198 A. D. an exchange of letters between Pope Victor, Bishop Narcissus of Jerusalem, Polycrates of Ephesus, shows that the feast had been for years in existence. Many references are found in Tertullian and writers of his time to this festival.

Connection of the Christian Festival with the Jewish. "The connection between the Christian and the Jewish feasts is both historical and ideal—historical because our Lord's death happened on the 15th Nisan, the first day of the Jewish feast; ideal, because what took place had been prefigured in the Old Testament by types, of which itself was the antitype. The Jewish rites and ceremonies (Exodus XII.) are referred to in the prophecies of the Messias. Thus, Isaias calls Him the Lamb chosen by God, who bears the iniquities of others. The Baptist called Jesus, the Lamb of God. The Evangelist refers to the typical character of the Passover rites, when he applies, 'a bone of it shall not be broken' (Exod. XII. 46), to Christ on the Cross. Justin and Tertullian see in the Christian sacrifice the fulfilment of the imperfect sacrifices of the old law. Hence, there is no doubt that the Jewish Passover was taken over into Christianity. Thereby its typical ceremonies found their due fulfilment.

"To the real and historical connection between Easter and the Passover is due the explanation of a striking peculiarity in the Church's year, viz., the moveable feasts of which Easter is the starting point. Easter falls on no fixed date, because the Jewish 15th Nisan, unlike the dates of the Julian and Gregorian Calendars, varied year by year.

"The preparation for Easter was the Lenten fasts. The fare on fast days consisted of water and soup made with flour; fruit and oil and bread were also eaten. The catechumens also fasted on Wednesdays and Fridays. Among the faithful there were some who ate nothing from their repast on Sunday until the following Saturday, e.g., for five days, and who all the year round took only one meal a day. Others abstained in Lent from all food for two consecutive days, but others fasted by taking nothing to eat all day, until the evening" (Kellner, *op. cit.* , p. 93).

The Easter celebrations were in the early ages chiefly noted for the great and solemn ceremonies of baptism conferred on a large number of catechumens, with solemn procession from the baptistry to the cathedral. The Easter Octave celebrates by festivals the supper at Emmaus, the appearance of our Lord (St. Luke xxiv.), His appearance by the sea (St. John xxi. 1-14), His appearance to Magdalen (St. John xx. 11-18), His appearance on the mountain (St. Matthew xxviii. 16-20), and His appearance just after He had risen (St. John xx, 1-9),

THE ASCENSION.

This day was kept as a festival in very early times, although it is not mentioned in the lists of Church festivals given by Tertullian (+220), nor by Origen (185-254). St. Augustine (354-430) (Epist. ad Januarium, 54, c. l.) attributes the institution of this festival to an apostolic ordinance or the injunction of a general council. But neither can be proved. But the festival dates from the days of the early Church, and as it was natural that the concluding act of our Saviour's life should be remembered and honoured, the celebration of the feast of His Ascension spread widely and rapidly. The feast was noted for the solemn processions held, to imitate and to commemorate our Lord's leading of the Apostles out of the city to the Mount of Olives.

WHIT SUNDAY.

Pentecost or Whit Sunday extends back to the early days of the Church. From Tertullian, it is plain that the festival was well known and long established. In the *Peregrinatio Silviae*, we read a detailed account of how the feast was kept in Jerusalem at her visit (385-388). "On the night before Whitsunday the vigil was celebrated in the church of the Anastasis, at which the bishop, according to the usual custom in Jerusalem on Sundays, read the Gospel of the Resurrection, and the customary psalmody was performed. At dawn, all the people proceeded to the principal church (Martyrium) where a sermon was preached and Mass celebrated. About the third hour, when the psalmody was finished, the people singing accompanied the bishop to Sion. There, the passage from the Acts of the Apostles describing the descent of the Holy Ghost was read, and a second Mass was celebrated; after which the psalmody was resumed. Afterwards, the archdeacon invited the people to assemble in the 'Eleona, ' from whence a procession was made to the summit of the Mount of Olives. Here, psalms and antiphons were sung, the Gospel was read and the blessing given. After this, the people descended again into the 'Eleona, ' where Vespers were sung, and then, with the bishop at their head, proceeded in a solemn procession, with singing, back to the principal church, which was reached towards 8 p. m. At the city gate the procession was met by torch bearers, who accompanied it to the Martyrium. Here, as well as in the Anastasias, to which the people proceeded in turn, and in the chapel of the Holy Cross, the usual prayers, hymns and blessings took place, so that the festival did not conclude until midnight. "

(Kellner, *op. cit.* , pp. 112-113). In most churches, the principal services were solemn baptism and processions. In some places it was customary to scatter roses from the roof of the church, to recall the miracle of Pentecost. In France, trumpets were blown in church, in memory of the great wind which accompanied the Holy Spirit's descent.

TRINITY SUNDAY.

The first Sunday after Pentecost, for centuries, was not called Trinity Sunday. Pope Alexander II. (circa 1073) was questioned about a feast in honour of the Holy Trinity and he replied that it was not the Roman custom to set apart any particular day in honour of the Trinity, which was honoured many times daily in the psalmody, by the *Gloria Patri.* But an Office and Mass, dating from a hundred years earlier than this Pope's time, were in use in the Netherlands and afterwards in England, Germany and France; and in 1260 were spread far and wide. In 1334, Pope John XXII. ordered uniformity and general observance of this feast on the Sunday after Pentecost. The Office in our Breviaries dates from the time of Pius V. It is beautiful and sublime in matter and in form. Whether this is a new Office or a blending of some ancient offices, is a matter of dispute. Baillet, *Les Vies des Saints* (Tom ix. c. 2, 158) thinks it a new Office. But Binterim, *Die Kirchichle Heortology*, Part I., 265, and Baumer-Biron, *Histoire du Breviaire*, 298, take a different view. The Roman rite follows the older form of enumeration, second Sunday after Easter and so forth, and not first Sunday after Trinity. The latter form of enumeration is adopted in the Anglican church service books.

THE PROPER OF THE SAINTS.

December. The Feast of the Immaculate Conception. The discussion of the question of this feast lasted for more than a thousand years. A feast of the Conception was celebrated in the Eastern Church in the early part of the eighth century and was celebrated on the 9th December (Kellner, *Heortology*, p. 242, *et seq.*). The feast was celebrated in England before the Norman Conquest (1066) (Bishop, *On the Origins of Feast of the Conception of the Blessed Virgin Mary*, London, 1904).

But there is an earlier codex than those mentioned by Bishop, and from it, it is argued that the feast is of Irish origin. In a metrical calendar, which is reasonably referred to the time of Alfred the Great

(871-901), there is the line "Concipitur Virgo maria cognomine senio"; and this calendar exhibits, says Father Thurston, S.J., "most unmistakable signs of the influence of an Irish character. " It was written, Dr. Whitely Stokes believed, by an Irishman in the ninth century or thereabouts. The script appears to him to be "old Irish, rather than Anglo-Saxon, and the large numbers of commemorations of Irish saints and the accuracy with which the names are spelt, point to an Irish origin. " This calendar places the feast of our Lady's Conception on the 2nd May. In the metrical calendar of Oengus, the feast is assigned to the 3rd May, and in his *Leabhar Breac*, the scribe adds the Latin note, "Feir mar Muire et reliqua, *i. e.*, inceptio ejus ut alii putant—sed in februo mense vel in Martio facta est illa, quae post VII. menses nata est, ut innaratur—vel quae libet alia feria ejus. " Again, in the martyrology of Tallaght, from which Gorman, a later martyrologist, says that Oengus, the Culdee, drew his materials, is found under date May 3rd, a mention of the celebration of the Conception of Mary. This evidence seems to show—although it is not perfectly conclusive—that the conception of the Blessed Virgin Mary was celebrated in the Irish Church in the ninth and tenth centuries, but not on the 8th December (see Father Thurston, S.J., *The Month*, May and June, 1904; Father Doncoeur, S.J., *Revue d'histoire ecclesiastique*, Louvain, 1907, p. 278, et seq. ; Baudot, *The Roman Breviary*, pp. 253-255; Kellner, *op. cit.*).

It is to be regretted that even in the new Breviary the lessons for the second nocturn of this feast are taken from the composition, *Cogitis me*, falsely attributed to St. Jerome, and rejected by critics, from the days of Baronius, as spurious (Baudot, *op. cit.* , p. 236).

February. The Purification.   Candlemas. According to the Gospel narrative, Mary fulfilled the commands of the Law (Lev. XII. 2-8), and on the fortieth day brought the prescribed offering to the Temple, where she met Simeon and Anna.

The first reference found in Christian writers to this festival is found in the famous *Peregrinatio Sylviae*, the diary of a Spanish lady who visited Jerusalem about 385-388. She tells us that the day began with a solemn procession, followed by a sermon on St. Luke II. 22 seqq., and a Mass. It had not yet a name, but was called the fortieth day after the Epiphany; and this naming shows that at Jerusalem the Epiphany was regarded as the day of Christ's birth. The lady's words show that the feast was not then observed in her own country. The feast was observed in Rome in 542; and Pope Sergius I. (687-701) ordered a procession on this festival. The opinion that is so often met with in pious books, that this feast with its procession of candlebearers was established by the Church to replace the riot and revels of the Pagan *Lupercalia*, is now rejected by scholars. For, processions, with or without lights, were so common amongst Pagans and Christians that any connection between these two feasts is negligible.

March. St. Joseph. In the Western Church the cultus of St. Joseph is not found in any calendar before the ninth century, although numerous traces of the esteem and veneration paid to him by individuals are found. The public cultus of St. Joseph was introduced by the private devotions of great servants of God, such as St. Bernard, St. Gertrude, St. Bridget of Sweden, John Gerson, St. Bernardine of Sienna, and other Franciscan preachers. The spread of the devotion in several countries led Pope Sixtus IV. (1471-1484) to introduce St. Joseph's feast, as a simplex, having only one lesson. Clement XI. (1700-1721) changed it into a feast of nine lessons. Two centuries previously the feast is found in Breviaries under date 19th March.

The Annunciation. Devotion to the Mother of God was continued by the apostles after the death of her Son. Fervent and widespread devotion is traceable in the Church's early days, but the organising of our Lady's feasts was a work of some time and difficulty. A great difficulty was the fear of blasphemy from pagans, and of error amongst pagan converts, so trained in myths and genealogies of the gods. Then the festivals commemorating the facts of the life, death and resurrection were primarily commemorative of the Redeemer and secondarily of His Mother. Long before the institution of her feast, the cultus of Mary was almost universal. The feast of the Annunciation falls on the 25th March with us. Its date depends entirely on the date of Christmas, but the birth of Christ was not always placed in calendars on the 25th December.

In early days the feasts of martyrs and other saints were not celebrated in Lent, and hence this feast of the Blessed Virgin was set down in some calendars as transferred, and was celebrated in Advent. In Spain, it was celebrated eight days before Christmas. In the East, the feast was generally celebrated on the 25th March, and gradually this date was fixed, and was sanctioned by several councils in the eleventh century.

May. The Finding of the Holy Cross. The history of the finding of the true cross by St. Helena is well known. The Alexandrine Chronicle gives the day as the 14th September, 320. This September feast of the holy cross is of earlier origin than the feast of May. The latter was established to commemorate the act of the emperor in 629, when he brought back to Jerusalem the true cross, from the Persian conquerors. On 3rd May, he handed it over to the Patriarch Zacharias, and, strange to say, this festival of May spread rapidly in the Western Church, whilst in the East only one feast, (the September one), of the finding of the cross was celebrated for centuries. In Milan, for instance, the September feast was received in the eleventh century, whilst the May feast was rooted in the Western Church very many years before that time.

The antiphons and hymns of this Office are, it is said, amongst the most beautiful and sublime prayers of our liturgy.

The Apparition of St. Michael. The cultus of the holy angels is of Jewish origin and existed in the Christian Church from the beginning. In St. Paul's Epistle to the Colossians (modern *Khonus on the Lycus*) he speaks of this devotion and of the attempts of a Gnostic sect to spread false doctrines on this point (Col. ii, 18). Although the evil wrought was long lived, true devotion to the angels was practised in Colossae and there the Archangel Michael appeared. In honour of this apparition, the festival of St. Michael in September was established. Devotion to the Archangel was of very early date in Rome and in the Western Church generally. Masses in his honour are found in the oldest Roman Sacramentary (483-492); and in these he is mentioned by name in prayers and prefaces. The May feast was instituted in the sixth century, to commemorate a second apparition near Sipontum on Monte Gargano, which took place on the 8th May, 520.

June 29. Feast of St. Peter and St. Paul. There always has been a constant tradition in Rome that these two saints suffered martyrdom on the same day, 29th June, and it is only natural that this day should be kept with great devotion and solemnity at Rome. In the East, feasts in honour of these martyrs were held at different seasons, Christmas, February and Epiphany. The day was kept in many places as a solemn holiday, servile works being prohibited. But in Rome, devotion was closely connected with the date and with the exact places of martyrdom. "Owing to the distance which separated the two churches of the apostles from each other, it was most fatiguing to celebrate Mass at both places, and so in course of time the festival was divided into two parts, and the Mass in honour of St. Paul took place on the 30th June. "

July. The Visitation. This feast was probably originated by the Franciscans in the thirteenth century. It certainly was preached and spread by their zeal. It is mentioned amongst Franciscan records bearing date 1263. It was kept in different places at different dates. In Paris it was kept in April. In 1850 Pius IX. raised this feast to the rank of a double of the second class, to thank God for having, on this day, 2nd July, freed Rome from the revolutionary yoke.

Feast of St. Mary Magdalen. Commentators on Sacred Scripture are not agreed whether Mary of Magdala was the sister of Lazarus or whether there were two or three Marys connected with our Lord — Mary the sister of Lazarus, Mary of Magdala, and Mary the sinner named in St. Luke's Gospel vii. 27. The Roman liturgy seems to favour the opinion that Mary of Magdala was the sister of Lazarus, and that she was a sinner and was possessed by seven devils. The history of Mary Magdalen after our Lord's death has been written, with large and varied additions of adventure, by pious mediaevalists. In the Western Church, traces of the saint's cultus are met with in Bede and his contemporaries. But devotion far and wide begins with mediaeval times. The many legends which have grown up around her name and history have so obscured historic truth that the Breviary gives no historic lessons on her feast day, but gives as a lesson part of a homily from St. Gregory. Some of the legends may be found in the Office of St. Martha (July, 29th).

August. The Assumption. "In all probability this is the earliest of our Lady's festivals" (Kellner, *op. cit.*, p. 235). Early writers mention the Garden of Gethsemani as the place of Mary's burial and the third year—some say the twelfth year—after our Lord's death as the year of her death. St. John Damascene relying on the writings of Euthymius tells us what we know of the Assumption. He tells that the wife of the Emperor Marcian (450-457) wished to transfer our Lady's relics from Jerusalem to Constantinople and was informed by Juvenal, Bishop of Jerusalem, that such relics were not in Jerusalem. The Blessed Mother had been buried there, in the Garden of Gethsemani, in the presence of the Apostles, Thomas alone being absent. On his arrival he wished to venerate the Mother of God; the tomb was opened for him, but nothing was found save the linen grave-clothes, which gave forth a sweet perfume. The Apostles concluded that Christ had taken to Heaven the body which had borne Him. The Emperor Maurice ordered the date, the 15th August, long and widely recognised, to be the date of this annual festival. However, some churches celebrated it on other dates. In the Gothico-Gallic missal of the eighth century, the feast is fixed for the 18th January. The festival was called sometimes *dormitio Mariae, pausatio Mariae*. It was celebrated in Rome at the end of the seventh century, but how long it had been in existence there, and in the West generally before that time, no one can say.

Feast of the Name of Mary. This feast owes its origin to the devotion of the faithful and was first authorised by the Pope in 1513. It was extended to the universal calendar in 1683, on the occasion of the deliverance of Vienna from the Turks.

Over the derivation and meaning of the name *Maria* much scholarship and conjecture have been lavished. It is said to mean (1) *stella maris* (Eusebius); (2) lady, from the Syrian *Martha* (St. John Damascene); this is the Breviary meaning, but the Breviary uses the first meaning, *stella maris*, too; (3) stately, imposing one (Bardenhewer); (4) from the Egyptian, *merijom*, friend of water, bride of the sea (Macke).

October. Feast of the Holy Rosary. It is not necessary to speak of the origin of the Rosary. This feast was established by Gregory XIII. in 1573, as a thanksgiving for the victory of Lepanto (October, 1571). Clement XI. extended the feast to all Christendom in consequence of the victory gained at Peterwarden by Prince Eugene in 1716.

November. Feast of all Saints. This feast was "instituted to honour all the saints, known and unknown, and, according to Urban IV., to supply any deficiencies in the faithful's celebration of saints' feasts during the year. In the early days, the Christians were accustomed to solemnize the anniversary of a martyr's death for Christ, at the place of martyrdom. The neighbouring dioceses began to interchange feasts, to transfer them and to divide them, and to join in a common feast;... frequently groups of martyrs suffered on the same day, which naturally led to a joint commemoration. In the persecution of Diocletian the number of martyrs became so great that a separate day could not be assigned to each. But the Church, feeling that every martyr should be venerated, appointed a common day for all. The first trace of it we find in Antioch on the Sunday after Pentecost.... At first only martyrs and St. John the Baptist were honoured by a special day. Other saints were added gradually, and increased in number when a general process of canonization was established; still, as early as 411 there is in the Chaldean calendar a 'commemoratio Confessorum' for the Friday after Easter.... Gregory IV. (827-844) extended the celebration on 1st November to the entire Church" (*Cath. Ency.*, art, "All Souls").

Feast of All Souls, "The theological basis for the feast is the doctrine that the souls, which, on departing from the body are not perfectly cleansed from venial sins, or have not fully atoned for past transgressions, are debarred from the Beatific Vision, and that the faithful on earth can help them by prayers, almsdeeds, and especially by the holy sacrifice of the Mass. In the early days of Christianity the names of the departed brethren were entered in the diptychs. Later, in the sixth century, it was customary in Benedictine monasteries to hold a commemoration of the deceased members at Whitsuntide, In Spain, there was such a day before Sexagesima or before Pentecost, at the time of St. Isidore (d. 636). In Germany, there existed (according to the testimony of Widukind, Abbot of Corvey, c. 980) a time-honoured ceremony of praying for the dead on 1st October. This was accepted and sanctified by the Church" (*Cath. Ency.*, art. "All Souls").

The psalms and lessons of this Office are especially well chosen, and the responses to the lessons—said to be the work of Maurice de Sully (d. 1196)—are greatly admired by liturgical experts.

It may be noted here, that, in the recitation of this Office, which is, for most priests, the only choral recitation of liturgy, care should be taken to select the proper nocturn or nocturns. "In the general rubrics of the Breviary (Tit. XIX. n. 2) it is stated that the invitatory is not to be said in *Officio Defunctorum* per annum, excepto die Commemorationis omnium fidelium defunctorum, ac in die obitus seu depositionis defuncti et quandocunque dicuntur tres nocturni. When, therefore, only one nocturn is recited, the invitatory is to be omitted except on the dies obitus seu depositionis. " In this latter case, even though the body is not present—for some special reason, such as contagious disease—the invitatory is not to be omitted.

"On any other occasion, no matter how solemn or privileged, such as the seventh, thirtieth, or anniversary day, when only one nocturn is recited, the invitatory must not be included. This is clear, not only from the rubrics of the Breviary and Ritual (Tit. VI., cap. IV.) but also from certain answers of the Congregation of Rites" (*Irish Eccles. Record*, December, 1913).

Dom Baudot's *The Roman Breviary* gives in an appendix, pp. 239-252, "tables showing the date at which each saint was inserted in the Roman Breviary, the rank given to his festival, and the variations it has undergone. It is often difficult to give precise dates. "

ROGATION DAYS, EMBER DAYS AND LITANIES.

"Litanies were solemn supplications instituted to implore the blessing of Heaven on the fruits of the earth. It was customary to recite them in the spring, that is, the season of late frosts, so much dreaded by the cultivators of the soil.... The people marched in procession to the spot, chanting the while that dialogue prayer which we call a litany, elaborated, according to circumstances, into a long series of invocations, addressed to God and to angels and saints. "

"The day set apart for this purpose at Rome was the 25th April, a traditional date, being that on which the ancient Romans celebrated the festival of the Robigalia....

"The most ancient authority for this ceremony is a formulary for convoking it, found in the Register of St. Gregory the Great, which must have been used in the first instance in the year 598" (Duchesne, *Christian Worship*, chap, viii., n. 9).

Ember days, a corruption from Latin Quatuor Tempora (four times). "The purpose of their introduction, besides the general one intended by all prayer and fasting, was to thank God for the gifts of nature, to teach men to make use of them in moderation, and to assist the needy. The immediate occasion was the practice of the heathens of Rome. The Romans were originally given to agriculture and their native god belonged to the same class. At the beginning of the time for seeding and harvesting religious ceremonies were performed to implore the help of their deities; in June for a bountiful harvest, in September for a rich vintage, and in December for the seeding.... The Church when converting heathen nations has always tried to sanctify any practice which could be utilised for a good purpose. " The fasts were fixed by the Church before the time of Callixtus (217-222). The spread of the observance of Ember days was slow; but they were fixed definitely and the fast prescribed for the whole Church by

Gregory VII. (1073-1085). (*Cf. Catholic Encyclopedia*, word, Ember Days; Duchesne *Christian Worship*, chap, viii. ; Dom Morin *Revue Benedictine*, L'Origine des Quatre Temps, 1897, pp. 330-347.)

NOTE A.

THE BREVIARY HYMNS.

Of all the many and varied branches of Christian art, there is none which offers to the researches of criticism a field so extensive as does the hymnography of the Roman Breviary. No other source of liturgical study, if we except the antiphonarium, has received such attention from studious men. But never, in any age, did this study receive such careful treatment and give rise to such patient and laborious research as in our own. (Pimont, *Les hymnes du Breviare Romain*, Introduction.)

In this note, an attempt will be made to define a hymn, to tell of the introduction of hymns into the Roman Breviary, and to note briefly the character of these hymns.

St. Augustine, commenting on Psalm 122, defined a hymn as a song with praise of God, cantus est cum laude Dei. It may, however, be more strictly defined as a spiritual song, a religious lyric (v. *Cath, Ency.* , art. "Hymn").

In the early Christian assemblies great use was made of the psalms and canticles in their congregational singing. St. Paul wrote: "Speaking to yourselves in psalms and hymns and spiritual canticles, singing and making melody in your hearts to the Lord" (Ephes. v. 18) "... teaching and admonishing one another in psalms, hymns and spiritual canticles, singing in grace in your hearts to God" (Col. iii. 16). The Jesuit, Father Arevalo, in his *Hymodia Hispanica*, cites many witnesses, such as Clement of Alexandria, the Apostolic Constitutions, Pliny the younger, to prove that hymns were used in the first and second centuries. But a much-debated question is, whether those hymns were really made part of the Office, as hymns stand there to-day. Some scholars deny that they were; others assert that they were certainly part of the Church's Office. All agree that they were certainly in use formally and substantially in the Office in the third and fourth centuries in the Eastern and in the Western Church. The Council of Antioch (269-270) wrote to the Pope that Paul of Samosate had suppressed some canticles recently composed in honour of Jesus Christ. St. Dionysius of Alexandria composed some hymns, to win over an erring bishop. In the fourth century the Council of Laodicea spoke of the introduction of some hymns, which were not approved; and St. Basil tells us that hymns were in universal use in the Eastern Church.

In the Western Church, St. Hilary of Potiers (370) composed a hymn book for his church. Its existence is known from the words of St. Jerome. St. Augustine states that St. Ambrose (340-397), shut up with his people in the church in Milan by the persecutors, occupied his flock by their singing of hymns which he himself had composed, and some of which are in our Breviaries. The Church of Milan certainly had hymns in its Office and in its Office books then, for St. Paulinus in his life of St. Augustine wrote: "Hoc in tempore, primum antiphonae, hymni ac vigilae in Ecclesia Mediolanensi celebrari coeperunt; cujus celebritatis devotio usque in hodiernam diem, non solum, in Ecclesia Mediolanensi verum per omnes pene Occidentis provincias manet. "

But the question arises, when did Rome introduce hymns into her liturgy? The learned Jesuit, Father Arevalo, held that the Roman Office had hymns as an integral part from the time of St. Ambrose, and he called the opinion of those who held that they were of later introduction an inveterate error, *errorem inveteratum (Hymnodia Hispanica* XVIII., n. 95). The introduction of antiphonal chanting was introduced into Rome at the time of St. Ambrose and liturgical hymn singing, too, was introduced about the same time. This we know from the Milanese priest Paulinus, St. Augustine, Pope Celestine I., and Faustus, Bishop of Riez. But formal, official and systematic hymnody was not introduced in Rome until centuries after the death of St. Ambrose. Mabillon (Suppl. ad IV. lib de div. off. Amalarii, t. 11) and Tomasi (In annot, ad Resp. et antip. Rom. Ecc.) place the date of the introduction of hymns into the Roman liturgy, in the eleventh or twelfth centuries. But scholars now agree that hymns were formally recognised in the liturgy of Rome in the latter half of the ninth century. "To judge of what Amalare of Metz says, there was no sign of it at the beginning of the ninth century, but from the middle of the same century onwards hymns must have been introduced into the Office used by the Churches of the Frankish empire, and shortly afterwards in Rome" (Baudot, *op. cit.* , pp. 67-68). Wilfrid Strabo agrees with Amalare. Rabanus Maurus testifies that hymns were in general usage in the second part of the ninth century.

(Migne, Pat. Lat. clx. 159, cxiv. 956). This is the opinion of Gueranger, Pimont, Blume and Baumer.

Dom Gueranger explains why Rome, the mother and mistress of all the churches, did not adopt the practice of hymn chanting in her liturgy for centuries; why she did not precede or quickly follow the Eastern and many parts of the Western Church in this matter of liturgical hymns. "The Church, " he says, "did not wish to alter by religious songs the simplicity, or the meaning, of her great liturgical prayer. Nor did she wish to adopt quickly any innovation in her liturgy or discipline" (*Inst. Liturg.* I. 1, pp. 170-171).

No part of the Church's liturgy has met with such persistent, abusive, and often ignorant criticism as her hymns have received.

The renaissance clerics, the Gallicans, the Jansenists, and the Protestants poured forth volumes of hostile and unmerited criticism on the matter and form of Rome's sacred songs. Becichemus, rector of the Academy of Pavia in the sixteenth century, in his introduction to the work of Ferreri, wrote of the hymns: "sunt omnes fere mendosi, inepti, barbarie refecti, nulla pedum ratione nullo syllabarum mensu compositi.... Ut ad risum eruditos concinent, et ad contemptum ecclesiastici ritus vel literatos sacerdotes inducant.... Literatos dixi: nam ceteri qui sunt sacri patrimonii helluones, sine scientia, sine sapientia, satis habent, ut dracones stare juxta arcam Domini. " The remarks of the rector recall the saying of Lactantius, "literati non habent fidem. " Ferreri, who had been commissioned by Pope Clement to revise and correct the Breviary hymns, wrote in his dedication epistle: "I have given all my care to this collection of new hymns, because learned priests and friends of good Latinity who are now obliged to praise God in a barbarous style, are exposed to laugh and to despise holy things. " Santeuil (1630-1697) characterised the Breviary hymns as the product of ignorance, the disgrace of the Latin language, the disreputable relics of the early ages, the result of lunacy.

Violent attack leads to violent defence. Both are generally born of ignorance, a partizan spirit, and exaggeration. Pious Catholic defenders write that the Roman Breviary has hymns far superior to the classic lyrics of ancient Rome; that they have an inimitable style; that they are far superior to Horatian poetry; that there is nothing to compare with their style and beauty in pagan classics, Indeed, zeal has led some holy men to censure Pope Leo X., Clement VII., and.

Urban VIII. for their attempts to correct these compositions, which they hold to have been perfect.

Truth seems to hold the place of the golden mean between the bitter critics and the over zealous defenders of our Breviary hymns. The following propositions, drawn from Father Barnard's *Cours De Liturgie Romaine*, may be taken as a fair and accurate statement of the views of scholars, views which may be safely held by all students of this portion of liturgy.

First Proposition: —Many of the hymns of the Roman Breviary have not the elegance of the Odes of Horace, of the hymns of Santeuil and of Coffin.

Proof: -(1) The holy Fathers had outlined in a rough sketch rather than perfected their hymns (Pope Urban VIII., Bull Quamvis, 17th June, 1644).

(2) Speaking of the new Hymnal of Ferreri, Pope Clement VIII. says that the new work could only add to the splendour of worship and help to the common interest, implying that the new hymns helped religion by their accuracy and grace of correct poetic forms.

(3) Pimont, the author of a classic work on the Breviary Hymns, in a number of comments, notes the crudities of the Breviary hymns, even in their revised forms. Thus, in the hymn for Prime, he notes apparent ruggedness. He passes similar comments on the hymns assigned to the little hours.

(4) Bacquez states that all the hymns do not join beauty of expression to the merit of the thought expressed, and that a certain number lack style and good prosody.

These opinions should not be extended to all, nor even to very many of the Breviary hymns. All serious critics agree about the beauty of such hymns as the *Aeterne rerum Conditor*, the *Somno refectis artubus*, *Splendor Aeternae gloriae*, *Verbum supernum prodiens*, and a good number of others.

The greater part of the Breviary Hymns are composed according to the rules of prosody, and their form is lyric, the popular form of Latin song, which preceded in Italy the prosodical system borrowed from the Greeks, and used by the classic pagan poets. The critics of the Renaissance period are very loud and very wrathful over the form of these hymns. Some of them accuse St. Ambrose, Prudentius and Gregory the Great of gross ignorance of the rules of Latin verse and, what to the critics was worse, ignorance of the ways of pagan classical models. But, was the rhymed, tonic accented lyric, which was to be sung by all sorts and conditions of men, in public, such an outrageous literary sin? Was it ignorance or prudence that guided the early hymn writers in their adoption of popular poetic form? It is not certain by any means that the early hymn writers wished to copy or adopt the classic forms of the Augustinian age. Nor is it clear that such men of genius as St. Ambrose, Prudentius, St. Gregory the Great, were ignorant of the rules and models of the best Latin poets. It seems that they did not wish to follow them. They wilfully and designedly adopted the popular lyric forms, so that they might give to their flocks in popular and easily remembered forms, prayers and formulas of faith.

Second Proposition: -The Breviary hymns have the principal elements of poetic beauty.

Briefly, these elements are sublimity of thought, beauty of sentiment, aptness of expression, unction of form. In these matters the Breviary hymns are not inferior to the classic poetry of paganism, nor to the much-belauded beauties of the Gallican Breviary hymns (*vide* Bacquez, *Le Saint Office*, notes vi. and viii. in finem).

The composition of the hymns is in perfect harmony with the end for which they are intended, that is, liturgical prayer, chanted prayer. Their phrases do not display the vain and superfluous literary glitter of the much-lauded Gallican hymns, but their accents go out from the sanctuary and live in the hearts of the people. Their language is, like the thought and expression of the psalms, the word of a soul praying to God and adoring Him in fervour, in simplicity, and in faith. Of the piety and expression of the French hymns, Foinard, an ardent apostle of the French liturgical novelties, wrote: "Il ne parait pas que ce soit l'onction qui domine dans les nouveaux Breviaries; on y a la verite, travaille beaucoup pour l'esprit; mais il semole qu' on n'y a pas travaille autant pour le coeur. " Letourneux, the fierce Jansenist, wrote to the Breviary-poet, Santeuil, his co-worker: "Vous faites fumer l'encens; mais c'est un feu estranger qui brule dans l'ensenoir. La vanite fait en vous ce que la charite devrait faire. " And the Catholic De Maistre, so famed for his fair-minded criticisms, wrote of the new hymn-makers' works: "They make a certain noise in the ear, but they never breathe prayer, because their writers were all alone (*i. e.*, unaided by the grace and guidance of the Holy Spirit) when they composed them. " Of the Roman Breviary hymns he wrote: "They always pray and excite the soul to prayer. " "Train your hearts to attention, and hear all their prayers. You will in them see the true religion, as clearly as you see the sunbeams. "

Fourth Proposition: —The characteristic of the Roman Breviary hymns is to express with lively sentiments and with unction the noble ideas and beautiful sentiments of the supernatural order, in a simple manner, without prosodical pretension, yet having ever a true rhythm which sometimes vies with better compositions.

The characteristic mentioned in this proposition, which comes as a corollary from the three preceding propositions, is one which is clearly noted in our Breviary hymns. For by their very position in the Breviary, side by side with the Psalms, Scripture extracts and words of the Fathers, the Church shows her esteem and her use of these lyrics of prayer and praise. Again, the Church's mind is shown by her retention of her hymns in her liturgy, notwithstanding the many efforts made to substitute a new hymnal. Up to the sixteenth century these Breviary hymns were universally esteemed. They were admired by St. Augustine. They are quoted and praised by St. Thomas in his Summa. Deays the Carthusian {1402-1471} wrote a beautiful commentary on them. Amongst all priests, secular and regular, the hymns were venerated and loved. Although there were many men of genius in every age and in every part of the Christian Church, the hymns escaped until the renaissance under Leo X. (1475-1521).

The lovers of everything classic and pagan were pained and exasperated at the venerable simplicity, the lack of prosody, the vagueness and crudity of the wording of the liturgical hymns. In 1531, Wimpheling, a priest of the diocese of Spire, produced a work, *Himni de tempore et de sanctis... secundum legem carminis diligenter emendati*. Leo X., yielding to his own taste and the wishes of the learned innovators who were ardent students of pagan antiquity, commissioned Ferreri to compose a new hymnal for liturgical use. His book was allowed for liturgical use, but was not prescribed. It omitted all the old hymns sanctioned by the Church for centuries, and sung with fervour by thousands down the ages. "There are found in the work of Ferreri, " wrote Dom Gueranger, "all the images and all the allusions to pagan beliefs and usages which we find in Horace. Sometimes, it is only fair to say, his hymns are beautiful and simple... but they follow generally and too servilely the pagan models... but they are the work of strong and clear inspiration, which under the mask of classic diction shows itself in every part. " (*Inst. Liturg.* t. I., p. 370.) During the reign of Pope Paul III. new hymnals were issued, but the Breviary hymns were not removed. St. Pius V. in his reform of the Breviary did not touch the Breviary hymns. Clement VIII. in his reform added new hymns but did not remove nor retouch the old ones. This work remained for Pope Urban VIII. (1623-1644).

Urban VIII., Maffeo Barberini, was a poet of no mean rank. Before his election to the papacy, he was a recognised lover of classical literature and an adept in following classic themes and classic forms. Our Breviaries contain some few of his compositions and they show correctness of form, poetic merit, and piety. They are the hymns, *Martinae celebri, Tu natale solum* (January 20); *Nullis te genitor, Regali solio fortis* (April 13). His great desire was the correction of the Breviary hymns. This work of correction was not beyond the personal power of the Pope himself, if we judge him by his hymns. His views are expressed in the Bull *Divinam Psalmodiam*, issued to promulgate the corrected hymns. It found a place in all copies of the Roman Breviary in the last century. To carry out the corrections outlined by the Pope, four Jesuits were appointed, and whether the result of the corrections is the Pope's or the Jesuits' is a highly and hotly disputed point. First of all, the task set to the Jesuits was a very difficult one, and one demanding much prudence as well as learning. It may seem to us that to begin the correction, mutilation and reconstruction of the works and words of men so great in church history and liturgy as Prudentius, Sedulius, St. Ambrose, St. Paulinus, was a work of rashness, a sort of sacrilege, attempting to remodel the glowing piety of their poems to the pattern of Horace's verse. But the Jesuits had got their commands and they were bound to obey. They were chosen on account of their classical scholarship, which was kept sharp by their daily teaching in college, and they were specially bound by a vow of loyal obedience to Papal orders. "It is only fair to give them the credit that out of respect for the wishes of Urban VIII, they treated these ancient compositions with extreme reserve and, while they made some impressions clearer, they maintained the primitive unction in a large number of passages" (Baudot, *op. cit.* , p. 185).

They corrected more than nine hundred false quantities found scattered through the Breviary, 58 in the psalter per hebdomadam, 359 in the proper de Tempore, 283 in the proper of Saints, and 252 in the common of Saints. They changed the opening words of more than thirty hymns. Some hymns were untouched—e. g., the three hymns of the Blessed Sacrament, the *Ave Maris Stella*, which is rhythmic prose, not verse, and the hymn of the Angels, which was sufficiently perfect. The metre of three hymns, *Tibi Christe splendor Patris*, and the *Urbs Jerusalem* and *Angularis fundamentum* were changed.

The Jesuits have been censured very bitterly for their work of correction. Perhaps they merited some censure, but surely they did not merit the censures heaped on them by hostile critics like Thiers, Henri Valois, and the Franciscan, Cavalli. They answered their critics splendidly and triumphantly by the works of Father Arevalo, S.J. But the wordy war lasts to the present day. Students who wish to see the unrevised and the revised hymnal of Urban VIII. may consult Daniel's *Thesaurus hymnologicus* for examples. Other examples are given in Monsignor Battifol's work, and others in Dom Baudot's. If the reader read in the Breviary, the hymn *Te lucis ante terminum*, he may note a difference in that, the revised form, and this, the unrevised: —

> Te lucis ante terminum,
> Rerum Creator poscimus,
> Ut solita clementia
> Sis praesul ad custodiam.
>
> Praesta pater omnipotens
> Per Jesum Christum Dominum
> Qui tecum in perpetuum regnat
> Cum Sancto Spiritu

Again, see Lauds for Passion Sunday, *Lustra sex*, second verse, unrevised reads: —

> Hic acetum fel arundo
> Sputa clavi lancea
> Mite corpus perforator
> Sanguis unda profluit
> Terra, pontus, astra, mundus
> Quo lavantur flumine.

Iste Confessor, unrevised reads: —

> Iste confessor domini sacratus
> Festa plebs cujus celebrat per orbem
> Hodie laetus meruit secreta
> Scandere coeli.
>
> Qui Pius, prudens humilis judicus,
> Sobrius, castus fuit et quietus
> Vita dum praesens vegetavit ejus
> Corporis artus.

The imitation of Breviary hymns has for centuries formed a notable part of sacred Latin poetry. A great amount of Latin poetry dealing with sacred themes finds no place in Missal or Breviary. Every nation has ancient Latin hymns, generally modelled on the then existing liturgical models; and these hymns are found in national hymnals and in works dealing with Christian antiquities, but they find no place in modern liturgy. Thus the Latin poetry of the ancient Irish Church is formed for private and not choral use. The oldest purely rhythmical Latin hymn is that of St. Sechnall (1448), "Audite omnes amantes Deum, sancta merita. " But neither it, nor any other of the old Latin hymns by Irish writers, finds place in the Breviary. Collections of Latin hymns by Irish writers of early Christian Ireland are to be found in Todd's *Book of Hymns of the Ancient Irish Church* (Dublin, 1885-1891); the *Irish Liber Hymnorum* (London, 1898), the *Antiphonary of Bangor* (Warren's Edition, London, 1893).

One of the most difficult works for a scholar to attempt and to carry out to his satisfaction is the translation of prose or poetry into another language. The work of translating the Latin of the Roman Breviary into English was attempted and completed years ago. The work was great and creditable, but not renowned as a feat of translation. The hymns of the Breviary have been translated by several authors in every country of Christendom, and with different degrees of success. The study of the Breviary hymns is a highly interesting one, and when it is supported by the different efforts of different translators, it yields new delights, and new beauties are discovered in verses which are sometimes said too rapidly for earnest thought and attention. In the list of books given in the bibliography below, there are given the names of books of translated hymns. Any one of them is of great interest.

NOTE B.

PARTICULAR EXAMEN ON THE RECITATION OF THE DIVINE OFFICE.

I. How preparation for saying the Hours is to be made: —

(a) Have we before commencing to recite the Breviary made a fervent act of faith in the presence of God and in the sovereign majesty of Him to Whom we are going to speak?

Have we endeavoured to purify our hearts by an act of contrition, in order that we may escape the terrible reproach which God addresses to the sinner—"to the sinner God hath said, 'Why dost thou declare my justices and take away covenant in thy mouth? '" (Psalm 49, v. 16)?

Have we taken particular care to clear off from our souls everything which can distract us, and above all others these things to which we are attracted and to which our minds may return during our prayer?

"Ante debes facere quod ait propheta: scopebam spiritum meum donec incalescat spiritus tuus ex devota meditatione et affectum et desiderium concipiat" (D. Gerhard Zutp. de spir. Ascen.). "Studeat oratione devota et recollectione animi interna divinum praevenire officium" (St. Bona. spec, di., p. 2, c. 7).

Have we recollected ourselves and remained silent for a time, particularly when passing from study or from a secular business, in order to banish vain or worldly thoughts, and to make ourselves ready to receive the Holy Ghost?

Have we united ourselves to Jesus Christ, Who is the perfect praise of God, the Father? Have we united ourselves in spirit to the Church, in whose name we are going to praise God? "In unione orationum ac meritorum Christi Jesu gratiam ad officium debite persolvendum petat" (St. Bona. *ibid.*)

Have we begged the Holy Ghost by the intercession of the Blessed Virgin and the saints, whose offices we read, that we may be allowed to join our praises to those which they give God?

Have we always formed intentions general and particular, not forgetting to form intentions embracing the intentions of Christ and His Church?

Have we adopted some pious thought prior to our reading, so that distractions may be excluded and fervour fostered during our recitation? Have we chosen suitable time and place to pray?

Have we taken pains to mark the places in the Breviary and looked over the rubrics? Has not negligence in these matters caused innumerable distractions?

II. Dispositions which we should have in saying the Office: —

Let us find out with what dispositions we recite the Divine Office, and if we say it in the manner in which the Church wishes it to be said, digne, attente, ac devote. (Orat. rec. ante offic.).

1. Have we considered well that God is present and that we speak to Him? Do we look on ourselves as instruments which need to be animated with God's holy spirit in order to bless His holy name? Have we said the Office with all the respect and all the veneration which His almighty majesty calls for? Cum timore et humilitate, tanquam Deo visibiliter presente, psallant (S. Bona, spec, discip., p. 1, c. 15).

2. In order to say it attentively have we taken great pains to put away all kinds of distractions?

"Munda cor meum ab omnibus vanis perversis et alienis cogitationibus" (*ibid.*).

Have we rejected even good thoughts which were unsuitable for the time of recitation, and above all have we banished idle or indifferent ones?

Have we tried, following the example of the saints, to excite in ourselves the different sentiments expressed by the Psalms, or to dwell on some perfection of God, or on some mystery of our Lord, or on some virtue of the saint whose office we read? Have we piously dwelt on these, or on some other subject proper to the Church's season or according to our needs?

"Si orat psalmus, orate; si gemit, gemite; si gratulatur, gaudete; si timet, timete" (St. Aug. in Ps. 30).

In order to say the Office devoutly, have we said it with love, having our hearts and souls fully alive to the advantages and the excellence and the beauties of the Divine Office?

Have we said it with fervour, abandoning ourselves to a good emotion, to holy affections, and to joyous transports, which the Holy Ghost usually works in fervent souls? Have we done this work with joy, taking a peculiar pleasure in this holy labour, recognising the great honour it is to be a partaker in the songs of praise offered to God by the heavenly company, whose hosts are filled with His glory?

III. How we must keep watch over ourselves in reading the Office: —

Let us examine ourselves to find out if in reading the Breviary we keep the rules of good recitation, as laid down by the saints— Distincte, integre, continue, reverenter, ordinate (St. Bonav., spec. discip. p. 1, c. 16).

1. *Distincte*, Do we recite distinctly, observing the ordinary pause at the middle and at the end of each verse, not hurrying the one on the other? Do we articulate every word, not adopting a careless or too speedy pronunciation?

"Non in gutture vel inter dentes, seu deglutiendo et syncopando dictiones vel verba" (Con. Basil, sess. 22).

2. *Integre.* Do we say the Office in its entirety, being scrupulously careful not to omit the smallest part, and taking great care that a part that we should wish or try to say by heart shall not slip out of our recitation altogether or be mutilated?

"Integre, ut de dicendis nihil omittant" (St. Bona., spec, discip., p. 1).

3. Continue. Do we say our Hours without interruption? Do we love this holy exercise? Or do we easily interrupt our prayer on any trifling pretext, and on the first opportunity?

"Interruptiones in eo non fiant, nisi urgente necessitate" (*ibid.*).

4. *Ordinate.* Do we say our Office with order, that is, order both in substance (not substituting one Office for another) and in manner, according to the rubrics arranging the several hours?

"Ordinate in substantia, tempore et modo" (St. Bona. spec., *ibid.*).

5. Have we said our Hours piously, with all the modesty and all the reverence which so holy an action demands? With becoming attitude, not lying prone, not crossing our legs; without saluting or speaking to those passing by?

"In officio curando magnopere reverentia et honestas, cum ubique sit eadem cui tune loquimur et adstamus Deitas et majestas" (*ibid.*). (From *Examens Particulers sur l'Office Divin,* par M. Tronson).

NOTE C.

BIBLIOGRAPHY.

Priests are provided in their text-books of College days with reliable guides dealing directly and indirectly with liturgy. Hence, some of the books quoted here may already be favourites with many readers; but, perhaps, some books in the list may be brought to the notice of students of liturgy for the first time, and may be useful in introducing priests and church students to easy, pleasant paths in liturgical studies. The prices quoted may be useful to book-buyers,

1. Dom Gueranger, *The Liturgical Year* (1895, Duffy, Dublin, 16 vols. £3 9s.)—This work is a favourite with all lovers of liturgy, It studies and comments on the Church's liturgy day by day, week by week. It gives readers of the Missal and the Breviary a new interest and an additional fervour in their daily prayers. It is a standard work and holds its own wonderfully against all competitors.

2. *Cours De Liturgie Romaine Le Breviare,* L'abbe Bernard, Sulpician (Paris. 1887, 2 vols, 7 francs). This is a text-book written with great care, showing fine scholarship and deep piety. It is the work of a skilled teacher.

3. *Le Breviare Romain, Commente* par L'abbe Maugere. Paris. 1887, 6 francs. —A very concise and useful work, which I have used often in compiling my book.

4. The articles in the *Catholic Encyclopedia,* on the Breviary and liturgy generally.

5. Duchesne, *Christian Worship* (London. 1904. 10s.). Very readable and serviceable to students of early Church history.

6. Battifol, *History of the Roman Breviary.* (London, 1912. 15s.)

7. Biron-Baumer, *Histoire du Breviaire.* (Paris. 2 vols. 11 francs.)

8. Baudot, *The Roman Breviary* (London. Cath. Truth Society. Price 4s. 6d.)

Monsignor Battifol's book is well and favourably known. It is in English, and has had a large circulation. It received searching and severe criticism from Dom Baumer, the author of *Geschichte des Breviers.* Baumer's work (translated into French by Biron) is a work showing wonderful industry, learning and critical acumen. The great German Benedictine was aided in several parts of his work by Mr. E. Bishop, the English liturgiologist, who intended to translate the work into English. Dom Baudot's book gives in concise form the results of the labours of Battifol and Baumer. The book is readable, accurate, and is excellent value for the price.

9. *The Calendar.* The introductory matter given in the Breviary suffices for the wants of the ordinary student of liturgy. But those who wish for an exhaustive study of times and seasons may safely read *Kalendarium Manuale,* Pars I. *Festa immobilia,* Editio secunda; price 9 lire; and Pars. II. *Festa Mobilia,* price 13 lire, by Rev. N. Nilles, S.J. Calendar study is highly interesting, and the articles in the *Catholic Encyclopedia* and Father Thurston's articles in the *Month* on Calendar affairs are always instructive.

The New Psalter (Myers and Burton. London. 1915. 3s. 6d.) is a very useful and practical help to the understanding and application of the new rubrics. I have quoted several times from its pages,

Heortology, a History of Christian Festivals from their Origin to the Present Day, by Dr. Kellner, Professor of Catholic Theology in Bonn, is a translation of a text-book written for German students preparing to pass Government examinations. It is a fine book, and if a student of liturgy knew its contents well he would have no poor knowledge of this and, incidentally, of other questions of liturgy. Gueranger,

Duchesne and Kellner constitute the beginnings of a student's liturgical library (London, Keegan, Paul. 1908. Price 10s. 6d.). An excellent little volume by Father McKee, dealing with the same subject, is published by Catholic Truth Society, London, 2s, 6d. It is introductory and elementary.

10. Thousands of works on the Psalms have been published. But any priest or student who studies Steenkiste's work on the Psalms learns nearly all that is needed to recite his psalms digne, attente ac devote. His work is a mine of useful, pious, and, in the main, accurate comment on the inspired text. Breviary students studying this commentary need little else to help them to admire, to understand and to use their psalmody in a prayerful manner. Steenkiste, *Liber Psalmorum* (3 vols, Bruges. 1886. Price 15s.).

The New Psalter of the Roman Breviary, by Fillon, S.S. (London, Herder. 1915. Price 6s.).

Father Fillon was consultor to the Biblical Commission. His notes are short and useful to those who, having studied the psalms, can recall their meaning by a few brief hints. Its comments are too brief, but it gives the Latin text, English translation, notes on psalms and newly added canticles, and is arranged in the order in which they stand in the Pian psaltery.

Sing Ye to the Lord, by Rev. R. Eaton (London, Catholic Truth Society. 2 vols. 4s. each).

In these books the leading idea or ideas of the Psalms are taken up, and beautiful explanations and spiritual readings given. The books are delightful reading, and give Breviary readers, old and young, fresh thoughts on psalms which through familiarity and constant repetition may have lost some of their pious meaning and prayerfulness.

Books of Scripture commentary by non-Catholic writers should be read with caution, and often ecclesiastical permission for their perusal must be sought. Neale and Littledale's *Commentary on the Psalms* (6 vols. London. 1867) is a compilation by two Anglican scholars, from the commentators of the Middle Ages. The wonderful piety of these men of old, saints and scholars, their beautiful comments, their glowing fervour, and above all their knowledge and love of the Bible text, surprise us all. Sometimes, of course, these mediaevalists run into far-fetched, outlandish comments, but the compilers give always the comments of the Masters, St. Thomas, St. Bede, etc.

Very many metrical arrangements of the Psalms by non-Catholic authors exist in English. Most of these metrical efforts are very poor, unreliable in giving the sense, and awkward and ungainly in poetic forms. An interesting book is Prothero's *Psalms in Human Life*. The author was a Protestant, hence his numbering of the Psalms may at first sight be confusing,

Sermons fresh and beautiful, full of unction, and full of texts, sublime and practical, are to be found in the Psalms. A work, little known in our islands, is Monsignor Doublet's fine work, *Psaumes etudies en vue de la Predication* (3 vols. 8th Edition. 12s.).

A charming booklet, dealing chiefly with the Psalms as prayers, is Rolland Gosselin's *Prieres et Meditations bibliques* (Paris. 1917. Bauchesne. 3s.).

10. Hymns. Immense labour has been devoted to the study of Latin sacred poetry. The *Analecta Hymnica* in 60 huge volumes testifies to the learning and zeal of its Jesuit authors. Ordinary mortals content themselves with lesser works, such as Pimont's *Hymnes du Breviare Romain* (Paris Poussielgne. 2 vols, 12-1/2 francs), or with *La Poesie du Breviaire, Les Hymns*, by l'abbe C. Albin. Price 6 francs. The opinions and judgments in neither book are infallible; and some of Pimont's findings have been roughly criticised and sometimes rejected. But both books give good, sound knowledge of Breviary hymns and thus help to make their recitation a pious and a rational exercise, not a mechanical, soulless labour.

Translation of poetry has ever been a study and a pastime. Every cleric is familiar with the prose translations which aided his boyhood's labours in rendering the poetry of Horace and Euripides into modern speech. But prose efforts are one thing, and poetical efforts are another, and just as many have laboured to present Virgil and Homer in modern language, in metre, in rhyme, in rhythm; so, many poets and verse-makers, in different ages and in different climes, have laboured to turn into modern poetic form and into their own national tongue the poems of the Breviary. The Breviary hymns have met with several good, kind, translating poets; but very often they have been rudely handled by well-meaning verse builders.

Passing over in charitable silence the indifferent efforts of those people, it may interest some students of the Breviary to read the efforts of well-known authors to translate the liturgy, its anthems, responses, collects, hymns, into good English.

(1) *The Day Hours of the Church.* —A translation of the Horae Diurnae, with the psalms, etc., arranged according to the reform of Pope Pius X. This is a good book, giving in parallel columns on the same page, Latin and English translations. It includes the very best hymn translations by Catholic authors, John Dryden, Cardinal Newman, Father Caswall, etc. (Burns & Gates. 8s.). This book is intended for the use of the laity, and, owing to the strict regulations issued for the printing of the new Roman Breviary, this book may not lawfully be used to replace the Breviarium Romanum. But, as it is a complete translation of the little Hours of the Church, it is a very useful aid to the attentive and devout recitation of the Hours. A look at its pages before each hour's recitation, or a glance to see the meaning of some verse of psalm or hymn will repay anyone. It is a wonderfully careful production, has a beautiful *format*, and is good value at the price marked.

(2) *Annus Sanctus*, by Orby Shipley (Burns & Oates. 1884). This book contains the work of many Catholic translators, and their translations of Breviary hymns vary in merit. It contains a good introduction, the translations attributed to Dryden, and it gives some things which are always interesting, the efforts of several minds, poets and verse-makers, to render the same Latin hymn into English verse. It includes verses from several Irishmen.

(3) *Hymns from the Roman Breviary*, translated (Catholic Truth Society, London. Price 1s. 6d). A good selection from Catholic and non-Catholic translators. The translations of Dr. Neale, Anglican—held to be superior in fidelity and in poetic form to that of any English translator—are given in this booklet. Neale's *Collected Hymns* (Hodder & Stoughton, 6s.) are useful for translators and composers of vernacular hymns. But his work is, I think, over-rated.

(4) Other translations of Breviary hymns are found in the collections of hymns used in Anglican churches: *Hymns, Ancient and Modern; The English Hymnal; The Hymner from the Sarum Breviary* (Plain-song and Mediaeval Society, London); *Songs of Sion*, by Woodward, etc.

For advanced study of liturgy, Dom Cabrol's *Dictionaire D'Archeologie Chrietienne Et Liturgie* (Paris: Letouzey et Ane) is indispensable. Its study delights and consoles those who possess it.

Lightning Source UK Ltd.
Milton Keynes UK
02 October 2009

144396UK00001BA/229/A